THE
BLACK DEATH
IN ENGLAND

PAUL WATKINS MEDIEVAL STUDIES
General Editor: Shaun Tyas ~ *Consultant Editor:* David Roffe

THE
BLACK DEATH
IN ENGLAND

edited by
W. M. ORMROD
and
P. G. LINDLEY

PAUL WATKINS
STAMFORD
1996

Typeset in Caslon
and published by
Paul Watkins (Publishing)
18 Adelaide Street
Stamford, Lincolnshire
PE9 2EN

ISBN
Paperback: 1 871615 56 9
Hardback: 1 871615 48 8

Printed by Woolnough Bookbinding Ltd., Irthlingborough

CONTENTS

PREFACE

The four principal contributions to this volume have their origins in a set of lectures delivered at a day school on the Black Death, organised by the Historical Association at the Tower of London in 1992. The success of that venture and of the discussion that flowed from it encouraged us to consider publication of the lectures in a more extended and developed form. For various reasons, the project has taken rather longer than originally expected: the chapters by Professors Harper-Bill and Ormrod were completed in 1993, those by Mr Bolton and Dr Lindley in 1994-95. A further Historical Association day school on the same theme held at the University of York in 1994, where the papers by Professor Ormrod and Dr Lindley were repeated, led the editors to invite Dr Goldberg to contribute an introduction to the emerging volume: they are deeply grateful to him for his swift and positive response and his valuable contribution to the project.

Time passes, and scholarship does not stand still. While this volume has been in preparation, a number of important articles and monographs on the Black Death and related topics have appeared, whose contribution to the on-going debate has had to be omitted altogether or merely confined to notices in footnotes. Above all, perhaps, we should note here the excellent collection of primary source materials now made available in *The Black Death*, ed. and trans. R. Horrox (Manchester, 1994), which appeared too late to be exploited properly here.

The editors wish to thank Dr Adrian Ailes, formerly of the Historical Association, who organised the original event from which this book sprang; to applaud Shaun Tyas, of Paul Watkins, for his customary patience, high standards and unfailing sense of humour; and to apologise to their respective families for the disruption and distractions created by their continuing preoccupation with matters pestilential.

W. M. Ormrod
P. G. Lindley
June 1995

Introduction

P. J. P. GOLDBERG

Only a few years ago the advent of AIDS and the threat of pandemic disease impervious to the powers of modern medical science caused a major panic in western Europe. Governments were forced to respond through propaganda campaigns, drawing upon Doomsday imagery, that were designed to inculcate the virtues of 'safe sex'. Broadsheet journalists saw a sea change in sexual mores, an end to the 'permissive' society and a return to traditional values. For some of the moral majority, AIDS was even divine punishment for sexual decadence and the 'perversion' of homosexuality. Only a few years on, we no longer share in this panic. Many lives have been lost and in some parts of the world the disease is indeed endemic, but it is law and order, the decline of the royal family, and animal welfare that sell papers and fill television time. It falls to historians of the future to tell whether society or sexual mores changed in response to the crisis, or were changing in any case. AIDS, of course, is not bubonic plague. Any historical analogy is likely to be misleading, not least because the Black Death itself was sudden and cataclysmic, but a few points are worth suggesting. Traumatic though the losses caused by plague might have been, it may be unwise to expect the survivors, let alone subsequent generations, to remain traumatised in ways that are readily recognisable many years after the first visitation. On the other hand, around the time of the plague itself, we do find evidence of panic responses and we do find contemporary chroniclers occupying the moral high ground, bemoaning the sins of the age and warning that plague represented divine admonition to repentance and moral reform. To try to understand the impact of the Black Death on English society, therefore, we must understand something of the contemporary discourses, but not mistake these discourses for an objective mirror of the age. Nor must we substitute our own assumptions of a traumatised and socially fragmented society for the absence of such evidence in the mundane records of the manor court or the chancery rolls.

Historiographically speaking, the Black Death came at an unfortunate moment. It heralds the final phase of the middle ages, an era famously characterised by Huizinga as 'the Waning of the Middle Ages', a *fin de siècle* time of decadence and misery, of empty show and vainglory, of pessimism and spiritual bankruptcy. This was a time when the triumphalism of papal monarchy was displaced by the uncertainties of the Great Schism and of Conciliarism, when the unity of Latin Christendom was challenged by warfare and the emergence of the nation state, and when a long period of expansion and economic growth subsided into an age of supposed

1

contraction and recession.[1] Even the more formal terminology of modern scholarship, which talks of the 'late' and 'later' middle ages, implicitly marks this as a period distinct from and fundamentally unlike the early modern era that followed. This remains true even though many elements of the received wisdom that underpinned the supposed transition from medieval to early modern have been questioned. Much of the more important recent scholarship on popular religion, for example, has stressed the vitality of late medieval Catholicism, thus challenging the notion that the Reformation came as 'rain to a dry land'.[2] Similarly the concepts of the 'new monarchy' or the Tudor 'revolution' in government no longer appear such useful tools for conceptualising English government before the age of Elizabeth.[3] Even the idea that the nuclear household or romantic love as a factor in marriage are essentially modern phenomena, quite unlike the large and loveless families of a 'feudal' age, has not gone unchallenged.[4]

Even though old orthodoxies have been challenged and continuities between the late medieval and early modern era increasingly tend to be stressed, this revisionist perspective has not done much to undermine the significance of the Black Death. The pandemic of 1348-49, rather than constituting the beginning of an end, is seen rather as the beginning of a new era within which the roots of capitalism, the birth of the modern family

[1] Harper-Bill, for example, sees a close correlation between the spread of Lollardy in England and the period of the Schism: below, p. 83.

[2] J. J. Scarisbrick, *The Reformation and the English People* (Oxford, 1984); N. P. Tanner, *The Church in Late Medieval Norwich, 1370-1532* (Toronto, 1984); C. Burgess, '"For the Increase of Divine Service": Chantries in the Parish in Late Medieval Bristol', *Journal of Ecclesiastical History* 36 (1985), 48-65; E. Duffy, *The Stripping of the Altars: Traditional Religion in England 1400-1580* (New Haven and London, 1992); P. H. Cullum and P. J. P. Goldberg, 'Charitable Provision in Late Medieval York: "To the Praise of God and the Use of the Poor"', *Northern History* 29 (1993), 24-39; G. Rosser, 'Going to the Fraternity Feast: Commensality and Social Relations in Late Medieval England', *Journal of British Studies* 33 (1994), 430-46. The quotation is from P. Heath, 'Urban Piety in the Later Middle Ages: The Evidence of Hull Wills', in *The Church, Politics and Patronage in the Fifteenth Century*, ed. R. B. Dobson (Gloucester, 1984), pp. 208-34, p. 229.

[3] D. Starkey *et al.*, *The English Court from the Wars of the Roses to the Civil War* (London, 1987).

[4] The best known protagonists of such views are E. Shorter, *The Making of the Modern Family* (London, 1976) and L. Stone, *The Family, Sex and Marriage in England 1500-1800* (London, 1977). For medievalists' contributions to this debate see, e.g., Z. Razi, *Life, Marriage and Death in a Medieval Parish: Economy, Society and Demography in Halesowen, 1270-1400* (Cambridge, 1980); R. M. Smith, 'Hypothèses sur la nuptialité en Angleterre aux xiiie et xive siècles', *Annales: économies, sociétés, civilisations* 38 (1983), 107-36; P. J. P. Goldberg, *Women, Work, and Life Cycle in a Medieval Economy: Women in York and Yorkshire c. 1300-1520* (Oxford, 1992), pp. 203-79.

and of the nation state, the flowering of vernacular literature, or the collapse of the old feudal order may individually and severally be traced.[5] To talk in such terms is to paint with a very broad brush. Change within the social and political fabric of the realm does not and did not occur suddenly. We may compare evidence from one period with that from another and observe change. But we would be foolhardy to locate that change in a specific moment in time. Thus we may compare the pre- and post-plague periods and observe change, but it is a more difficult matter either to explain this change as a consequence of plague or to locate it specifically in the aftermath of the plague itself. Thus Lindley observes that a shift from the late Decorated to the Perpendicular style of architecture may be observed over the course of the fourteenth century, but rejects the simplistic notion that the change was solely a consequence of plague and followed immediately from the events of 1348-49. Rather, he offers a more subtle interpretation allowing for a degree of evolution that in origin pre-dated the plague, but was accelerated by the consequences of plague.[6]

For the medievalist, the problem of locating and explaining change in the past is compounded by the sources. All too often a source will relate specifically to one moment in time, or will only survive from the period before or (more often) the period after the plague. This makes comparison more difficult, but may also suggest a purely illusory degree of change. The records of presentments under the Ordinance and Statute of Labourers (1349 and 1351 respectively), for example, provide an invaluable source for wage rates and terms of employment during the later fourteenth century, and, as Penn has remarked, suggest a significant level of participation of women within the waged labour-force.[7] But no equivalent source survives from before 1349 and thus we cannot know how remarkable the proportions of female labourers found after the plague really are. Likewise, the proliferation of wills from the latter part of the fourteenth century has facilitated a significant literature on lay piety, much of it fairly upbeat in tone.[8] It would be too easy, however, to regard this as essentially new or in any significant sense a consequence of the plague merely because many fewer wills (and from a much narrower social range) survive from before the

[5] For a recent discussion of continuities over the period see J. M. Bennett, 'Medieval Women, Modern Women: Across the Great Divide', in *Culture and History 1350-1600*, ed. D. Aers (London, 1992), pp. 147-75, pp. 147-9.

[6] See Lindley, below, pp. 137-38, 141-43.

[7] S. A. C. Penn, 'Female Wage-Earners in Late Fourteenth-Century England', *Agricultural History Review* 35 (1987), 1-14. Penn's data is biased towards seasonal work, particularly harvest employment, and women may thus be disproportionately represented as they constituted a supplementary source of hired labour when demand was most acute.

[8] See n. 2 above.

Black Death. Similarly, we may wonder whether the supposed proliferation of religious guilds from the later fourteenth century is an optical illusion created on the one hand by this same survival of wills, from which so many guilds are noticed, and on the other by the particular obsessions of the Cambridge parliament of 1388 which resulted uniquely in the inquest into guilds and their assets.

If long-term, structural change is neither easy to locate in time nor to explain in relation to what contemporaries called 'the great pestilence', then a methodologically more sure approach is to explore more immediate changes that may be tied more confidently to the advent of plague. The first and most striking of these is the high level of mortality associated with the first pandemic. This is graphically illustrated in Harper-Bill's discussion of clerical mortality, but is analysed more clinically in Bolton's chapter.[9] Bolton's suggestion that 'the first wave of the Black Death carried off somewhere between 30% and 40%' of the population may err on the side of caution. Though calculated mortality rates, using manor court rolls and bishops' registers, are invariably biased towards better-off adult males and show considerable local fluctuation, a mean mortality rate of 45% occurs with considerable frequency. If one allows for a certain level of 'natural' mortality (that is, people who would have died even had there been no epidemic), this still suggests a level of plague mortality well in excess of the one third regularly cited in the older literature. Such a high level of mortality accords rather well with the tone of the contemporary chronicles whose *leitmotif* is that the survivors were scarcely sufficient in number to bury the dead.

The first pandemic was followed by a succession of lesser epidemics. The plague of 1361-62, sometimes known as the Grey Death, seems to have been particularly virulent, an observation strengthened by Ormrod's anecdotal evidence for the numbers of deaths among senior officers of the crown.[10] Later epidemics became increasingly regional in their impact, and none appears to have been of the same scale of severity as these first two, but by the beginning of the fifteenth century the disease had probably become endemic. Chroniclers were only able to observe sudden surges in the mortality rate in particular localities associated with epidemic disease. High levels of background mortality may nevertheless have had at least as great an impact on population levels in any decade as one or two epidemics within the same period.[11] It is noteworthy that the seasonality of mortality

[9]   See Harper-Bill, below, pp. 84-87, and Bolton, below, pp. 22-26.
[10] See Ormrod, below, p. 152.
[11] J. M. W. Bean, 'Plague, Population and Economic Decline in England in the Later Middle Ages', *Economic History Review*, 2nd ser., 15 (1963), 423-37, has argued that the impact of plague waned from the beginning of the 15th century as the disease became increasingly localised and urbanised. His analysis is primarily based upon chronicle evidence, itself biased towards

suggested from probate evidence is, for males at least, skewed towards a late summer/early autumn peak until the later fifteenth century.[12] Such a pattern, though hardly conclusive, is at least suggestive of endemic plague. As Bolton shows, moreover, recent work on the monks of Christ Church, Canterbury, and of Westminster indicates that high rates of mortality were nearly as much a phenomenon of the later fifteenth as of the epidemic years of the later fourteenth century.[13] If we take on board my own, albeit somewhat speculative, hypotheses concerning depressed patterns of nuptiality and fertility in the century following the Black Death, then demographic recession can be seen as a long-term phenomenon continuing at least until the second half of the fifteenth century.[14]

The sudden and catastrophic fall in the numbers of people had an immediate and demonstrable impact upon the supply and cost of labour. Wages paid to agricultural labourers and building workers alike rose swiftly as employers found themselves in competition for a scarce resource.[15] This was the context for the Ordinance of Labourers of 1349, a measure seen as an emergency response to a temporary problem. But the question that has not hitherto been posed is why the demand for labour did not contract in line with the population as a whole. Had this been the case then any local dislocation caused by differential levels of mortality would quickly have been resolved and there would have been little need for employers to offer better terms and conditions, albeit to a depleted labour force. Patently, this was not the case. The grain that had been sown before the plague still needed harvesting, the buildings that were begun before still needed completing. In practice, the surviving labour force was insufficient to meet

---

epidemic disease, and ignores the effect of endemic disease. For a perspective that takes account of endemic disease and challenges the view that plague became an essentially urban phenomenon by the 15th century, see R. S. Gottfried, *Epidemic Disease in Fifteenth Century England* (Leicester, 1978), pp. 126-42.

[12] *Ibid.*, pp. 107-17; P. J. P. Goldberg, 'Mortality and Economic Change in the Diocese of York, 1390-1514', *Northern History* 24 (1988), 38-55, p. 41.

[13] The work of Hatcher on Canterbury and Harvey on Westminster is discussed by Bolton, below, pp. 30-31.

[14] Goldberg, *Women, Work, and Life Cycle*, pp. 345-55; Bolton, below, pp. 34-40.

[15] The most useful indices of wages and of the purchasing capacity of money wages are those by Phelps Brown and Hopkins which in this period are primarily concerned with the wages of Oxford building craftsmen. There is little reason to believe that trends in the wages of such craftsmen differed markedly from those of other waged workers, though it should be remembered that workers were seldom remunerated solely in cash. See H. Phelps Brown and S. V. Hopkins, 'Seven Centuries of Building Wages' and 'Seven Centuries of the Prices of Consumables, Compared with Builders' Wage-rates', in *Essays in Economic History*, ed. E. M. Carus-Wilson, 3 vols (London, 1954-62), II, pp. 168-96.

these needs. Chroniclers tell of harvests rotting in the fields for lack of harvest workers and building works seem frequently to have been interrupted.[16] It was, however, much easier for cathedral chapters and the heads of religious houses to curtail or scale down building works which were not strictly essential than it was for peasant agriculturalists to abandon their livelihoods simply because a much reduced population meant a much reduced demand for grain.

From the perspective of individual peasant farmers in arable regions, the logic of higher labour costs was not to limit, but to maximise production, even by taking up lands left vacant by the plague, in order to meet increased overheads. Only those whose profit margins were tenuous even prior to the plague, when labour was cheap and grain prices buoyant due to pressure of population, were forced to abandon intensive arable cultivation in the face of the sudden increase in the cost of labour. It is thus in parts of midland England that we find a marked shift away from arable cultivation towards less labour-intensive forms of mixed husbandry and pastoralism and a corresponding exodus of the young and mobile whose employment prospects were consequently undermined.[17] This pattern was further repeated from the 1370s as grain prices, which had remained surprisingly buoyant for the first two decades or more after the Black Death, finally slumped in response to the fall in demand.[18] The contraction in the scale of grain production, and hence the demand for agricultural labour, in response to the fall in the population thus occurred only gradually and as a consequence of hard economic shocks. Those peasant grain producers who enjoyed particularly fertile soils were able, sometimes by judicious purchase of additional lands, to ride out these shocks. Similarly, peasant farmers who made their livelihood even before the plague primarily from sheep or from stock rearing were able to set increased prices, a product of growing demand for wool, leather and meat, against any increase in their more modest wage bills. Pastoralists, moreover, made

[16] Henry Knighton, for example, observed that 'many crops rotted in the fields for lack of men to gather them': translated in R. B. Dobson, *The Peasants' Revolt of 1381*, 2nd edn (London, 1983), p. 61. See also Lindley, below, pp. 139-43.

[17] For the distribution of deserted medieval villages, the most extreme manifestation of this shift, see M. W. Beresford and J. G. Hurst, *Deserted Medieval Villages* (London, 1971). For a discussion of the factors determining the movement of labour see Goldberg, *Women, Work and Life Cycle*, pp. 280-304.

[18] The decades immediately following the Black Death had seen a number of years of poor harvests due to the vagaries of the climate. The last quarter of the 14th century, however, saw a run of good harvests that prompted a downward trend in grain prices: C. Dyer, *Standards of Living in the Later Middle Ages* (Cambridge, 1989), pp. 261-3, 272-3.

significant use of servant labour, remunerated primarily in terms of bed and board rather than money wages.[19]

The agrarian economy was slow to respond to the changed needs of a greatly reduced population. By the time it did, the labour requirements of the non-agrarian sector of the economy had probably grown. We know all too little about the vitality of towns, where industry was primarily concentrated, before the plague. Much has been written about the cloth industry and the wool trade, mainly in terms of overseas markets, and a certain amount about port communities, again in respect of overseas trade.[20] Comparatively little has been written about internal trade and manufacture for the domestic market, but the impression is that the market was essentially determined by the needs of the landed aristocracy and ecclesiastical institutions, this being where surplus wealth was concentrated.[21] There was thus a significant demand for luxury goods (plate, jewelry, hangings, high quality cloth, spices, etc.), numbers of which items were in fact imported. It may thus be that, though numbers of merchants and specialist craftsmen enjoyed a degree of prosperity through the patronage of such wealthy consumers, towns as a whole were not especially prosperous places. Certainly, we should not be deceived by the rather sketchy evidence for the size of the resident population. From at

[19] Arable agriculture was characterised by a very seasonalised demand for labour which was best met primarily through the use of waged day labour. The less seasonalised labour requirements of a pastoral economy, however, could be more readily met by retaining a dependent labour force through the year. As the cost of wage labour rose after the Black Death, but the cost of grain declined from the mid 1370s, moreover, so the economic benefit of servant labour over wage labour was enhanced: Goldberg, *Women, Work, and Life Cycle*, pp. 159-60.

[20] E. Power, *The Wool Trade in English Medieval History* (Oxford, 1941): A. R. Bridbury, *Medieval English Clothmaking* (London, 1982); T. H. Lloyd, *The English Wool Trade in the Middle Ages* (Cambridge, 1977). Whereas there is a modern literature on trade and the economic fortunes of such towns as York, Hull, Boston, Lynn, Yarmouth, Colchester, Exeter, Bristol, and Chester, there is no equivalent literature for such important inland towns as Nottingham, Leicester, Coventry (before the end of the 15th century), or Winchester. For the suggestion that trade passing through a port may not have had such a great impact on the economy of the port community itself, see O. Coleman, 'Trade and Prosperity in the Fifteenth Century: Some Aspects of the Trade of Southampton', *Economic History Review*, 2nd ser., 16 (1963), 9-22.

[21] R. H. Britnell, *The Commercialisation of English Society 1000-1500* (Cambridge, 1993) offers the best recent overview of economic trends before and after the agrarian crisis of the earlier 14th century. For aristocratic patterns of consumption, see Dyer, *Standards of Living*, pp. 49-85. See also the household accounts in *Household Accounts from Medieval England*, ed. C. M. Woolgar, 2 vols (Oxford, 1992-3).

least the later thirteenth century towns probably housed significant proportions of dispossessed rural migrants, a phenomenon vividly illustrated by Hilton's portrait of the small town of Halesowen.[22] The plague of 1348-49 and the epidemics that followed it transformed this picture by changing patterns both of supply and of demand, but particularly within the countryside.

The haemorrhaging of peasant landholders as a consequence of the plague ensured a greater availability of land for the survivors. This was increased still further from the end of the fourteenth century by the tendency of lords to lease out the demesne, even to farm out entire manors, in the face of declining rental incomes and profits from direct management. Such available lands tended to be taken up by those who were already landholders or who expected to hold land rather than the landless or near landless. On the other hand, the landless, who made their livelihood from selling their labour to those who had more land to work than might be worked by family labour alone, be they lords or substantial peasant agriculturalists, were generally able to enjoy a higher standard of living and greater security of employment for the reasons already described, because the proportion of peasant agriculturalists dependent on buying in labour may have increased, and also because urban and rural industry was an increasingly important source of competition for available labour. Although some labourers probably used their enhanced standard of living to invest in leisure, many would have taken the opportunity to purchase items of clothing, basic utensils, furnishings and so on. We know, for example, that metal cooking vessels came to displace earthenware at this period and that the population as a whole tended to enjoy both higher standards of nutrition and a more varied, less exclusively cereal-based diet.[23] Peasant agriculturalists likewise benefited from the greater availability of land and the growing market for wool, hides and livestock required to meet the new demand for cloth, shoes and meat and in turn contributed to the demand for manufactured goods and services and hence to the demand for labour to supply these. Much the same can be said of craftworkers themselves, who both employed labour in their workshops and contributed to the demand for foodstuffs and manufactured goods.

This essentially benign model of economic growth was sustained by continued demographic recession ensuring that the labour supply always fell short of demand. During the later fourteenth century towns do not seem to have had difficulty drawing in rural migrants. This is suggested by

[22] R. H. Hilton, 'Lords, Burgesses, and Hucksters', *Past and Present* 97 (1982), 3-15. For a critique of Hilton's interpretation see P. J. P. Goldberg, 'The Public and the Private: Women in the Pre-Plague Economy' in *Thirteenth Century England III*, ed. P. R. Coss and S. D. Lloyd (Woodbridge, 1991), p. 85.

[23] Cf. Dyer, *Standards of Living*, pp. 151-60.

the movement of urban rental values and by the high levels of admissions of freemen shown where registers survive.[24] It was achieved, however, despite the availability of both land and, some arable regions excepted, work in the countryside. The implication is that towns were able to offer sufficiently attractive employment prospects for artisans and labourers alike for them to be able to compete with rural labour markets. It is noteworthy that only in the second half of the fifteenth century do we find guilds regulating against the employment of unskilled labour.[25] The implication is that hitherto the demand for labour in towns was such that all rural migrants, regardless of skills, were welcome. This observation shows also that the benign model described here did not go on indefinitely. By the earlier fifteenth century, labour supply, though significantly augmented by female and servant labour, may simply have fallen too far to meet the needs of a growing economy. The renewal of the war in France under Henry V could only have exacerbated this situation. Falling population levels further into the century may also have meant that, despite generally higher standards of living and hence purchasing power, there were simply not enough people entering the market place to sustain economic growth. Any contraction in overseas markets could only have added to a growing climate of recession from about the middle of the fifteenth century.

The significant, though short-lived, departure from the pattern just outlined is the experience of the less productive arable regions of midland England and of London. The former seem to have suffered severe dislocation when rampant labour costs devoured slender profit margins. We may suppose a marked exodus of labour either into regions better able to adapt to the new economic circumstances or into the towns and cities. There is reason to think that London was particularly hard hit, being unable to absorb the sudden influx of migrants from the home counties. The capital may well have witnessed a decade or two during which numbers of able-bodied migrants looked in vain for work or made a precarious living out of petty crime, vagrancy, or prostitution. In 1351, for example, the city authorities sought the arrest of 'misdoers who had flocked' to the city 'after the cessation of the pestilence', and in 1359 a

---

[24] A. F. Butcher, 'Rent, Population and Economic Change in Late-Medieval Newcastle', *Northern History* 14 (1978), 67-77; S. R. Rees Jones, 'Property, Tenure and Rents: Some Aspects of the Topography and Economy of York', University of York D.Phil. thesis (1987); R. B. Dobson, 'Admissions to the Freedom of York in the Late Middle Ages', *Economic History Review*, 2nd ser., 23 (1973), 1-22.

[25] It is the contention here that guild ordinances were revised in response to changing economic concerns and do not simply represent codifications of established practice. Implicitly prior to the later 15th century the shortage of labour was sufficiently acute that employers were content to take and train unskilled migrant labour.

proclamation was issued requiring unemployed migrants to leave the city immediately.[26] It may be that this London perspective informed contemporary labour legislation in much the same way as London was to influence Tudor parliaments.

As we have seen, the plague had profound economic repercussions, but they were not necessarily those that contemporaries chose to comment upon. The changing ratio of labour supply to labour demand was understood only in terms of an idle, greedy, disobedient, and truculent workforce. When labourers, who before the plague had made do with a spartan diet of bread and cheese and but the barest of essentials, demanded a cooked meal of meat or went to the ale-house at their dinner hour and then failed to return in the afternoon secure in the knowledge that they would still find employment on the morrow, this was seen as evidence of the sins of sloth, gluttony, pride, and avarice. Such, indeed, is the language of the Statute of Labourers.[27] Artisans and substantial peasants, or even persons of lesser rank, who used their enhanced standard of living to purchase good cloth or even furs were deemed to be flouting the divinely sanctioned order of society as manifested through dress. The desire to correct this perceived provocation of divine wrath likewise lay behind the short-lived sumptuary legislation of 1363.[28] Lastly, we may detect patriarchal disquiet at the enhanced role played by women in the public economy of the labour-starved decades of the later fourteenth and earlier fifteenth centuries. This is suggested, for example, by the circulation of a text such as *How the Goodwife taught her Daughter*, but more particularly in the harsh reaction against the independent working woman observed by the later fifteenth century.[29]

If the plague was universally understood as divine punishment for sin in society, it may be that the perspective of the legislators, drawn primarily from the landed elite, and the chroniclers, an educated and predominantly clerical cadre whose sympathies lay with the ruling order of society, represents only one interpretation of the nature of that sin. Unfortunately, it is to the chroniclers that we must continually return since alternative discourses are largely unrecorded. Even more conventionally literary sources than chronicles tend to share similar prejudices. Gower and

---

[26] *Calendar of Letter Books of the City of London: Letter Book F*, ed. R. R. Sharpe (London, 1904), p. 210; *Memorials of London and London Life in the XIIIth, XIVth and XVth Centuries*, ed. H. T. Riley (London, 1868), p. 304.

[27] Dobson, *Peasants' Revolt of 1381*, pp. 62, 64.

[28] *Statutes of the Realm*, 11 vols (London, 1810-23), I, pp. 380-2. See F. E. Baldwin, *Sumptuary Legislation and Personal Regulation in England* (Baltimore, 1926).

[29] F. J. Riddy, 'Mother Knows Best: Reading Social Change in a Courtesy Text', *Speculum* (forthcoming); Goldberg, *Women, Work, and Life Cycle*, pp. 198-201, 331-3, 337-40, 347, 354-6, 361.

Chaucer reflect the perspective of the court and the well-to-do, and even Langland, for all his sympathies with peasant society and the lot of the poor, demonstrates an essentially conservative, London-oriented view that may betray his own gentle pedigree: the shepherd's garb he adopts at the beginning of his poem is but a literary guise. We must look elsewhere for a peasant discourse or discourses.

The Peasants' Revolt of 1381 is perhaps one context in which we may locate such alternative discourses. This is implicit in Ormrod's discussion of the resentment of village elites at the intrusion of gentry-dominated peace sessions into local government.[30] This intrusion was a breach of the cherished principle of self-policing, rooted in the Statute of Winchester (1285), but it was also disruptive of the communal order and essentially partisan and unjust in that those who enforced the law were seen to operate beyond the law. The Statute of Labourers in particular was used, not as originally framed against all who paid or received wages in excess of the level that applied before the plague, but against small employers and the labourers whom they employed, giving lords an unfair advantage in the operation of regional labour markets. This may well have been seen as an abuse of authority on the part of those whose rank in society might be justified only in terms of the responsibilities that went with it. Certainly, local constables could be ambivalent or even antagonistic towards the statute, as in Essex, where lords competed with substantial numbers of peasant agriculturalists and rural artisans for labour.

The disruptive and essentially unjust intrusion of royal government into village society was likewise experienced in relation to the third poll tax. Ormrod argues that particular problems arose not so much with the level of tax or even the extension of the tax burden to persons who by tradition were exempt from taxation, but rather with the imposition of outsiders over the heads of local tax collectors to inquire into underpayment of the third poll tax.[31] But there was a deeper grievance that may also be identified. The complexities of the third poll tax, with its requirement that an average of a shilling a head be levied, but that the better-off should subsidise the poor down to a minimum of only 4*d.*, seems to have met with a variety of responses from local tax officers. A common response, however, was to turn a blind eye to numbers of less affluent adults who could not readily be charged the full shilling, but who equally could not be subsidised without placing an excessive burden on their more prosperous neighbours.[32] This appears to have been the case in Essex, one of a number of counties where exchequer concern at the high level of

[30]   Ormrod, below, pp. 155-59.
[31]   Ormrod, below, pp. 165-67.
[32]   P. J. P. Goldberg, 'Urban Identity and the Poll Taxes of 1377, 1379, and 1381', *Economic History Review*, 2nd ser., 43 (1990), 194-216, pp. 202-8.

under-enumeration compared to earlier returns resulted in the sending of a commission of inquiry. According to the *Anonimalle* chronicle, a commission came to Brentwood with the specific purpose of collecting from the neighbouring hundred tax 'in default'. The chronicler's narrative is particularly telling at this point. He (erroneously) talks of raising 'a new subsidy', but describes how the people of Fobbing answered 'that they would pay nothing at all because they had an acquittance ... for the said subsidy'.[33] Although there are obvious flaws in the *Anonimalle* account, it may here give a clue to the actual response of the peasant elite in rural Essex, that the tax had already been paid and that the commission was thus acting beyond law and justice.

The response of the lower echelons of society to the moralising of the ruling order, to legislation designed to regulate aspects of behaviour that had never previously been the concern of royal government, to the unprecedented and apparently disruptive intrusion of external control into the government of local communities, and to the misconduct of social superiors who neither respected the law nor, through their mismanagement of the war in France, protected those who tilled their fields and paid their rents, was, as we know, sometimes violent, but it was often quite articulate. Most villages would have had a core of substantial peasant agriculturalists well used to litigation in the customary court, and to holding manorial, guild, or local government office. Artisans likewise, as managers of workshops and employers of labour, were well able to hold their own. The aspirations of these groups can be seen in much the same moral terms of a return to a golden age as that of their social superiors. It was merely that they constructed a different golden age. Indeed, the most radical slogan of the Revolt of 1381 – 'When Adam delved / And Eve span / Who was then the gentleman?' – was a demand for the social equality (but implicitly the gender divisions) of the Garden of Eden. Wat Tyler's followers at Smithfield likewise demanded 'that no lord should have lordship in future, but it should be divided among all men', and that there be an end to villeinage 'that all men should be free and of one condition'. Within this restored Eden there would be but one law, namely (we are to understand) the Statute of Winchester.[34]

Society changed following the Black Death. For certain groups, such as women below the rank of the aristocracy, the young, artisans and wage labourers, the changes were marked, although not necessarily lasting. The higher profile of women within the public economy before the middle of the fifteenth century did little to challenge an essentially patriarchal order and nothing to protect them when the economic tide changed later in the

---

[33] Dobson, *Peasants' Revolt of 1381*, p. 124.
[34] *Ibid.*, pp. 164-5. The rebels did not challenge the authority of the king.

century.[35] Nor did the rebels of 1381, despite the radical demands of some
of their leaders, precipitate the collapse of feudal power structures.
Villeinage withered away only over time as a consequence of a retreat from
direct management of the demesne and irrespective of the Peasants'
Revolt. The only lasting achievement was the abandonment (at least
during the medieval era) of the poll tax and a return to the system of
subsidies established from 1334. Artisans gained a degree of political clout
in many towns, but their influence always remained subordinate to
mercantile elites.[36] The young of both sexes, drawn into positions as
servants away from their natal homes, may have enjoyed a degree of
economic and emotional autonomy from their families, and, in the case of
older servants, may thus have enjoyed a certain freedom of courtship and
choice of marriage partner; but it would be unwise to overstate the extent
of this phenomenon, nor is there any evidence that household or marriage
structures were substantially changed as a consequence.[37]

These are still real changes. The problem that arises is how far we can
explain them in terms of the plague. That is very much the theme of this
present collection of essays. What emerges is the need always to explore
new avenues of research. Thus Bolton points to the diversity of local and
regional experiences, Harper-Bill to the destabilising influence of the Great
Schism, Ormrod to changes in the structure of government, and Lindley to
the actual impact of mortality on known workshops. Repeatedly we find
that the plague was not an autonomous agent of change, but worked in
tandem with other processes. Neither the participation of women in the
labour force nor of youngsters in life-cycle service was a product of the
Black Death, but the labour shortages created by the plague stimulated
demand for both these sources of labour. In Tuscany, by contrast, labour
shortage encouraged parents to retain adult sons within the household and
to allow the heir to marry within the natal home.[38] This was likewise
merely an acceleration of a traditional pattern. The nature of the response
was thus culturally determined, the level of mortality shaping only the
extent of the response. Likewise, though the Perpendicular predated the
plague, high labour costs, diminishing purchasing power, evolution of
fashion, and the availability of master masons all combined to popularise

[35] See n. 29 above.
[36] Cf. A. F. Butcher, 'English Urban Society and the Revolt of 1381', in *The English Rising of 1381*, ed. R. H. Hilton and T. H. Aston (Cambridge, 1984), pp. 84-111. For a particularly emphatic statement of the continuing authority of mercantile elites, see H. Swanson, 'The Illusion of Economic Structure: Craft Guilds in Late Medieval English Towns', *Past and Present* 121 (1988), 29-48.
[37] Smith, 'Hypothèses sur la nuptialité', pp. 128-31; Goldberg, *Women, Work, and Life Cycle*, pp. 158-279.
[38] *Ibid.*, pp. 340-5.

the new style in the decades following the Black Death. We may speculate that the style would have evolved independently of the plague, but we would be hard put to it to explain how it would have evolved. We can, however, move away from a discourse that constructs the plague as an autonomous agent of change.

Bolton shows how Postan described an economy, already sapped by the agrarian crisis, waning further in tandem with years of demographic attrition. For Meiss, as Lindley argues, artists and patrons were working in a world traumatised by plague, haunted by images of mortality, and searching for a simpler spirituality. Harper-Bill, in this present collection, argues that morbidity and pessimism permeated religious life after the plague. Within such a discourse it becomes possible to suggest, for example, that the Perpendicular displaced the Decorated because, according to Prior, craftsmanship deteriorated following the plague or, according to Wilson, the Perpendicular better suited a 'soberer and more spiritual' age. Similarly Rubin, following Mollat, is able to argue for a hardening of attitudes to the poor at the same time as a greater emphasis on funerary pomp.[39] Alternative discourses eschew such emotive language and seek more mundane explanations for change. The lower construction costs of the Perpendicular, for example, unencumbered by the elaborate carvings that characterise the Decorated, accord with the needs of religious institutions faced with the twin effects of rampant labour costs and declining rental incomes. As Lindley shows, artistic styles changed because numbers of established masters died in the pestilence and new workshops came to the fore in their place.[40] Likewise, Ormrod is able to explain a shift in the language of resistance to royal taxation from an emphasis on plague-induced poverty and hardship to a more active criticism of the costs of the royal household in purely pragmatic terms free from the moral impedimenta of the contemporary rhetoric.[41]

If we are to look beyond this rhetoric of pestilence, poverty, and moral decay so readily to be found in the contemporary discourse of chroniclers, clerks, and the aristocratic elite, for whom plague indeed brought a diminution in personal fortunes, so we must be alert to alternative discourses. Though Langland and the framers of the Statute of Labourers articulated a common hostility towards the sturdy vagrant, the wall paintings at Trotton (Sussex) or the glass at All Saints, North Street, York depicting the Seven Corporal Acts of Mercy tell a different story, one that is repeated in hundreds of surviving wills and in the proliferation of almshouses or maisonsdieu from the later fourteenth century.[42] The

[39]   M. Rubin, *Charity and Community in Medieval Cambridge* (Cambridge, 1987), esp. pp. 289-99.
[40]   Lindley, below, pp. 137-39.
[41]   Ormrod, below, pp. 167-71.

14

religious guilds that seem to have been so popular from much the same time were in part burial clubs, but their welfare function, drawing upon the same gospel rhetoric of the Seven Works, was no less a part of their purpose and popularity.[43] Thus, an era that saw a marked fall in recruitment to religious houses also saw a flowering of lay devotion reflected in guilds, the circulation of devotional literature and the use of primers (books of hours), patronage of parish churches, religious drama, and the growing devotion to the Holy Kindred.

As Harper-Bill observes, much can be traced back to the Fourth Lateran Council rather than the Black Death. But much can also be explained by a redistribution of wealth away from the landed aristocracy in favour of merchants, artisans, peasant agriculturalists, and even labourers, resulting in a shift of patronage from the large impersonal and institutional structures of the monastery and the hospital towards the more modest, but more intimate, structures of the parish, the guild, and the maisondieu. This same redistribution of wealth prompted Bridbury to describe the post-plague era as an age of economic growth. I have likewise painted a generally up-beat portrait of the later medieval economy by stressing the way in which higher standards of living for women and men alike stimulated demand for goods and services. Nor need we characterise artistic production, including the vast numbers of parish churches augmented or rebuilt, as intrinsically inferior to that which went before the plague, though because so much patronage was from persons of comparatively modest means the quality of what was produced was likewise often modest. The Wilton Diptych, the cloisters of Gloucester Abbey, the Lytlington Missal, the Dunstable Swan, and the glazing of Winchester College demonstrate that wealthy patrons could still obtain craftsmanship of the very highest order. We do not need to impose the shadow of death over English society after the plague. The 'great pestilence' killed on a terrible scale, but it did not necessarily destroy also the spirit of the survivors.

---

[42]   P. H. Cullum, '"For Pore People Harberles": What was the Function of the Maisondieu?', in *Trade, Devotion and Governance: Papers in Later Medieval History*, ed. D. J. Clayton, R. C. Davies and P. McNiven (Stroud, 1994), pp. 36-54; M. K. McIntosh, 'Local Responses to the Poor in Late Medieval and Tudor England', *Continuity and Change* 3 (1988), 209-45; Cullum and Goldberg, 'Charitable Provision in Late Medieval York', pp. 24-39; E. Clark, 'Social Welfare and Mutual Aid in the Medieval Countryside', *Journal of British Studies* 33 (1994), 381-406.

[43]   Here I differ from Harper-Bill who sees only the chantry function of guilds as central to their purpose: below, p. 113. Cf. Rosser, 'Going to the Fraternity Feast', pp. 430-46.

'The World Upside Down'
Plague as an Agent of Economic and Social Change

JIM BOLTON

INTRODUCTION: THE DEBATE

> Of all the forces that were changing the face of English society in the late middle ages, the most wide ranging in its effects was the drop in population following the visitation of the fourteenth-century plagues.[1]

So begins the best recent general survey of social change in late medieval England. There is virtually no disagreement amongst modern historians that the advent of endemic plague had profound consequences for both the economy and for society after 1348. Yet there is continuing disagreement about the centrality of the plague in causing change and, indeed, about the changes apparently brought about by radical depopulation. There is nothing new about this debate. Essentially, it began in the late nineteenth century when Bishop Stubbs, J. R. Green and William Denton painted as black a picture of post-plague England as could be. Simultaneously, J. E. Thorold Rogers, in his magisterial studies of prices and wages, saw the fifteenth-century wage earner as enjoying a standard of wellbeing the like of which his ancestors had never known and his descendants would never again enjoy until England ceased to be primarily an agricultural country.[2] This was the essential parting of the ways. By the mid-1920s Kingsford could write of late medieval England as a place where all those who stayed out of politics lived lives of increased ease and comfort – whilst Huizinga, in his classic study *The Waning of the Middle Ages*, saw the middle ages dragging out their last years in gloom and decay, an interpretation that successive studies of great estates in England, showing the landlords facing ruin and the peasantry deserting villages on a large scale, only seemed to confirm.[3]

[1]　M. Keen, *English Society in the Later Middle Ages, 1348-1500* (London, 1990), p. 27.

[2]　The best summary of 19th-century views on the 15th century is to be found in A. R. Bridbury, *Economic Growth: England in the Later Middle Ages* (London, 1962), pp. 13-17; W. Stubbs, *Constitutional History of England*, 3 vols, 4th ed. (Oxford, 1890), III, p. 638; J. R. Green, *A Short History of England* (London, 1880), pp. 282-84; J. E. Thorold Rogers, *Six Centuries of Work and Wages* (London, 1884), pp. 326ff; *idem, A History of Agriculture and Prices in England, 1259-1793*, 7 vols (Oxford, 1866-1902), I, pp. 688-94, IV, pp. 753-60; W. H. Denton, *England in the Fifteenth Century* (London, 1888), pp. 118-19.

[3]　C. L. Kingsford, *Prejudice and Promise in Fifteenth-Century England* (Oxford, 1925), *passim*; J. Huizinga, *The Waning of the Middle Ages* (Harmondsworth, 1955), pp. 27-29, 134-46; Bridbury, *Economic Growth*, p. 18 and especially n. 13.

17

Then, in the late 1930s, Professor M. M. Postan began his attempts to reconcile these two conflicting interpretations and in so doing produced the first of the general explanations of the post-plague economy around which current debate turns. Postan saw late-medieval England as a country where stagnation was tinged with gloom. The severe decline in the population led at one and the same time to falling demand for food and higher labour costs. Prices fell and wages rose, as labour shortages began to bite, and those shortages were exacerbated by the movement of previously landless labourers to vacant tenements, as land became readily available at low rents. Landlords, faced with falling profits from sales of agricultural produce, rising labour costs and, from the 1380s, a growing inability to enforce manorial discipline, gradually opted out of direct farming for the market and sought refuge in leasing out their estates. But land values, and therefore rents, were so low that this meant declining incomes, and it was the attempt to offset this decline which led to the scramble for office and ultimately to the civil wars of the 1450s and '60s. Collapse at the top did mean some redistribution of incomes, however, in favour partly of the middle classes, but mainly of the peasantry. There was enough land for all. Holdings could be enlarged and worked by families whose aim became self sufficiency. As a result, the overall fall in demand consequent upon a decline in the population was made even worse, and those who supplied the market – townsmen, traders, manufacturers – suffered accordingly. Even the expansion of the cloth industry could not offset the decline in the non-agrarian sectors of the economy. Exports of broadcloths rose, but they did not equal in value the raw wool exports of the late thirteenth and early fourteenth centuries until the very end of the fifteenth century.[4]

Few general historical explanations have commanded so much respect and agreement for so long. Yet Postan's thesis was bound to be challenged, and that challenge came most brilliantly from Dr A. R. Bridbury, in his short book, *Economic Growth: England in the Later Middle Ages*, first published in 1962. Bridbury would have none of the gloom. For the survivors, he argued,

> the fourteenth century famines and pestilences were no doubt, on personal grounds, inexpressibly grievous. But they unlocked a cornucopia. England was given a sort of Marshall Aid on a stupendous scale ... Land was not merely abundant; it was equipped, and stocked, and often,

[4] M. M. Postan, 'The Fifteenth Century', *Economic History Review*, 1st series, 9 (1938-39), 160-67; *idem*, 'Some Economic Evidence of Declining Population in the Later Middle Ages', *Economic History Review*, 2nd series, 2 (1949-50), 221-46; *The Cambridge Economic History of Europe*, ed. M. M. Postan, I, 2nd edn (Cambridge, 1966), pp. 595-600, 630-32; M. M. Postan, *The Medieval Economy and Society: An Economic History of Britain, 1100-1500* (Harmondsworth, 1972), pp. 41-44, 154-59, 194-202, 217-30; J. L. Bolton, *The Medieval English Economy 1150-1500* (London, 1985), pp. 208-09.

perhaps, enriched rather than impoverished by the husbandry of generations of peasants.[5]

A prosperous, mobile peasantry was able to enlarge its holdings and increase their productivity. Fortified by ample tenancies and long leases, the peasantry entered into its own, and, since at least three quarters of the population consisted of peasant farmers and farm labourers, the economy itself was bound to flourish. Indeed, Bridbury's thesis centres around the argument that late-medieval towns remained rich and vigorous by supplying the sustained demand for non-agrarian goods and services. His comparison of the taxation assessments for 1334 and 1524 suggested that urban wealth formed a far greater proportion of total lay wealth in the early sixteenth century than it had in the early fourteenth. Prosperous towns serviced the demand from an equally prosperous countryside. The booming textile industry supplied both the home market and sent for export broadcloths which, in terms of their raw wool equivalent and added labour costs, far outstripped in value the raw wool exports of the late thirteenth century. Moreover, this industry was based firmly in and around towns, old and new, whilst English merchants began to challenge long-established alien supremacy in the export trade.[6]

Bridbury's arguments have only one point of common ground with Postan's, namely that whilst aggregate wealth may have declined, per capita wealth increased. The two seem irreconcilable, but they have engendered vigorous controversy and a debate which, in the last decade or so, has moved from the general to the particular. New areas needing investigation have been identified, and new techniques deployed for the analysis of evidence. Above all, new historical interpretations of the causes of change in pre-industrial early-modern economies have been advanced and applied to England in the century and a half after the arrival of the Black Death. Demographers have grappled with the problem of why – indeed, if – there were such high death rates from the first waves of the plague, and with the possibility that other diseases, and perhaps famines, should be taken into account when trying to explain the most difficult of all the problems: namely, why the population did not recover and replace itself in the later fourteenth and through most of the fifteenth century. Here, in particular, they have focused on the question of whether we should look not simply to the mortality schedule, but also to problems of nuptiality and fertility, of marriage and childbearing, to explain this difficult phenomenon. Medical historians have supplied much new evidence on the aetiology, or nature, of plague and on differential male and female death and survival rates, with the interesting implication that there may have been more women than men in late-medieval England. If that were the

[5] Bridbury, *Economic Growth*, p. 91.
[6] Bridbury, *Economic Growth*, pp. 70-82, 25-38.

case, then it might have had important, if only temporary, consequences for the status of women in society. Urban historians have engaged in endless, and perhaps sterile, quarrels about the fortunes of towns great and small, old and new, though such debates have at least had the merit of helping to establish urban history as a discipline in its own right. Historians of the countryside (for it no longer seems apposite to call them simply agrarian historians) have begun to look at the fortunes of village communities rather than those of great landlords. Did these communities lose their social cohesiveness after the Black Death, as individualism and enterprise replaced communal effort, and was it simply depopulation which led to the shrinkage or desertion of villages themselves? They have also raised important questions about the regionality of change and the possibility of a growing division between north and south, in both economic and political terms.

But it is the final emergence of 'social' history, in its varying forms, which has brought the most stimulating challenges to orthodoxies. As a result of the work of the *Annales* school of French historians and their disciples in England, most notably Professors Hilton and Dyer, the study of all aspects of the lives of peasants, workers and women, and other underprivileged groups in society, has become widely accepted as a legitimate area for historical investigation. Aided by a mass of new information from archaeologists and increasingly from building historians, the question of substantial changes in living standards is now being thoroughly explored. So is the anatomy of popular revolutions, resulting in a growing awareness that the Peasants' Revolt had diverse origins rather than one single cause. They – the 'social' historians – have also begun to argue that the structure of society itself established and maintained inequalities, and that the wealth of the aristocracy was derived as much from its military, political and judicial domination of a subordinate peasantry as from the direct economic exploitation of the land. Lordship allowed the few to exploit the resources of the many, through labour services or cash payments in lieu, through legal control over land transfers, through rent payments, through courts, or, in other words, through 'feudal' means. The majority of society was constantly being deprived of resources by the demands of lords. That held back individualism, enterprise, the ability to use resources to invest and reinvest in agriculture or industry. Capitalism could only emerge if the feudal structure of society was challenged.[7] There might be many reasons for such a challenge, beyond a simple readjustment of people to resources as a result of endemic plague. Changes in the money supply, it is argued, had as profound an effect on

[7] For an excellent discussion of recent trends in historical investigation see C. Dyer, *Standards of Living in the Later Middle Ages. Social Change in England c.1200-1520* (Cambridge, 1989), pp. 3-7.

prices and wages as did population decline. According to monetary historians it was the shortage of bullion throughout Europe which caused a dearth of coin in England and the deflation responsible for the collapse in prices and rents which so troubled the greater landlords.[8] War, and the taxation to pay for it, are also often seen as agents of social change, as is religious debate, and without doubt orthodox religion faced severe challenges in the post-plague period.[9]

Certainties, therefore, seem to have been replaced by uncertainties. Recent research has even cast some doubt on the centrality of plague in explanations of the change from medieval to early-modern, pre-industrial England. In 1350 society was still structured around the three orders of *bellatores, oratores* and *laboratores*: those who fight, those who pray and those who work to support them. By 1500 that homogeneity had been challenged. Esquires, gentlemen, yeomen, husbandmen jostled with knights for place; merchants and lawyers joined, or perhaps sought to join, a society which was infinitely more fluid and infinitely more English in both speech and attitude.[10] Could all this have resulted from the advent of endemic plague? It is also fairly obvious that long-standing 'general' theses of depression or growth are in need of serious re-evaluation. The purpose of this essay, then, is to try to provide such a general re-evaluation. It will do so by considering first the impact of plague in both demographic terms and in the light of new arguments about the causation of economic change. The conclusion will be that depopulation, for whatever reason, remains a key factor in the debate. Against that background, the immediate and long-term consequences for late fourteenth- and fifteenth-century England will be examined. In this context, most recent work, aside from that on the causes of the Peasants' Revolt, has concentrated on changes in peasant and gentry society, on the fortunes of towns and townsmen, and on the status of women in society. It is on these areas that discussion will be focused, to determine whether such changes were structural, that is permanent, or merely conditional on a temporary decline in the population. That, indeed, is the first of the two crucial issues which have to be resolved: whether the Black Death, over a period of some 150 years, altered for good and all the structure of English society. The second is whether the calamitous year 1348 did usher in a period of unrelieved gloom or an age of prosperity and

8 J. Day, 'The Great Bullion Famine of the Fifteenth Century', *Past and Present*, 79 (1978), 3-54; see also his collected essays, *The Medieval Market Economy* (Oxford, 1987); H. A. Miskimin, 'Monetary Movements and Market Structures: Forces for Contraction in Fourteenth- and Fifteenth-Century England', *Journal of Economic History*, 24 (1964), 470-95; P. Spufford, *Money and its Use in Medieval Europe* (Cambridge, 1988), pp. 339-62; *L'Economie Médiévale*, ed. P. Contamine (Paris, 1993), 299-328, pp. 314-18.

9 Cf. Harper-Bill, below, pp. 118-19.

10 Keen, *English Society in the Later Middle Ages*, pp. 1-5, 303.

ambition, of relative affluence for all those who survived that most awful of all pestilences, from which at least one contemporary chronicler doubted any of the race of Adam would escape.[11]

THE PLAGUE

The First Outbreak, 1348-50

The arrival of plague in southern England in the summer of 1348, scarcely more than a year after it had reached southern Europe from the Crimea, brought two years in which 'England's population was dealt a blow of enormous force with loss of life on a scale that has not since been experienced.'[12] Chronicles vividly recorded its onset and its inexorable progress across the country, and modern research has confirmed their accounts. From its initial point of entry, at Melcombe Regis near Weymouth in Dorset, it fanned out to the south west, towards Bristol, and north-eastwards towards London, to reach much of the rest of England by the summer of 1349. Yet the bald listing of dates conceals in some ways the suddenness with which the plague struck at communities which must have known it was on its way. At Kibworth Harcourt in Leicestershire, the year 1348, as seen through the court rolls, was uneventful: a death, a marriage, a case of maladministration of a tenant's land during a vacancy. By the end of April 1349, 42 deaths had been registered; two more followed in August, and no further courts were held until 1350. The deaths recorded in the court rolls were those of landholders only, and to this number must be added an unspecified number of women, children and landless men, before the scale of the catastrophe which struck this Midland village can be appreciated. In the archdeaconry of Coventry (diocese of Coventry and Lichfield), comprising much of north-east Warwickshire, the first recorded death of a parish priest from the plague was on 6 April 1349. The pestilence then raged in Warwickshire and Staffordshire from May to early June, moving to Derbyshire and Cheshire in mid-June and early September, with the peak period for deaths of parish priests in the five archdeaconries coming as early as 16 June in Coventry, 15 July in Stafford, 28 July in Derby, 8 August in Shrewsbury and 10 August in Chester.[13]

[11] 'Cronaca Senese di Agnolo di Tura del Graso' in *Cronache Senese*, ed. A. Lisini and F. Iacometri, Rerum Italicarum Scriptores, 15, vi (Bologna, 1939), p. 556.

[12] R. M. Smith, 'Human Resources' in *The Countryside of Medieval England*, ed. G. Astill and A. Grant (Oxford, 1988), 188-212, p. 209.

[13] Good surveys of chronicle and other contemporary evidence are given in P. Ziegler, *The Black Death* (Harmondsworth, 1970), pp. 120ff; R. S. Gottfried, *The Black Death* (New York, 1983), pp. 58-67; J. L. Bolton, 'The Black Death', *The Historian*, 39 (Autumn 1993), 3-8, pp. 3-4; and, most recently, *The Black Death*, ed. R. Horrox (Manchester, 1994). C. Howell, *Land, Family and Inheritance in*

In their search for aggregates, their attempts to calculate how many people died in the first wave of plague, modern historians tend to overlook the fact that this was a largely rural society, living in villages or scattered settlements, waiting for the pestilence to arrive. Sometimes it came by road, passing from village to village, sometimes by river, as in the East Midlands, or by ship, from the Low Countries or from other infected areas within England, which seems to have been the case in East Anglia and Durham.[14] When it struck, there appears to have been no way of knowing how many would die, since death rates seem to have been so variable. On the vills of the bishop of Worcester's estates in the west midlands they ranged between 19% of manorial tenants (by no means all the population within villages) at Hartlebury and Hanbury to no less than 80% at Aston. Similar variations can be seen in the north east where 21% of Durham Priory tenants died at Monkton but 78% at Jarrow. Death rates in towns were very similar, but no more severe, as has often been argued. At Norwich, England's second or third city, with a pre-plague population of some 10-12,000, the plague arrived in January 1349 and raged until spring 1350. Perhaps 40-45% of the lay population died. In the other great East Anglian town, Bury St Edmunds, perhaps 50% of the population of some 7,000 perished, but that actually compares favourably with 60% in the surrounding villages, a death rate also found at Coltishall in Norfolk, some six miles from Norwich itself.[15]

It is very difficult for us to imagine the impact of plague on these small rural communities, where a village might have no more than 400 or 500 inhabitants. Few settlements were totally depopulated, but in most others whole families must have been wiped out, and few can have been spared some loss, since the plague killed indiscriminately, striking at poor and rich alike. Great Waltham in north Essex was a large township, with 187 male

---

Transition: Kibworth Harcourt 1280-1700 (Cambridge, 1983), p. 42; R. A. Davies, 'The Effect of the Black Death on the Parish Priests in the Medieval Diocese of Coventry and Lichfield', *Historical Research*, 62 (1989), 85-90, p. 86.

[14] Gottfried, *Black Death*, p. 65; R. Lomas, 'The Black Death in County Durham', *Journal of Medieval History*, 15 (1989), 127-40, p. 128.

[15] The problems of calculating death rates from contemporary evidence are fully discussed by J. Hatcher in his *Plague, Population and the English Economy, 1348-1530* (London, 1977), pp. 21-30 and in a subsequent article 'Mortality in the Fifteenth Century: Some New Evidence', *Economic History Review*, 2nd series, 39 (1986), 19-38, pp. 19-22. C. Dyer, *Lords and Peasants in a Changing Society: the Estates of the Bishopric of Worcester, 680-1540* (Cambridge, 1980), pp. 237-38; Lomas, 'Black Death in County Durham', p. 129; Gottfried, *Black Death*, p. 66; R. S. Gottfried, *Bury St Edmunds and the Urban Crisis 1290-1539* (Princeton, NJ, 1982), p. 51; B. M. S. Campbell, 'Population Pressure, Inheritance and the Land Market in a Fourteenth-Century Peasant Community' in *Land, Kinship and Life Cycle*, ed. R. M. Smith (Cambridge, 1984), 87-134, pp. 96-97.

inhabitants over the age of 12 in 1348. By 1350 there were only 104 left, a death rate of 44.4%, which surely must have been matched to a lesser or greater extent among the women and children in the parish. Here, as elsewhere, fields would have been left unploughed, stock untended, and the physical act of burying the dead would have posed considerable problems: at Belford, in Northumberland, the cemetery had to be enlarged to accommodate the dead of half a dozen adjacent hamlets. Contemporary accounts may be highly coloured but they certainly reflect the immense shock to society from what was clearly seen as a great catastrophe.[16]

Nor can there be much doubt that it was plague that had caused the disaster. Various attempts have been made in the past twenty years to question this assumption, and to suggest that the demographic disaster of 1348-49 was the result of other diseases. J. D. Shrewsbury argued that, since the first outbreak of the pestilence was mainly bubonic in nature, its overland movement would have been hampered or even halted by the concentration of the population in nucleated villages separated by extensive tracts of land and devoid of the outlying farms essential for providing the link in the transmission of rat plagues from one village concentration of rats to another.[17] But there are at least three major flaws in this argument. The first plague, for which we have the best evidence, was certainly both bubonic and pneumonic in nature, raging as it did through both summer (bubonic) and winter (pneumonic). It is pneumonic plague which is the real killer, and as long ago as 1910 it was shown that at Curry Rivel in Somerset no deaths were reported at the manor court in October 1348, but 18 were notified in December, 5 in February 1349 and 10 in March.[18] That was pneumonic plague, and the fact that the pestilence raged through two winters, those of 1348-49 and 1349-50, must surely confirm that it was a combination of the two varieties which caused the high death rates. Secondly, most local communities were not isolated, either from each other or from nearby markets in towns small and large. By 1300 society was well and truly 'commercialised', with peasants

---

[16] L. R. Poos, 'The Rural Population of Essex in the Later Middle Ages', *Economic History Review*, 2nd series, 38 (1985), 515-30, p. 522; *idem*, *A Rural Society after the Black Death: Essex 1350-1525* (Cambridge, 1990), pp. 104-08; Smith, 'Human Resources', pp. 192, 208-09; E. Miller, 'Introduction: Land and People' in *The Agrarian History of England and Wales*, III, *1348-1500*, ed. E. Miller (Cambridge, 1991), 1-33, p. 3. For a discussion of the age- and gender-specific nature of plague, see below, pp. 35-37.

[17] J. D. Shrewsbury, *A History of Bubonic Plague in the British Isles* (Cambridge, 1970), pp. 21-22.

[18] J. F. Chanter, 'Court Rolls of the Manor of Curry Rivel in the Year of the Black Death', *Somerset Archaeological and Natural History*, 46 (1910), 85-135, pp. 92-98; E. Miller, 'The Occupation of the Land: the Southern Counties', *Agrarian History of England and Wales*, III, 136-51, pp. 139-40.

participating fully in the market economy. Rats and fleas could be carried in loads of grain and bales of cloth and, in the case of fleas, on humans. Plague clearly moved along major routes and fanned out from them via local markets and fairs.[19]

Finally, and most importantly, it is a mistake to think that it is only the rat which can carry the plague bacillus and transmit it to the human via the bite of the flea. Modern medical research on plague in the United States has shown that it can have a variety of other vectors. In California it is the ground squirrel which carries the plague, whilst in remote and mountainous north Colorado it is in the burrows of the black-tailed prairie dog that the plague bacillus persists, to be transmitted to humans not by the rat flea, *X. cheopis*, but by *oropsylla hirsuta* or the hirsute flea. In New Mexico, 119 cases of plague in cats were discovered in 1977-88, 53% certainly bubonic, 10% pneumonic and 8% septicaemic, and in 1984, in Oregon, plague was transmitted to a ten-year-old girl by a scratch wound from an infected cat. This is important. It is quite possible that plague in 1348-49 – and later – moved across the countryside from colony to colony of wild animals, independent of man, to infect other household and barnyard animals, since all of these save the horse can act as secondary carriers from which the prime carrier, the flea, can transmit the disease to the tertiary carrier, or rather victim, the human.[20] More recently than Shrewsbury, Twigg has suggested that because of the swiftness of the disease's transmission in 1348-49, it must have been an airborne pathogen, possibly anthrax. But that is a disease which strikes at humans and at cattle, and there is as yet no substantiated evidence of high death rates amongst livestock in these years.[21]

[19] Two recent studies stressing the high degree of commercialisation in late medieval society are R. H. Britnell, *The Commercialisation of English Society 1000-1500* (Cambridge, 1993) and C. Dyer, 'The Consumer and the Market in the Later Middle Ages', *Economic History Review*, 2nd series, 42 (1989), 305-26.

[20] R. Epstein, 'A Persistent Pestilence', *Geographical Magazine*, 63 (1991), 18-22, *passim*; *Robbins Pathological Basis of Disease*, ed. R. S. Cotran, V. Kumar and S. L. Robbins, 4th edn (Philadelphia, 1989), p. 362; M. L. Beard, S. T. Rose, A. M. Barnes, J. A. Montieri, 'Control of *Oropsylla hirsuta*, a Plague Vector', *Journal of Medical Entomology*, 29 (1992), 25-29; M. Eidson, J. P. Thilsted and O. J. Rollag, 'Clinical, Clinicopathological and Pathological Features of Plague in Cats: 119 Cases', *Journal of the American Veterinary Association*, 199 (1991), 191-97; B. G. Weniger, A. J. Warren, V. Foreseth, G. W. Shipps, T. Creelman, J. Gorton and A. M. Barnes, 'Human Bubonic Plague Transmitted by a Domestic Cat Scratch', *Journal of the American Medical Association*, 251 (1984), 927-28. In this case the fleas transmitting the disease were of the species *Diamanus montanus*. I owe these references to Dr R. E. Bolton. Gottfried, *Black Death*, p. 7.

[21] G. Twigg, *The Black Death: a Biological Reappraisal* (London, 1984), pp. 200-22; review of Twigg by B. M. S. Campbell, *Journal of Historical Geography*, 11

None of this is to deny that other diseases, along with famine, could and did contribute to high death rates. Indeed, there is a long-standing argument that it was the great famines of the early fourteenth century, and not the Black Death, which began the long demographic decline of the later middle ages. In central and northern Essex, where there was a decline of 15% in the population as a result of the famines, followed by three decades of sustained decline before the Black Death, this may have been the case, but so far this evidence has not been widely repeated elsewhere. Perhaps taking the argument to the opposite extreme, Razi, in his study of Halesowen in the west midlands, has suggested that the famines were followed by a baby-boom, the result of the earlier marriage allowed by the sudden availability of land, although his techniques of family reconstruction have been the subject of much vigorous criticism by other demographers.[22] Nonetheless, that there was sustained population decline nationally before 1349 seems to be an unproven case, whilst, even given the variable death rates at a local level, there seems to be general agreement that the first wave of the Black Death carried off somewhere between 30% and 40% of a population of somewhere between five and six millions in England and Wales.[23]

The Plague Persists: 1360 – c.1500

What has continued to surprise historians, however, is the speed with which recovery set in, after the initial panic. Holdings were filled, manorial discipline re-imposed, or even imposed, largely, it seems, because there was a pool of landless men waiting to take up vacant tenements. That

---

[22] (1985), 313-14; Smith, 'Human Resources', p. 208.

The best recent surveys of the arguments about demographic and economic decline before 1348 are B. F. Harvey, 'Introduction: the Crisis of the Early Fourteenth Century' and R. M. Smith, 'Demographic Developments in Rural England 1300-1348: a Survey', both in *Before the Black Death. Studies in the 'Crisis' of the Early Fourteenth Century*, ed. B. M. S. Campbell (Manchester, 1991), 1-77; Poos, 'Rural Population of Essex in the Later Middle Ages', pp. 521-23; Z. Razi, *Life, Marriage and Death in a Medieval Parish. Economy, Society and Demography in Halesowen, 1270-1400* (Cambridge, 1980), pp. 27-32, 47-50. A great debate rages between Smith and Poos on the one hand and Razi on the other over family reconstruction techniques; see L. R. Poos and R. M. Smith, 'Legal Windows onto Historical Populations? Recent Research on Demography and the Manorial Court Roll in Medieval England', *Law and History Review*, 2 (1984), 128-52; Z. Razi, 'The Use of Manorial Court Rolls in Demographic Analysis: a Reconsideration', *Law and History Review*, 3 (1985), 191-200; L. R. Poos and R. M. Smith, '"Shades Still on the Windows"; a Reply to Z. Razi', *Law and History Review*, 3 (1985), 409-29. It is not, however, for the faint-hearted.

[23] See below, p. 28 and n. 29, for further discussion of population totals pre- and post-plague.

take-up rate was high in the bishop of Durham's townships, at 69% of the vacancies, but less than that at Halesowen, where 82% of the vacancies were quickly filled, or Kibworth Harcourt, where new tenants were quickly found for all but four of the 44 vacant tenements.[24] Yet by 1377, when the evidence of the first poll tax becomes available, it is obvious that there had been a very substantial fall in the population indeed. This time there seems to be little doubt about the cause: namely, subsequent and successive outbreaks of the plague in 1360-62, 1367-69 and 1373-75.[25] Plague, once it had arrived, was not to go away. It remained in reservoirs of infection among the animal population, breaking out again both nationally and locally at fairly regular intervals. We know far less about death rates from these subsequent epidemics, and the evidence we do have is often distorted as a result of vast administrative upheavals, which can lead to both under- and over-recording of people and of property transfers, and by migration as people began to move more readily from one village to another, or further afield to towns.[26] But at Coltishall (Norfolk), Campbell estimates that there was a further decline in tenant numbers of 55% between 1359 and 1370, and that in the space of two decades the manor's population was reduced by 80%. Here it was not only plague which led to depopulation, but severe food shortages in 1367 and 1368 which reached famine conditions in 1369, the dearest year since 1321, and the fourth dearest in the period 1280-1405, with food prices remaining high until 1373. This seems to be an extreme case. Halesowen was also visited by the three epidemics of 1361-62, 1369 and 1375, but the death rate amongst males over 20 seems to have been only about one third of the 1349 rate, although still 4.5-6 times the average for the first half of the fourteenth century. The death rate as a whole in the period 1350-1400, at 2.04% *per annum*, was lower than in the earlier period, but that was in relation to a much depleted population as a result of the first plague. Death rates from the second and third visitations also seem to have been lower in Lancashire and Yorkshire, but in the Forest of Knaresborough they were still three or four times higher than normal.[27]

Yet aggregate death rates probably conceal a much more serious problem. The plagues of 1361-62 and 1369 were referred to specifically by chroniclers in England, France and Spain as striking at infants and young men. The *Anonimalle* and Meaux chroniclers (both from northern England)

[24] Lomas, 'Black Death in County Durham', p. 131; Razi, *Life, Marriage and Death*, p. 110; Howell, *Land, Family and Inheritance*, p. 42.

[25] Hatcher, *Plague, Population and the English Economy*, p. 57, provides the best list of 'national' epidemics.

[26] See above, p. 23, n. 15 and below, pp. 28, 37-38, 72-73.

[27] Campbell, 'Population Pressure, Inheritance and the Land Market', pp. 96-97; Razi, *Life, Marriage and Death*, pp. 124-28; Miller, 'Introduction: Land and People', pp. 3-6.

called the outbreak of 1361-62 the plague of children, and Thomas Walsingham described it as a great pestilence which affected men more than women. A London chronicler recorded that it struck particularly at young men and children and was less fatal to women. This opinion was repeated by John of Reading, the *Brut* and the *Polychronicon*, by de Chauliac in France, and as far afield as Poland. It was repeated again and again by commentators on later outbreaks of plague. Walsingham referred to the outbreak of 1369 as a pestilence of men and the larger animals, and certain outbreaks in the later 1370s and 1380s were said to have raged chiefly among children.[28] Modern medical and epidemiological research tends to confirm the gender-specific nature of plague, and Razi argues strongly that at Halesowen the later plagues took a terrible toll of children. Families were also much smaller than they had been before 1348 and it seems quite possible that in the 1360s and the late 1370s and early 1380s plague had become both gender- and age-specific. Aggregate death rates may have been lower, but the fact that young men and children were especially at risk may well have had profound consequences for the reproductive cycle. The population may barely have been able to replace itself. By 1377 the scale of the disaster becomes all too clear. Whereas at the end of the thirteenth century there may have been between 5 and 6.5 million people in England, by the time of the first poll tax there may have been as few as 2.5 to 3 million, with the best estimates probably tending towards the lower figure. The population had been almost halved.[29]

Nor was there to be any rapid recovery. By the mid-fifteenth century, it has recently been argued, there had been a further fall in the population, to about 2 to 2.5 million; only by the 1520s were there any real signs of recovery in most areas. These are again approximations, but the specific evidence from Essex confirms this pattern:

> At Great Waltham and High Easter, resident adolescent and adult males in the third quarter of the fifteenth century totalled slightly fewer than one half their average in the same community in the last quarter of the

[28] *Chronicon Monasterii de Melsa*, ed. E. A. Bond, 3 vols, Rolls Series, 43 (London, 1866-68), III, p. 159; *The Anonimalle Chronicle of St Mary's Abbey, York*, ed. V. H. Galbraith (Manchester, 1927), p. 50; Gottfried, *Black Death*, p. 130; Hatcher, *Plague, Population and the English Economy*, pp. 58-59; *L'Economie Médiévale*, ed. Contamine, p. 332; Bolton, 'Black Death', p. 7.

[29] See below, p. 37, for a further discussion of the gender-specific nature of plague; Razi, *Life, Marriage and Death*, pp. 104, 124-35, 143. There is no general agreement amongst historians as to the size of the population in either 1300 or 1348, and those given here may be regarded by some as conservative estimates. The best general discussion of the evidence, with full reference to recent work, is Smith, 'Human Resources', pp. 189-96. See also *idem*, 'Demographic Developments in Rural England, 1300-48: a Survey', 25-77 *passim*; Miller, 'Introduction: Land and People', p. 6; and above, p. 26, n. 22.

1200s.[30]

Poos warns us to be careful. Essex did not mirror all of England during this period. Yet recent studies of the north east in particular have only confirmed his argument that for most of the fifteenth century the population of both these areas achieved a remarkably stable equilibrium within its environment and local economy at broadly one half the level it had previously been, and one half the level it would reach again in the early 1600s.[31]

A Stagnant Population? Mortality and Life Expectancy

The question, of course, is why the population level should have stagnated for so long. In theory there should have been a rapid recovery. The age of marriage in peasant society, it is argued, is controlled by the availability of land. If it was easy to find a 'niche', a place within the existing socio-economic framework of the village (which in crude terms means a holding able to support the family), then marriage would take place at a relatively early age, perhaps between 18 and 20 for men and somewhat earlier for women. If the economic prospects of the marriage were also good, offering relatively abundant food, adequate housing and clothing, or the opportunity to add to income by occasional wage labour at high rates, or, indeed, of earning a comfortable living by working for others when wage rates were high (the proletarian or real wage model of marriage), then this would also encourage an earlier age of marriage. The earlier the marriage, the greater the fertility of the woman within the marriage, the more children born of it: which, in the harsh conditions of the middle ages, meant more surviving children. Such conditions certainly seem to have obtained immediately after the first plague and, it has been argued, led to the observed recovery of the population between 1350 and 1361-62 or perhaps up to 1369.[32] But long-term recovery manifestly did not occur. Instead, after 1377 there was at best equilibrium, at worst continuing slow decline, with little sign of recovery before 1460.

As ever, there is no easy answer to the question and much disagreement amongst historians. The most obvious and most persistent argument is that subsequent outbreaks of plague, both nationally and

---

[30]   Poos, A Rural Society, pp. 109-10.

[31]   A. J. Pollard, North-Eastern England during the Wars of the Roses. Lay Society, War, and Politics 1450-1500 (Oxford, 1988), p. 48; R. Lomas, North East England in the Middle Ages (Edinburgh, 1992), p. 160. P. J. P. Goldberg suggests that the population recovery was beginning in York and the West Riding from about the 1460s: 'Mortality and Economic Change in the Diocese of York, 1390-1514', Northern History 24 (1988), 38-55, pp. 52-53.

[32]   Poos, A Rural Society, pp. 141-43; Howell, Land, Family and Inheritance, p. 57; Razi, Life, Marriage and Death, pp. 63, 110-11; and see Bolton, Medieval English Economy, pp. 61-64, for a general discussion of this problem.

locally, acted as a constant brake on the recovery which might otherwise have occurred. It is reasonably certain that in little more than a century there were severe outbreaks of plague at a national and local level, in 1379-83, 1389-93, 1400, 1405-07, 1413, 1420, 1427, 1433-34, 1438-39, 1457-58, 1463-64, 1467, 1471, 1479-80 and 1485. Hatcher has calculated, from his study of the monks at Christ Church, Canterbury, that between 1395 and 1505 the crude death rate rose above the crisis level of 40 per 1000 on 27 occasions, 17 times between 1375 and 1450 and ten times after 1450. Before 1450 there were more frequent, but by the standards of the day relatively moderate, surges in the death rates; in the latter period, the peaks were less frequent, but distinctly more sharp, with much higher death rates. Disease was less frequent, then, but more deadly, and at the same time there seems to have been a significant fall in life expectancy. At the age of 20 members of the group or 'cohort' of monks that entered the monastery between 1445 and 1475 had a life expectancy (expressed as e_{20}) eight years less than that of their predecessors who had entered between 1405 and 1430. At age 25 (e_{25}) it was six years less. The seasonal distribution of mortality also seems to have shifted significantly into late summer and early autumn peaks, typical of outbreaks of bubonic plague.[33] This pattern of mortality has been amply confirmed by Harvey's recent study of the monks of Westminster Abbey. There were 13 crisis years between 1399 and 1528, but no fewer than five of these fell in the decade 1499-1508. The peaks of mortality in these years, in the summer and autumn, again suggest that bubonic plague was the main cause of death, although the monks at Westminster were affected as much as those at Canterbury by enteric diseases, the 'sweating sickness' and, interestingly, by tuberculosis. Monks entering the monastery in the first half of the fifteenth century, like those at Canterbury, also lived longer than their successors, since there was a sharp decline in life expectancy. Between 1475 and 1499 e_{20} was some 10 or 11 years lower than it had been for the cohorts of monks professed between 1395 and 1419. It was also the younger monks who suffered most severely during the crisis years. If the patterns discerned in both monasteries were repeated nationally, then both Hatcher and Harvey seem agreed that it would have taken quite exceptional increases in the fertility rates to compensate for them.[34]

Monks, of course, cannot provide us with entirely reliable evidence on which to base national demographic projections. The size of the sample

---

[33] Hatcher, *Plague, Population and the English Economy*, p. 57; *idem*, 'Mortality in the Fifteenth Century', pp. 27-29.

[34] B. F. Harvey, *Living and Dying in the Middle Ages* (Oxford, 1993), pp. 122-29, 142-45. Hatcher is more cautious, but the idea that a massive increase in the fertility schedule would have been needed to offset continuing high mortality is surely implicit in his arguments in *Plague, Population and the English Economy*, pp. 55, 57, 61, 72 and in 'Mortality in the Fifteenth Century', p. 19.

itself is very small, with the total population under observation at Westminster Abbey amounting to only 328 monks for the whole period and that at Christ Church, Canterbury, to some 414. Moreover, in spite of the fact that every feature of monastic life contained health hazards (from the typhus transmitted in the communal dormitories by lice bred in straw mattresses changed only once a year to enteric disease caused by often 'fragile' sanitary arrangements), monks were undoubtedly better fed and housed than the majority of the population. Yet late-medieval peaks in mortality at Christ Church seem to have mirrored those within the city of Canterbury itself (and by implication within Kent generally), and at Westminster Abbey those in the vill of Westminster, although the crisis years there were not the same as those within the plague-ridden city of London. Therefore, both studies appear to provide us with substantial evidence of frequent outbreaks of disease, with lower death rates in the first half of the fifteenth century, less frequent but more virulent outbreaks in its latter part, and falling life expectancy, which would explain why there was no recovery before the mid-century and even prolonged stagnation thereafter.[35] Such a 'regular' pattern is not immediately observable elsewhere. But local and regional studies, which have shown a considerable degree of variation in the frequency of outbreak and the virulence of epidemic disease, have largely modified rather than confounded Dr Hatcher's general thesis that continued high levels of mortality from plague and other diseases acted as a brake on recovery. Two such studies are those of Colchester in Essex and of the 28 rural townships of the bishop of Durham in the north east. High mortality affected Colchester in 1369, 1375, 1380, 1384 and 1386, and in the four years between autumn 1390 and autumn 1394. None of the later peaks of mortality approached the severity of those during the earlier crises of 1348-49 and 1361, but Colchester could only maintain its population by in-migration. There were further outbreaks in 1412-13, 1420-21, and probably in 1426-27, 1433-34 and 1439, but then a period of respite until the exceptionally severe crises of the early 1460s. There was further severe loss of population during Henry VII's reign, at the same time as plague crises at Bury St Edmunds, where there were epidemics in 1499-1500 and another in 1509. From this, Britnell concludes that from 1348 to about 1415 epidemics were so rapidly followed by recovery that the population of Colchester actually grew; that between 1415 and 1450 recovery was barely sufficient to maintain steady numbers; but that after 1450 recovery from epidemics was not sufficient to prevent the population from declining.[36]

---

[35] Hatcher, 'Mortality in the Fifteenth Century', pp. 25, 35-36; Harvey, *Living and Dying*, pp. 129-42.

[36] R. H. Britnell, *Growth and Decline in Colchester, 1300-1525* (Cambridge, 1986), chapters 6 and 13, *passim*, and pp. 159-60, 262-3; Gottfried, *Bury St Edmunds*

Plague, it is often argued, had become an urban disease by the fifteenth century, and so the evidence from Colchester ought not to be projected nationally, any more than that of the mortality rates and life expectancy of monks. But Lomas's recent work on the north east suggests strongly that such projections can properly be made. On the bishop of Durham's 28 townships, largely in Teesdale, there were significant increases in property transfers after the death of customary tenants in 1375, 1385, 1389, and 1398, but of these, only 1385 and 1398 are known plague years in the north. Similar surges in tenancy changes can be seen in 1413, 1429-30, 1437-38, 1444, 1452 and 1480, and of these only 1413, 1437-38 and 1468-69 coincided with national outbreaks of plague. 1437-38 were also years of devastating famine in the north, which Pollard has argued was probably more important than the plague in its long-term consequences and began an economic and political divide between north and south which was to last well into the early modern period. All the available evidence suggests that on the bishop of Durham's estates the population in 1500 was only half what it had been in 1348.[37]

Clearly, in the rural north east, it was a combination of national and local epidemics which prevented population recovery, but they did not always precisely coincide with those which ravaged the south. The epidemic of 1479 was as severe in the north east as elsewhere, but the region seems to have escaped the 'flux' or dysentery in the hot summer of 1473 which was exceptionally severe in East Anglia; and the 'sweating sicknesses' of 1485 and 1489 do not seem to have been notably deadly in the diocese of York. The outbreak of plague at Newcastle in 1432, which carried off substantial numbers of citizens, seems to have been purely localised, and whilst East Anglia was relatively free from disease between 1466 and 1468, death rates in the diocese of York seem to have peaked in the same period. A similar phenomenon of national and local outbreaks of plague has been noted in the west midlands, and whilst Poos's study of Essex has not entirely confirmed Hatcher's evidence of declining life expectancy, it does show how miserable the prospects were. At the age of 12 (e_{12}) for both sexes it was about a further 40 years, and at birth (e_0) no more than 32-34 years, significantly lower than that for the early modern period.[38]

and the Urban Crisis, p. 64.

[37] Lomas, 'Black Death in County Durham', pp. 137-39; *idem, North East England during the Middle Ages*, p. 160.

[38] Pollard, *North-Eastern England during the Wars of the Roses*, p. 48; R. S. Gottfried, *Epidemic Disease in Fifteenth Century England: The Medical Response and Demographic Consequences* (New Brunswick, NJ, 1978), pp. 144-49; Goldberg, 'Mortality and Economic Change in the Diocese of York', p. 47; Dyer, *Lords and Peasants in a Changing Society*, pp. 223-25; Poos, *A Rural Society*, pp. 118-20.

It might seem, then, that our understanding of the effects of plague has been considerably modified by new evidence and new interpretations. Increasing stress has been laid on the importance of regional outbreaks in both town and countryside, and on the consequences of enzoötic plague resulting from local reservoirs of infection. Investigation has begun into death rates from other diseases, notably tuberculosis (where more work is needed to follow up Hatcher's significant findings), dysentery (flux), and malaria in coastal districts.[39] Above all, for the north east, it is now argued that the consequences of famine were as important as those of plague in causing economic decline. Yet the argument still centres for the most part on mortality, on the simple excess of deaths over births. To take Scarborough as an example: between 1414 and 1442 deaths in the years of pestilence and other epidemics more than offset the tendency in normal years for births to exceed deaths. Births fluctuated between 30 and 68 *per annum*, but in the crisis years of 1438-39 death rose from an average 30 *per annum* to 161.[40] The result was continuing population decline caused by periodic epidemics, with no real signs of recovery before the early sixteenth century. But the significant problem remains. For the majority of the population, the rural dwellers, there were unparalleled opportunities for early marriage, and thus for more children to be born of the marriage and survive. So, in spite of recurrent outbreaks of epidemic disease, the population ought at least to have replaced itself after the devastation of 1348-75, at best to have recovered, and even to have grown slightly, not perhaps to the levels of 1300 but certainly above those of 1086. It did not; and the question remains, why? Here it is necessary, as Dr Goldberg has suggested to us, to move away from the relentless pursuit of 'national' epidemics and trends in mortality to a fuller appreciation of the interplay of all demographic variables. In so doing, recent writers have raised a series of tantalising possible explanations for the failure of the population to recover.[41] In reviewing these explanations, it must be stressed that at this stage they are still only possibilities, and that they propose variables which worked with the mortality and with each other to produce the stagnant population profile of the fifteenth century.

[39]   Hatcher, 'Mortality in the Fifteenth Century', pp. 29-31; Harvey was unable to confirm Hatcher's findings, given the nature of the evidence, but discusses the likelihood of tuberculosis at Westminster Abbey, *Living and Dying*, pp. 129-35; P. Franklin, 'Malaria in Medieval Gloucestershire: an Essay in Epidemiology', *Transactions of the Bristol and Gloucestershire Archaeological Society* 101 (1983), 111-22, *passim*; J. H. Bayliss, 'Epidemiological Considerations of the History of Indigenous Malaria in Britain', *Endeavour* 9 (1985), 191-97, pp. 191-92.

[40]   Pollard, *North-Eastern England during the Wars of the Roses*, pp. 47-8.

[41]   Goldberg, 'Mortality and Economic Change in the Diocese of York', p. 55.

Age and Sex Structures: Marriage and Fertility

The first possibility is that there was an ageing population. It has already been noted that plague was age-specific, striking particularly at the young. Russell and Heillener argue that recurrent outbreaks of plague had both short- and long-term consequences, the former preventing recovery, the latter altering the age structure of the population, thus depressing birth rates in succeeding decades. In his study of life expectancy, marriage and death rates in the large west midland parish of Halesowen, Razi concluded that after 1350 the plague did indeed alter the age structure. It significantly depressed birth rates, so that by the end of the fourteenth century the population of the parish was overwhelmed by the middle aged and elderly and doomed to a long period of stagnation and decline. The methodology of this study has been much criticised and the results await repetition elsewhere, but they need to be considered, especially in the light of what is now being said about age of marriage, numbers of children, and family size generally.[42] However, the life expectancy figures produced for the monks of Christ Church, Canterbury, and Westminster raise an even more intriguing question. If life expectancy did deteriorate as rapidly as Hatcher and Harvey suggest, and if their calculations can be projected across the late medieval population generally, then fertility rates would have to have been some 50% higher than they were in the late Stuart period for England to have achieved even zero population growth. This was highly unlikely if the population was quite as middle aged and elderly as Razi suggests. But Poos's calculations for the rural population of Essex do not entirely confirm Hatcher's findings. They do show that life expectancy was lower than in late sixteenth- and early seventeenth-century England, but not significantly lower, and he argues that in the later period the English population did begin to replace itself and even grow again, after the disasters of the late middle ages. His conclusion is that if unfavourable mortality was not altogether of a wholly different order from that which early modern England expected at times, then it was unlikely to have been the entire reason for the prolonged late medieval depression in population. Rather, the fertility side of the equation demands our attention.[43]

[42] J. C. Russell, *British Medieval Population* (Albuquerque, 1948), pp. 188, 230-31, 260-70, 375-77; K. Heillener, 'The Population of Europe from the Black Death to the Eve of the Vital Revolution', *The Cambridge Economic History of Europe, IV: The Economy of Expanding Europe in the Sixteenth and Seventeenth Centuries*, ed. E. Rich and C. H. Wilson (Cambridge, 1967), 1-95, pp. 10-11; Razi, *Life, Marriage and Death*, pp. 114-15, 150-51, but see above, p. 26, n. 22 for criticisms of this study; Hatcher, *Plague, Population and the English Economy*, pp. 61-62.
[43] Poos, *A Rural Society*, pp. 119-20; *ibid.*, pp. 111-14.

The problem is that direct evidence for fertility is so scarce as to be almost non-existent. As will be seen, the only reasonably convincing figures are those produced by Poos himself, for one large Essex parish. But there is a series of observable phenomena which, taken together, and only if taken together, help to establish a thesis that high death rates were paralleled by birth rates sufficient only to maintain the low population levels caused initially by the plague.[44] The first of these is the lack of children to survive their parents and grow to maturity. The later fourteenth and fifteenth centuries were an age when fewer children were produced of marriages, and sometimes no children at all. Campbell noted that at Coltishall (Norfolk) the replacement rate, in this case the ratio of inheriting sons to deceased fathers, which had stood at 1.2 between 1280 and 1348, fell to 0.56 between 1351 and 1375, rising only slightly to 0.69 in 1376-1400. These figures were roughly comparable to replacement ratios at Halesowen where the result was a low survival rate for peasant families, with only 24% of those noted in the court rolls surviving from 1410 to the 1490s, compared with 60% between 1310 and the 1390s. In part this was due to migration, but it also seems to have been the result of there being no direct male heir to take over the holding, or no heir at all.[45] This lack of male heirs in the fifteenth century has been widely noted, and perhaps three other examples will suffice. On seven manors in southern England, below a line stretching from the Wash to the Thames valley, in Suffolk, Buckinghamshire, Hampshire, Norfolk and central Essex, the demographic conditions which prevailed in the late fourteenth and early fifteenth centuries made it highly likely that men would not have had male offspring alive at their own deaths, to serve as heirs. Over 50% of men would have been without surviving sons and 30% of men would have been without surviving sons or daughters. Langridge has noted a similar pattern at Chartham in Kent, and Razi at Halesowen, although here again migration has to be taken into account.[46] Secondly, in a fascinating study, Payling has argued vigorously and convincingly that the same pattern obtained in noble and gentle landed society. From the reign of Henry III to the Black Death 72% of male tenants-in-chief left sons as heirs, 10% daughters or the issue of daughters and 18% no heirs at all, reflecting the sustained population growth in that

---

[44] See below, pp. 39-40.

[45] Campbell, 'Population Pressure, Inheritance and the Land Market', pp. 98-99; Z. Razi, 'The Myth of the Immutable English Family', *Past and Present* 140 (1993), 3-44, pp. 28-33.

[46] R. M. Smith, 'Coping with Uncertainty: Women's Tenure of Customary Land in England *c.*1370-1430', in *Enterprise and Individuals in Fifteenth-Century England*, ed. J. Kermode (Stroud, 1991), 43-67, pp. 46-47; A. M. Langridge, 'The Population of Chartham from 1086 to 1600', *Archaeologia Cantiana* 101 (1984), 217-44, p. 231; Razi, 'The Myth of the Immutable English Family', pp. 31, 37, 39-41.

period. Between 1348 and 1400 this was dramatically reversed, with only 57% leaving sons as heirs, 15% leaving daughters and 29% leaving no heirs at all, and it was not until after 1450 that the pattern reverted to that which had obtained before 1348.[47] Finally, in the towns the situation was no better. Kowaleski's study of Exeter, Holt's of Gloucester and Kermode's of York, Beverley and Hull have all confirmed Thrupp's long-stated observations on the merchant class of medieval London, that few families survived beyond one or two generations. Either there were no male heirs, or no heirs at all.[48]

These 'general' figures suggest, first and most obviously, that the size of families must have fallen compared with the period before the Black Death; and secondly that there would have been a distinct imbalance between males and females in the population. Both propositions have been confirmed by recent research. In three very different areas of rural England, the north east and the east and west midlands, family sizes seem to have shrunk. In the north east they fluctuated between just under four and just over five, whilst at Kibworth Harcourt (east midlands) they fell from 4.84 in 1280 to 3.72 in 1379 (although here again Howell suggests that migration must be taken into account as a factor controlling household size). At Halesowen (west midlands) the average was 2.8 children per household before the plague but 2.1 in the 1380s and 1390s, with no apparent recovery in the fifteenth century.[49] Razi also argues that chiefly as a result of migration, rather than changes in replacement or fertility rates, the old bond between land and family was broken and that the extended familial system which had obtained before the plague broke down, to be replaced by the small nuclear family often held to be typical of early modern rather than late medieval England.[50] If that were the case, then both the demographic and the socio-economic implications are of great importance. But equally important are the data recently produced from poll tax returns

[47] S. J. Payling, 'Social Mobility, Demographic Change, and Landed Society in Late Medieval England', *Economic History Review*, 2nd series, 45 (1992), 51-73, pp. 52-56.

[48] M. Kowaleski, 'The Commercial Dominance of a Medieval Provincial Oligarchy: Exeter in the Late Fourteenth Century', *Medieval Studies* 46 (1984), 355-84, pp. 378-79; R. Holt, 'Gloucester in the Century after the Black Death', *Transactions of the Bristol and Gloucester Archaeological Society* 103 (1985), 149-61, pp. 154-55; J. Kermode, 'Merchants, Overseas Trade and Urban Decline: York, Beverley and Hull c.1380-1500', *Northern History* 23 (1987), 51-73, p. 68; S. Thrupp, *The Merchant Class of Medieval London* (Chicago, 1948), pp. 198-206.

[49] Pollard, *North-Eastern England during the Wars of the Roses*, p. 46; Howell, *Land, Family and Inheritance*, p. 235; Razi, *Life, Marriage and Death*, p. 143; see also Dyer, *Lords and Peasants in a Changing Society*, pp. 232-34.

[50] Razi, 'The Myth of the Immutable English Family', pp. 31, 37, 39-41, 42-43; and see below, p. 51, 53-55, for further discussion of this issue.

on male:female ratios within society. Goldberg has calculated adult sex ratios (the number of males to 100 females), of 85.7 for Carlisle, 91.9 for Colchester and 86.1 for Hull in 1377; of 92.9 for Sheffield and 93.4 for Lynn in 1379; and of 85.6 for Shrewsbury in 1381. Poos has also calculated a ratio of 93.4 for rural Essex in 1381. The figures for urban populations contrast sharply with the male:female ratio of 108:100 calculated by Smith for other rural areas at about the same time, but the reason for this may be the higher degree of female migration from town to countryside, leaving rural areas markedly short of young females.[51]

Why do there appear to have been more females than males in late medieval society, and what might be the demographic implications? The answer to the first of those questions seems to be purely medical, in that young males seem to be the age group most susceptible to the plague. The chronicles noted this and modern medical and epidemiological research has tended to confirm their observations. During the severe outbreak of plague at Sydney (Australia) in 1900, more males than females contracted the disease simply because it struck most heavily in the wharf and business districts, areas of high male employment. Even so, the case mortality rate among males was significantly greater than the general rate, at 35.56 compared to 33.99, and deaths among teenage and young adult males between the ages of 13 and 27 were particularly high. Of those who caught the plague in Sydney, it was clearly the young males who suffered most. In the United States in the 1980s the pattern of infection itself is even clearer: more male children and young adults catch the disease than females, the ratio being 2:1.[52]

The cumulative evidence does therefore suggest that there was a shortage of males, and particularly of young males, in fifteenth-century England. From this it might be argued that fewer males must have meant fewer marriages and, per se, fewer children. But the causal relationship does not seem to have been as straightforward as that. It is possible that the shortage of males provided unusual and perhaps unique opportunities for female labourers in fifteenth-century England, both as live-in servants (who had to remain unmarried) and in commercial and industrial occupations. This seems to have been especially true in urban society and may have caused female migration to towns in search of employment and the independence, both financial and marital, which it brought. Young women

[51]   P. J. P. Goldberg, 'Urban Identity and the Poll Taxes of 1377, 1379, and 1381', *Economic History Review*, 2nd series, 43 (1990), 194-216, pp. 198-201; Poos, *A Rural Society*, p. 154; Goldberg, 'Urban Identity', pp. 212-13, for information from Dr R. M. Smith.

[52]   P. Curson and K. McCracken, *Plague in Sydney: the Anatomy of an Epidemic* (Kensington, New South Wales, 1989), pp. 131-33, Figure 5.9 and Table 5.3; T. Butler, 'The Black Death Past and Present, I, Plague in the 1980s', *Transactions of the Royal Society of Tropical Medicine* 83 (1989), 458-60, p. 459.

could postpone marriage and even seek partners of their own rather than accept those imposed by their parents – something which itself may have led to a later age of marriage. The deposition evidence from Yorkshire towns suggests that in the fifteenth century marriage was regularly delayed until the couples were in their mid to late twenties, perhaps as much as a decade later than before the plague. In Essex, mobility was at its most marked among the rural population in the late teens and early twenties. Those who stayed where they were and worked the land, the agriculturalists, married earlier, but significant numbers of labourers and rural craftsmen, perhaps up to half the population in 1381, married much later, if at all. Marriage rates hovered around 60%, strikingly similar to those in the early modern period and in what has been called the 'north European marriage pattern', a model which postulates later marriage, or no marriage at all, fewer children, and more live-in servants to help with domestic and other work previously performed by the younger members of the family.[53]

Successive studies have noted this phenomenon of later marriage or of no marriage at all. At Kibworth Harcourt the age of marriage, based on a limited sample of landholders between 1349 and 1363 and a much larger one in the mid-fifteenth century, ranged from 22.8 to 27.9 years (with neither sample supporting the argument that men regularly married between the ages of 16 and 25). Penn and Dyer, in their important discussion of wages and earnings in later medieval England, speculate interestingly on why the increased earning capacity of young people did not encourage them to marry earlier and thus produce larger families (the proletarian or real wage model of marriage), but conclude, firmly, that they did not do so. Campbell draws parallels between late medieval Coltishall and early modern Colyton to argue that both demonstrated patterns of later and less frequent marriage, whilst Miller very tentatively suggests that there may have been deliberate delay in marriage or indeed deliberate limitation on fertility within marriage by the forms of contraception known to have been practised in the middle ages.[54]

---

[53]   Goldberg, 'Mortality and Economic Change in the Diocese of York', p. 51; *idem*, 'Female Labour, Service and Marriage in the Late Medieval Urban North', *Northern History* 22 (1986), 18-38, p. 25; Poos, *A Rural Society*, pp. 131-43, 154, 170, 179; M. Kowaleski, 'The History of Urban Families in Medieval England', *Journal of Medieval History* 14 (1988), 47-63, pp. 53-55; for a discussion of the European marriage pattern see Smith, 'Human Resources', pp. 207-08, 210-11 and below, pp. 72-75.

[54]   Howell, *Land, Family and Inheritance*, p. 225; S. A. C. Penn and C. Dyer, 'Wages and Earnings in Late Medieval England: Evidence from the Enforcement of the Labour Laws', *Economic History Review*, 2nd series, 43 (1990), 356-76, pp. 374-75; Campbell, 'Population Pressure, Inheritance and the Land Market', p. 128; Miller, 'Introduction: Land and People', p. 8;

Given this albeit tentative evidence for a fall in reproductive rates, and taking with it the other evidence for death rates, life expectancy and the nature of the family, nuclear rather than extended, it is possible to advance a general explanation for the continuing low population levels of the fifteenth century by drawing comparisons with the early modern period. The demographic phenomena correspond most nearly to those to be found in the late seventeenth century, when population was stagnant. So, it is argued, they would have produced a similar population profile in the fifteenth century, and for the same reasons, most notably the fall in fertility caused by late marriage.[55] These are arguments from generalities rather than specifics and not all medieval historians are happy to accept such tempting comparisons with the early modern period. Yet the one specific piece of evidence for fertility certainly confirms that such speculations are worth considering. It comes from the churching records for the large parish of Walden in Essex explored by Poos. Churching was a ceremony of purification undertaken by women after childbirth, usually within one month, for which the parish charged a fee collected by the churchwardens, usually one penny, but sometimes a halfpenny or twopence. The sums collected cannot therefore be multiplied to give the precise numbers of women churched *per annum*, but they can be used to calculate a rough birth rate per 1000, given that Walden had a population of somewhere between 1400 and 1500. This birth rate equalled about 30 per 1000 *per annum*, close to the rate that Schofield and Wrigley have calculated nationally, from much better evidence, for the late seventeenth and early eighteenth centuries, a period when birth and death rates were in rough equilibrium. So, Poos argues, a combination of life expectancy at birth (due to high mortality) of about 32 years, plus fertility levels no higher than those which England possessed in the late seventeenth century, meant zero population growth in the fifteenth century.[56]

Essex was a relatively densely populated county, with probably a more prosperous and more mobile society than many if not most other areas of England. But it does offer the tantalising evidence, which links the general

Hatcher, *Plague, Population and the English Economy*, pp. 55-56; P. P. A. Biller, 'Birth Control in the West in the Thirteenth and Early Fourteenth Centuries', *Past and Present* 94 (1982), 3-26; J. Riddle, 'Oral Contraceptives and Early-Term Abortificants during Classical Antiquity and the Middle Ages', *Past and Present* 132 (1991), 3-32; *idem, Contraception and Abortion from the Ancient World to the Renaissance* (Cambridge, 1992), pp. 2-19 and chapters 2 and 13, *passim*; A. McLaren, *A History of Contraception from Antiquity to the Present Day* (Oxford, 1992), pp. 119-28.
[55] Poos, *A Rural Society*, chapters 5 and 6, *passim*, but particularly his conclusions, pp. 290-91; Smith, 'Human Resources', p. 207; Campbell, 'Population Pressure, Inheritance and the Land Market', p. 128.
[56] Poos, *A Rural Society*, pp. 121-29.

to the specific, to suggest that whilst we should leave mortality at the centre of the debate, we should also take into account the other variables themselves resulting from the plague. Of these, the most important was probably the shift in the fertility schedule due either to later marriage or to no marriage at all or to the avoidance of difficult and dangerous childbirth in an age when infant mortality rates were so high and when there were new opportunities for female independence.[57] The debate will certainly continue; as will that on when recovery began or, indeed, whether there was any recovery in the fifteenth century at all. On the one hand, Goldberg argues that population recovery had begun in the diocese of York by the 1460s as a result of increasing fertility rates; yet Pollard, on the other, sees few grounds for supposing that the population in the north east began to grow again much before the early sixteenth century and cautions historians against seeking too early a date for its recovery there.[58] The evidence is not conclusive, the recovery uncertain, but there are few if any willing to argue that there were as many people in England in 1600 as there had been in 1300.[59]

Alternative Explanations: The 'Bullion Famine', War and Weather

The Black Death had apparently done its best, or its worst. Or had it? In the same way that there has been a re-evaluation of the role of other diseases in the mortality schedule, and of famine, in causing sharp economic distress in the north east, so other ingredients still have to be added to the recipe for the cause of structural change, or of depression, in the fifteenth century. The three most notable are: fluctuations in the money supply; war and its costs; and the possible consequences of climatic change.

As to the first, it has been argued that the main determinant of the supposed economic depression of the later middle ages was what is known as the great European bullion famine, caused by the drain of gold and particularly silver to the Near East and by the failure of European mines and the closure of European mints. The volume of English currency in circulation sank from perhaps £1.5 million in 1300 to £639,000 in 1417. English mint output reached its nadir in 1448 and then remained low until the late 1460s, when some £700,000 of coin, gold and silver, was in circulation after the recoinage of 1464-71. In 1445 a commons' petition spoke of the lack of small change in circulation which particularly affected the poor, and the crown responded by ordering the striking of more

---

[57]   See below, pp. 70-77.

[58]   Goldberg, 'Mortality and Economic Change in the Diocese of York', p. 53; Pollard, *North-Eastern England during the Wars of the Roses*, p. 48; Hatcher, *Plague, Population and the English Economy*, pp. 63-67.

[59]   Smith, 'Human Resources', pp. 190-91; Hatcher, *Plague, Population and the English Economy*, figure 2, p. 71; and see above, p. 28, n. 29.

halfpennies and farthings, though apparently with little effect. With less money in circulation there would be fewer buyers and sellers. Demand would fall, markets stagnate, manufacturing decline; there would be general economic malaise.[60]

The other consequence of a shortage of bullion would be a sharp rise in its value and therefore in the value of the silver (or gold) content of each coin. A silver penny would be 'worth' more, because it would buy more, and prices would respond to the increased value of the coinage by falling.[61] To take two hypothetical examples, one penny might buy a quarter of grain, but if the value of the penny doubled because of the change in the intrinsic worth of its silver content, then it would buy two quarters of grain, and the price per quarter would fall from one penny to a halfpenny. The rent of a piece of land which had stood at one shilling *per annum* would similarly fall to sixpence. Those who lived by the sale of produce or from rents would find their incomes severely depressed. They would have less to spend, and so manufacturers would suffer, as would towns which lived by trade and industry. The combined result both of shortage of coin and of an increase in its value would thus be a quite vicious downspiral of deflation unless ways could be found to ease the shortage of money. Increased use of credit transactions might be one answer. Money was always in short supply in the English countryside and systems of both credit and barter and payments of rent in kind were always important, but their importance may possibly have increased during the bullion famines of the mid-fifteenth century.[62] Yet one historian has recently argued that in international trade

[60]   J. Day, 'The Great Bullion Famine', *passim*; the best general accounts of this debate are Spufford, *Money and its Use*, chapter 15, *passim* and *L'Economie Médiévale*, ed. Contamine, chapter 8, *passim*, and particularly pp. 314-18; M. Mate, 'The Economic and Social Roots of Popular Rebellion: Sussex in 1450-1451', *Economic History Review*, 2nd series, 45 (1992), 661-76, p. 662; P. Nightingale, 'Money Contraction and Mercantile Credit in Later Medieval England', *Economic History Review*, 2nd series, 43 (1990), 560-75, pp. 561-62; Britnell, *Commercialisation of English Society*, pp. 179-81 and esp. Table 5; *Rotuli Parliamentorum*, 6 vols (London, 1783), V, pp. 108-09; W. Robinson, 'Money, Population and Economic Change in Later Medieval Europe', *Economic History Review*, 2nd series, 12 (1959-60), 63-76, *passim*, and M. M. Postan, 'Note', *ibid.*, pp. 77-82.

[61]   Nightingale, 'Money Contraction and Credit in Later Medieval England', p. 561, Table 1, illustrates this point; see also J. L. Bolton, 'Inflation, Economics and Politics in Thirteenth-Century England', in *Thirteenth Century England*, IV, ed. P. R. Coss and S. D. Lloyd (Woodbridge, 1992), p. 4, n. 12.

[62]   C. Dyer, 'The Consumer and the Market in the Later Middle Ages', p. 322; Britnell, *Commercialisation of English Society*, pp. 183-84; R. H. Britnell, 'The Pastons and their Norfolk', *Agricultural History Review* 36 (1988), 132-44, pp. 134, 137-39; C. E. Moreton, *The Townshends and their World. Gentry, Law and Land in Norfolk c.1450-1551* (Oxford, 1992), p. 147.

the availability of credit itself expanded and contracted in line with the supply of new bullion brought to the mint by overseas trade. When the supply was reduced, then the extent to which credit could finance industrial or commercial expansion was dependent on the extent to which merchants could mobilise cash from other resources. If they could or would not do so, for fear of undermining their own financial probity, then credit evaporated. Credit could not take the place of coin for long and thus offset what had become a crippling shortage of bullion by the mid-fifteenth century, the result being a marked fall in both imports and exports.[63]

What applied to overseas trade should also have applied to the economy generally. Professor Mate has noted, for instance, increased use of barter and payment by goods and services rather than by money in mid-fifteenth century Sussex, and there is some very limited evidence of the use of tokens as alternative money to overcome the shortage of coin.[64] So, it is argued, the stagnation of the English economy by the mid-fifteenth century was as much, if not more, the result of monetary deflation consequent upon the shortage of bullion and therefore of coin, as of depopulation caused by plague. Such arguments cannot be ignored, but the supposed bullion famine may have aggravated, rather than caused, the illness; and there are in any case good reasons for treating the monetary arguments with some caution. If prices fell, then why did wages not move with them? Monetarists might argue that the labour shortage would keep them artificially high, but the theory either works as a whole or does not work at all. There must also be considerable doubts as to whether the amount of coin per head in circulation did fall. Britnell argues, tentatively, that the ratio per head rose from between 3s. and 4s. in 1324 to 6s. in 1467.[65] There were only half the people in England in 1450 that there had been in 1300, but probably more than half the amount of coin in circulation. This may explain why, in spite of vociferous complaints about the lack of money, there were no major debasements of the coinage in fifteenth-century England to produce 'white money' (coins with a markedly lower silver content) or 'black money' or billon (copper coins with a very

[63] Nightingale, 'Money Contraction and Credit in Later Medieval England', p. 574; Britnell, *Commercialisation of English Society*, p. 181; but Kermode, 'Merchants, Overseas Trade and Urban Decline', pp. 63ff, stresses the importance of other variables, including plague, in the contraction of credit.

[64] Mate, 'Economic and Social Roots of Popular Rebellion', p. 662; M. K. McIntosh, *Autonomy and Community: The Royal Manor of Havering, 1200-1500* (Cambridge, 1986), pp. 167-70; Dyer, 'The Consumer and the Market', p. 322; Britnell, *Commercialisation of English Society*, p. 181, but noting that they were more common in the late 14th than in the 15th century.

[65] Britnell, *Commercialisation of English Society*, pp. 184-85; he also argues that the relationship between declining circulation and declining prices was weak, p. 182.

low silver content indeed), nor the widespread use of tokens or jettons as substitute coins as there was on the continent.[66] As to arguments about the contraction of credit, it must be pointed out that international trade comprised only a small (albeit valuable) sector of the economy generally, and that problems faced by English merchants may well have been the result as much of structural weaknesses in the English money market as of lack of coin. More importantly, we simply have no idea of the total value of credit – rural, urban, mercantile – either in the mid-fifteenth or in the thirteenth century. Comparisons are impossible. We do not know if it rose or contracted in line with the money supply or with the population. Finally, what really mattered was not whether there was more or less money in circulation but whether the majority of the population was better or worse off – and that remains to be seen.

Nor can war be seen as imposing oppressive burdens on the English population through heavy taxation as it had in the late thirteenth and fourteenth centuries. Professor Ormrod demonstrates conclusively that the great economic and social upheavals which threatened between 1348 and 1381, partly as a result of demands for war, were healed in the fifteenth century. Not even Henry V's exactions reached those of the 1370s, fifteenths and tenths became less frequent and the principle that assessment was linked to economic capacity to pay was restored. This may have posed problems for government, but not for society in general.[67] Occasional attacks on the south coast and in the north may have caused considerable local destruction, but recovery, especially in the north east, seems to have been rapid. Fear of Scottish raids probably caused more dislocation than the raids themselves. It may be that we have underestimated the long-term consequences of Glyndwr's rebellion in the Marches of Wales and of the Wars of the Roses for some major towns, and there can be little doubt that both war and the diplomacy of the Hundred Years War on occasion severely affected international trade. But, as with the supposed shortage of coin, the case for warfare as a contributory cause of general economic decline remains unproven.[68]

---

[66]   Spufford, *Money and its Use*, pp. 323-36, and esp. p. 331.

[67]   J. R. Maddicott, *The English Peasantry and the Demands of the Crown, 1294-1341*, *Past and Present Supplement*, no. 1 (1975), *passim*; below, pp. 173-75.

[68]   M. Mate, 'Economic and Social Roots of Popular Rebellion', p. 672; Pollard, *North-Eastern England during the Wars of the Roses*, pp. 44-46; J. A. Tuck, 'War and Society in the Medieval North', *Northern History* 21 (1985), 32-52, pp. 34, 42-43; D. M. Palliser, 'Urban Decay Revisited' in *Towns and Townspeople in the Fifteenth Century*, ed. J. A. F. Thomson (Gloucester, 1988), 1-21, p. 6; J. A. Tuck, 'The Northern Borders' in *The Agrarian History of England and Wales*, III, 34-41, pp. 36-38; D. H. Owen, 'Wales and the Marches', *ibid.*, 92-106, pp. 99ff.; Bolton, *The Medieval English Economy*, pp. 259, 292-94.

There remains, as ever, the weather. It is a commonplace that the European climate became wetter and colder in the later middle ages, heralding a supposed mini-ice age.[69] It was the three wet summers from 1438 to 1440 that brought harvest failure and famine to England, and especially in the north, with the lasting consequences there that Professor Pollard has described. That was mainly a northern crisis (although both London and Sussex were affected by food shortages), yet pastoral farming generally seems to have been affected by the wetter weather of the fifteenth century.[70] So were some coastal areas and lands along estuaries. The main reason for the desertion of the village of Eske in Humberside was the deterioration in climate and drainage which reduced the viability of the settlement, and Dr Bailey has drawn our attention to the severity of storms, and the consequences, in the late thirteenth and early fourteenth centuries.[71] Yet there were only two decades, the 1360s and the 1430s, when there seem to have been major disasters due to the weather, and their long-term economic consequences seem to have been mainly regional. In all but the worst years the productive capacity of the land seems to have been well able to cope with demand from the much reduced population.

The Black Death, then, remains central to the debate on economy and society in late medieval England, although not simply because of the high mortality it caused. Other variables working with the appalling death rates must now be given due consideration: the fall in life expectancy; changing sex ratios; the age of marriage; the fertility of the marriage; and attitudes to marriage itself and to child bearing. All these were direct consequences of the plague. Together with the high mortality, they caused demographic catastrophe, a population scarcely greater in size than it had been in the

[69] M. L. Parry, *Climatic Change, Agriculture and Settlement* (Folkestone, 1978), pp. 65-66, 97-99; H. H. Lamb, *Climate, History and the Modern World* (London, 1982), pp. 82-93, 186-90; Dyer, *Standards of Living*, pp. 258-73; but for more sceptical views see E. Le Roy Ladurie, *Times of Feast, Times of Famine* (London, 1972), pp. 11, 244-87 and P. Brandon, 'Late Medieval Weather in Sussex and its Agricultural Significance', *Transactions of the Institute of British Geographers* 54 (1971), 1-17, p. 7.

[70] A. J. Pollard, 'The North-Eastern Economy and the Agrarian Crisis of 1438-40', *Northern History* 25 (1990), 88-105; Goldberg, 'Mortality and Economic Change in the Diocese of York', pp. 45-6; Mate, 'Economic and Social Roots of Popular Rebellion', p. 661; *The Great Chronicle of London*, ed. A. H. Thomas and I. D. Thornley (London, 1938), pp. 173-74; M. Mate, 'Kent and Sussex' in *The Agrarian History of England and Wales*, III, 119-36, pp. 122-23; M. J. Stephenson, 'Wool Yields in the Medieval Economy', *Economic History Review*, 2nd series, 41 (1988), 368-91, pp. 381-83.

[71] B. English and K. Miller, 'The Deserted Village of Eske, East Yorkshire', *Landscape History* 13 (1991), 5-32, p. 13; M. Bailey, '*Per impetuum maris*: Natural Disaster and Economic Decline in Eastern England, 1275-1350' in *Before the Black Death*, ed. Campbell, 184-208, pp. 205-8.

early twelfth century and subtle changes to the nature of the family and to patterns of inheritance. These were bound to have severe economic and social repercussions, for both good and ill, and it is to those that we must now turn.

ECONOMY AND SOCIETY

The Peasants' Revolt

The first and most obvious long-term consequence of the arrival of endemic plague was the Peasants' Revolt of 1381, the only truly popular uprising in English medieval history. The causes of the revolt have long been the subject of historical debate, and there is now fairly general agreement that they were cumulative, the result of the severe depopulation after four major outbreaks of plague; of the enactment and enforcement of the labour laws; of the 'feudal reaction' as landlords sought to maintain their incomes by asserting all their seigneurial rights over unfree peasants; of the disturbed political conditions at the end of Edward III's reign; of the intense religious debate in which ideas of equality were being preached; and of the progressive and crippling burden of taxation. The third poll tax may have sparked off the revolt, but it was, as it were, the flame which lit the fuse to set off the main explosive charges.[72] Recent research, however, has both added to our knowledge of certain aspects of the revolt and, significantly, questioned our interpretation of others. That there was a 'feudal reaction' cannot be in any doubt, yet its severity on the estates of the bishop of Durham was quite extraordinary, and Dr Britnell's study has shown the acute pressures and dilemmas that the unfree tenants had to face there. Villagers were forced to take up vacant holdings where no suitable heir was available, whether willing or not, whilst lands, mills and ovens were also committed to townships to hold corporately. The bishop was able to use all his extensive secular and palatine powers of lordship to obtain reports from coroners on potentially rebellious runaway villeins. The coroners were also enlisted to assist in the recapture of fugitives or to distrain upon their goods and to enforce the labour laws through the palatinate courts. Villagers were forced to cooperate with the bishop simply to survive. At the halmote courts the jurors had little alternative but to single out tenants who were able to take on extra land since failure to do so might have made them personally liable for such holdings; they also had to

---

[72] There is a vast literature on the Peasants' Revolt but the most useful recent works are *The English Rising of 1381*, ed. R. H. Hilton and T. H. Aston (Cambridge, 1984) and E. B. Fryde, 'Peasant Rebellion and Peasant Discontents' in *The Agrarian History of England and Wales*, III, 744-819. R. B. Dobson, *The Peasants' Revolt of 1381* (London, 1970), provides an excellent collection of original source material in translation.

assist in the recovery of fugitives. The threat, potential and real, of the village community having to take on collective responsibility for the increasing acreage of vacant land was too great. Only a successful revolt against the principle of committing land could have freed the villagers from the need to protect themselves through cooperation with the bishop, but by accepting that principle the communities consistently validated episcopal authority. Villagers were thus turned against their neighbours, rather than against the bishop, but there was no open revolt, as in the south. The critical difference seems to have been that the lay poll taxes were not levied in the palatinate, and the spark to light the fuse was thus not struck. But this study of the north east shows us starkly the dichotomy facing many villagers: that they had to cooperate with their lord to survive, whether they liked it or not.[73]

It also shows us something that is perhaps currently underemphasised, namely that the plague did bring a real crisis of lordship and that the response of many lords was to assert or reassert their powers in any ways they could. This was certainly the case in the south east, on the estates of Christ Church, Canterbury, in Essex and Kent, which lay in the very epicentre of the revolt. Once the immediate panic and dislocation had passed, harvest services were reimposed on all the house's manors. Unlike the bishops of Coventry and Lichfield, and the monks of Ramsey Abbey and Durham Cathedral Priory (whose estates were held separately from the bishop's), the monks of Canterbury successfully maintained their rights on most of their lands through the 1370s. In parts of Essex and east Kent this meant heavy and obviously resented burdens for the peasantry. When these are taken into account with the consequences of the labour laws, then some of the reasons for the outbreak of the revolt in the south east become more readily intelligible. Professor Mate is in no doubt that the Statute of Labourers was rigorously enforced in Kent. Money wages in the thirty years after the Black Death were not determined solely by economic factors, and the Statute of Labourers, although somewhat 'spotty' in its enforcement, definitely seems to have kept them lower than they might otherwise have been.[74] Indeed, there is now a growing body of evidence, in addition to that first provided by Bertha Putnam in 1908, that the statute was effectively enforced in some areas, both before the Great Revolt and indeed after it, when the Statute of Cambridge of 1388 again laid down the maximum annual rates of pay that servants should receive. Since at least one-third of all the population of late medieval England gained all or part of their living

---

[73] R. H. Britnell, 'The Feudal Reaction after the Black Death in the Palatinate of Durham', *Past and Present* 128 (1990), 28-47, pp. 29, 32-47.

[74] M. Mate, 'Labour and Labour Services on the Estates of Canterbury Cathedral Priory in the Fourteenth Century', *Southern History* 7 (1985), 55-67, pp. 60-66.

by earning wages, we can more readily understand why any attempts to control such wages would cause great resentment. But Penn and Dyer's recent study has shown that there were deeper reasons for such hostility. What was particularly disliked was the insistence on the full performance of annual contracts, which were in the employers' interests. Such contracts often involved live-in servants whose wages were paid partly in kind, in bed and board, and, since food was cheap, they offered the prospect of stable wage costs over the year. Short-term contracts meant higher wages, as labourers played off one employer against the other. Such short-term contracts were what labourers, both male and female, preferred, but not necessarily for the obvious reason of cash in hand. Some did want the freedom to move around, to select the most remunerative work; but others wanted the opportunities for time off and increased leisure simply to enjoy themselves. Yet the Statute of Labourers, for all its patchy enforcement, seems to have worked. Employers were able to recruit full-time servants on annual contracts if they so wished, as the poll tax returns and manorial accounts both show, though at what seems to have been a high cost in terms of social tension.[75]

Who were these 'employers'? Here recent research has taken different lines and has challenged the older, monolithic idea that there was only one set of employers, the greater landlords. All sorts and conditions of men and women employed labour, from live-in servants to ploughmen, pigmen, harvest gangs, and journeymen artisans in craft and industrial occupations. Nor were the labour laws themselves without precedent. In the thirteenth century, village bylaws had attempted to control labour supply, in the interest not only of manorial lords but also of the wealthier tenants, since peasants, and particularly wealthy peasants, also needed to hire labour. After the Black Death this became even more true, as holdings were enlarged and competition for labour intensified at all levels. The village elites, who controlled local government at its basic level, might well have found that the Statute of Labourers offered a sanction of social and economic control which helped them maintain their relative economic position. Elements within local communities were thus co-opted into the machinery for enforcing the labour laws, and proceedings under the statute betray a complex web of interests, and not simply those of the 'feudal'

[75] B. H. Putnam, *The Enforcement of the Statute of Labourers during the First Decade after the Black Death, 1349-59* (New York, 1908); Penn and Dyer, 'Wages and Earnings in Late Medieval England', pp. 366-70; C. Dyer, 'The Rising of 1381 in Suffolk: its Origins and Participants', *Proceedings of the Suffolk Institute of Archaeology and History* 36 (1985), 274-87, p. 276 for an attack on Sir John Cavendish in 1381; E. Clark, 'Medieval Labor Law and English Local Courts', *American Journal of Legal History* 27 (1983), 330-53, p. 345; Penn and Dyer, 'Wages and Earnings in Late Medieval England', pp. 372-75.

landlord class.[76]

If this is so, then village communities generally may have experienced tensions similar to those caused by the bishop of Durham's feudal repression, a resentment at the exercise of lordship coupled with the need to cooperate in its workings. Village elites have long been seen as leaders of the revolt and Professor Ormrod shows below why they found themselves increasingly at odds with the ruling elites at a local and at a county level. The Black Death speeded up the process of social stratification and drew a sharper distinction between county and parish gentry, something which the increasing property qualifications for office-holding in the later fourteenth and fifteenth centuries tended to emphasise. Indeed, Professor Ormrod sees these property qualifications as a deliberate attempt to create a pyramidal structure within the elite, with the leaders of village communities firmly at the bottom.[77] The revolt of 1381 was therefore in part the reaction of classes that found their status and interests threatened by changes within the structure of government; and the most radical changes were those involving the Statute of Labourers and its enforcement and the assessment and collection of taxation. Wage labourers who found their earning capacity and their freedom of movement restricted and who might well be branded as fugitives were clearly resentful at lordship exercised in this way. So were village elites who objected to the ways in which the gentry, as landlords, enforced the various statutes in order to secure their own labour supply.

On the one hand, then, we have clear evidence of village elites using the labour laws for their own purposes, on the other of their resentment at the erosion of their traditional authority by the gentry, acting as both justices of labourers and justices of the peace. Just as the villagers on the bishop of Durham's estates found that they had no choice but to cooperate with the bishop, so village elites may have found it necessary to cooperate in the workings of the labour laws, although the enforcement of such laws was now taken out of their hands and given over to the gentry. Their resentment was compounded by the poll tax itself, and, as Professor Ormrod shows, by the way in which the tax was levied, which again eroded their standing within the village.[78] If the Peasants' Revolt was anything, it was a revolt against the exercise of lordship in all its various forms, seigneurial and royal. It was the revolt of the free and the unfree, of the

---

[76]   Clark, 'Medieval Labor Law', p. 332; Penn and Dyer, 'Wages and Earnings in Late Medieval England', p. 359; L. R. Poos, 'The Social Context of the Statute of Labourers Enforcement', *Law and History Review* 1 (1983), 27-52, pp. 36-37, 40, 50-52.

[77]   C. Dyer, 'The Social and Economic Background of the Rural Revolt of 1381' in *The English Rising of 1381*, ed. Hilton and Aston, 9-24, pp. 15-19; Ormrod, below, pp. 153-55.

[78]   Ormrod, below, pp. 165-67.

wage labourer and the village worthy, but a revolt, a challenge to lordship, only because the exercise of that lordship was generally being called into question by the cumulative depopulation caused by the plague.

That the revolt did not answer the question is of course well known. Resistance continued, not only in the decades immediately after 1381, but also well into the fifteenth century. Professor Mate has recently shown that behind the rising of 1450-51 in Sussex there were serious social and economic grievances not dissimilar to those which caused the Peasants' Revolt, one of them being the continued and oppressive exercise of seigneurial lordship in the county. But change came, almost inexorably, and it did so because the economic events of the last quarter of the fourteenth century, and especially those resulting from the sudden decline in population, gave peasant tenants an irresistible bargaining position. The bishop of Durham's estate officials, like those of many other lords, may have tried to ensure that none of his rights should be lost, but in the end the feudal reaction was only an opening gambit. By the late 1380s it had largely failed, in the face of tenant resistance and economic realism.[79]

The Plague as an Agent of Change

What then came of this new economic realism caused by long-term depopulation? It was suggested in the introduction to this essay that, whilst some attempt has to be made to resolve the long-standing debates on national or regional prosperity or depression, it might be more fruitful to adopt other approaches and to ask whether the demographic circumstances of the late fourteenth and fifteenth centuries produced conditions which led to structural changes in both the economy and society. Subsequent discussion of the demographic evidence has helped to identify some of the key issues in this context, namely changes in the nature and size of the family (from functionally extended to nuclear), the impermanence of families, and the break between land and family caused by high mortality and lack of heirs. The consequences of late marriage, greater personal independence and physical mobility also have to be explored if there is to be any answer to those important questions: did the Black Death act as an agent of structural change in the economy and society, rural and urban; did that change foster individualism and enterprise, the capitalism and the capitalist attitudes which are held to characterise English society in the early modern period; and was that change of a type which could not be reversed when the population began to recover? We face again the difficulty that whilst the full demographic effects of plague are now being grasped, the concomitant consequences for the economy and society have only partially been explored. There are, and for once genuinely, no sure

[79] Fryde, 'Peasant Rebellion', pp. 784-88, 793-809; Mate, 'Economic and Social Roots of Popular Rebellion', pp. 666-74; Britnell, 'Feudal Reaction after the Black Death in the Palatinate of Durham', pp. 46-47.

answers to important questions, so that no sustainable general thesis of structural change has yet emerged. The purpose here, as already indicated, will be to consider the fortunes of four main groups in lay society, the peasantry, the gentry, townsmen and, by gender, women, to see if any tentative answers can be given to those questions, any general conclusion reached as to the extent and durability of change in society. One group will not be considered separately, the lay nobility, not because their social, economic or political importance was in any way diminished in the fifteenth century, but because little new published work on them has appeared in the last ten years. They remained, as Bishop Russell described them in 1483, firm land and rocks in a perilous sea, a pivotal point in society, and certainly not as impoverished as Professor Postan would have had us believe.[80] Yet the starting point for this discussion must be that, in spite of persistent attempts, they could not enforce their lordship over their peasant tenants, and especially over their customary tenants. That was the crucial difference between the thirteenth and the fifteenth centuries. Lordship had lost its coercive power in the face of depopulation and, it has been argued, of the long term opposition of a restless peasantry intent on acquiring freedom and pursuing its own fortunes by hard work and individual enterprise.[81]

The Fortunes of the Peasantry

Whether the peasantry achieved this nirvana, or simply temporary improvements in their status and standard of living which would disappear when the population recovery began in the sixteenth century, remains the central question. There was, apparently, an end to villeinage. Labour services could no longer be enforced, customary payments were refused and a bewildering collection of new forms of tenure emerged. There were *tenancies at will* held on a year to year basis, for as long as it pleased the lord; *leaseholds*, sometimes communal (with the peasantry on a manor leasing the customary tenures as a whole and contributing individually towards the commutation payment) but more often individual, for short terms and attractive both to tenants seeking to enlarge their holdings and to labourers wishing to supplement their wages or to improve their diet; and the *copyhold*, where the peasant took over his holding for a life or term of lives, to hold by custom of the manor. These all stood alongside *freehold*, which had long existed to a greater or lesser extent everywhere in England.[82] All

[80] J. R. Lander, *Conflict and Stability in Fifteenth-Century England* (London, 1969), p. 176; for a general discussion of the fortunes of the nobility see Bolton, *The Medieval English Economy*, pp. 220-29.

[81] Bridbury, *Economic Growth*, pp. 91-92.

[82] Miller, 'Introduction: Land and People', pp. 16-17; Pollard, *North-Eastern England during the Wars of the Roses*, pp. 68-69; Howell, *Land, Family and Inheritance*, pp. 51-53; Lomas, 'The Black Death in County Durham', pp.

this is commonplace, as is the fact that these tenures were a response to a new mobility in the rural population occasioned by the plague. Mobility here is not to be understood simply in terms of freedom to move around the countryside, in search of better land, better terms on which to take up that land, or simply enhanced wages (particularly, in certain areas, in the rapidly expanding rural textile industry). It must also be understood in terms of the changed demographic circumstances of the late middle ages. There was no certainty of inheritance. Sons did not succeed fathers, either because there were no sons, or because they no longer wished to do so. They had no need to wait until their fathers died in order to come into their lands, when holdings could be obtained almost anywhere. Non-inheriting children had no need to live with their parents for want of other support, nor did they do so for longer than was necessary. The functionally extended family of the pre-plague period which, it is argued, acted as a drag on economic activity (because, in protecting its members, individual initiative was stifled) was replaced, finally, by the more dynamic nuclear family. Simplified structures of family and household predisposed the individual towards self-reliance, enterprise and the relentless quest for profit, all the characteristics to be found in a pre-capitalist or capitalist society.[83]

The bond between land and family was thus broken, to be replaced by a new mobility in society, not necessarily to move around, since most stayed where they were or migrated no more than five or ten miles from their 'home' village, but mobility for men and women to make the best provisions they could for themselves when death now seemed even more certain than life. But mobility did not bring security. Of all the various

---

134-35; R. Faith, 'Berkshire: the Fourteenth and Fifteenth Centuries' in *The Peasant Land Market in Medieval England*, ed. P. D. A. Harvey (Oxford, 1984), 106-77, pp. 111, 121-58, *passim*; A. Jones, 'Bedfordshire: Fifteenth Century', *ibid.*, 178-251, pp. 192-94, 233-34; P. D. A. Harvey, 'Conclusion', *ibid.*, 328-56, pp. 328-38; for a general discussion of the various forms of tenure see Bolton, *The Medieval English Economy*, pp. 238-40.

[83] Penn and Dyer, 'Wages and Earnings in Later Medieval England', pp. 363, 373; Campbell, 'Population Pressure, Inheritance and the Land Market', pp. 100-01; Howell, *Land, Family and Inheritance*, pp. 44-47; R. K. Field, 'Migration in the Later Middle Ages: the Case of the Hampton Lovett Villeins', *Midland History* 8 (1983), 29-48, pp. 29-43; Langridge, 'Population of Chartham from 1086 to 1600', p. 233; Pollard, *North-Eastern England during the Wars of the Roses*, p. 69; Poos, *A Rural Society*, pp. 131, 159-79, *passim*; for female migration to towns, see below, pp. 72-76. The critical question of the emergence of the nuclear family and the break in the land/family bond are discussed extensively by Razi, 'The Myth of the Immutable English Family', pp. 28, 33-36, 39-42, which follows on from his previous work on Halesowen, *Life, Marriage and Death*, pp. 117-24, 139-50; C. Dyer, 'Were There any Capitalists in Fifteenth-Century England?' in *Enterprise and Individuals*, ed. Kermode, 1-24, p. 5; and see below, pp. 53-54 and n. 89 and pp. 61-63.

forms of tenancy, the only one which had any substantial protection at law, in the royal courts, was freehold. The others all contained a degree of uncertainty and impermanency. Tenancies at will could be revoked; and when leases fell in, their terms might well then be reviewed and revised. Most importantly, copyhold, which had largely replaced villeinage as the main form of peasant tenure in the manorialised areas, could ultimately be challenged. It was a form of hereditary tenure. The land could be passed to the right heir, often for two lives, and as pressure on land began to increase in the very late fifteenth century this may have led to an increased demand for copyhold because of the security it offered. But it was essentially a form of tenure worked out on an *ad hoc* basis, its terms differing from manor to manor and from county to county. It was distinctive only in a purely local context. For the most part the question of whether it offered any long-term security of tenure had not been tested in the royal courts. In the fifteenth century there was no need to do so; paradoxically, the fact that members of the gentry frequently held copyhold lands amongst their enlarged estates made such a challenge less likely. So, by 1500 formerly unfree tenants had acquired a species of hereditary tenure, but one which lacked adequate protection against landlords whenever the latter were determined to get rid of unwanted tenants. For Brenner it was this failure by the peasantry to gain complete legal title to their holdings, and the security of tenure it brought with it, that marked a critical stage in the emergence of agrarian capitalism. Peasants had lost their struggle with their lords who would, when they so wished, be able to expropriate them to enclose and engross their holdings and so create the large farms suitable for capitalist enterprise and large-scale commodity production. But he sees this failure purely in terms of legal structures and as having little or nothing to do with demographic change and the consequent availability of land and growth of the market. The strength of lordship, buttressed by the power of the state, was all. Yet a more balanced view must surely be that the peasantry had in the long run failed to benefit from the social and economic mobility brought about by plague.[84]

[84] Harvey, 'Conclusion', pp. 328-37; the general debate on the transition from feudalism to capitalism is succinctly summarised by Dyer, 'Were There any Capitalists in Fifteenth-Century England?', pp. 1-10; for the specific debate see *The Brenner Debate: Agrarian Class Structure and Economic Development in Pre-Industrial Europe*, ed. T. H. Aston and C. H. Philpin (Cambridge, 1985); J. E. Martin, *Feudalism to Capitalism. Peasant and Landlord in English Agrarian Development* (Basingstoke, 1983); R. J. Holton, *The Transition from Feudalism to Capitalism* (London, 1985); R. W. Hoyle, 'Tenure and the Land Market in Early Modern England: or a Late Contribution to the Brenner Debate', *Economic History Review*, 2nd series, 43 (1990), 1-20; M. Mate, 'The East Sussex Land Market and Agrarian Class Structure in the Late Middle Ages', *Past and Present* 139 (1993), 46-65.

For the openings were there for those who could exploit them. A thrusting peasant could grasp the opportunities to enlarge his holdings, to take up lands by copyhold or by leasehold in its various forms, or, if sufficiently wealthy, to buy freehold. Small farms of 60-100 acres were created, worked partly by family labour but increasingly by live-in servants with the assistance, when necessary, as at harvest time, of very expensive hired labour. So there emerged the English yeoman, who is often held to typify the English peasantry generally in the fifteenth century.[85] That is not the case. All recent studies have strongly suggested that this class was numerically very small indeed. Some 3,400 persons were assessed for the land tax of 1436 as having freehold lands, rents or annuities valued at between £5 and £9 *per annum*. Below this there lay the class of 40s. freeholders who did not pay this tax, but who can scarcely have numbered fewer than a further 3,400. In addition, there was a substantial but totally unquantifiable number of wealthy peasants who were not freeholders. But even if this group was as large as the previous two combined, the 'yeomanry' would still only consist of about 14,000 households, containing around 40,000 persons, or between 1.5% and 2% of a total population of about 2.5 million.[86] Yeomen there certainly were, but not that many of them; nor did they, as is often assumed, automatically found lasting dynasties that were to thrive into the sixteenth century. Demography was simply against them. In Berkshire such families lasted for no more than one or two generations before holdings were split up again into their component copyhold and leasehold parts. The emerging yeomanry of the late middle ages was soon supplanted there by the new men of the Tudor period, and the same pattern has been observed elsewhere.[87]

Nonetheless, opportunities for individual enterprise, which had always been possible in the free areas of eastern England, certainly did exist. The ambitious yeoman could run more sheep (albeit in a depressed market for

[85] Pollard, *North-Eastern England during the Wars of the Roses*, pp. 64-67; Dyer, *Lords and Peasants in a Changing Society*, pp. 241-42; Campbell, 'Population Pressure, Inheritance and the Land Market', p. 103; Langridge, 'Population of Chartham from 1086 to 1600', pp. 234-36; B. F. Harvey, *Westminster Abbey and its Estates in the Middle Ages* (Oxford, 1977), pp. 266-67, 288-90; Poos, *A Rural Society*, pp. 181-223, for servants; for the persistence of customary tenures in East Sussex, see Mate, 'The East Sussex Land Market and Agrarian Class Structure', pp. 60-61. *The Agrarian History of England and Wales*, III, chapter 7, 'Tenant Farming and Tenant Farmers' (various authors), 587-743, provides the most comprehensive summary of the size of holdings and farming practices in all areas of England and is essential reading.

[86] Calculated from the figures given by H. L. Gray, 'Incomes from Land in England in 1436', *English Historical Review* 49 (1934), 607-39, p. 610.

[87] Faith, 'Berkshire: the Fourteenth and Fifteenth Centuries', pp. 173-77; Harvey, *Westminster Abbey and its Estates*, p. 290; Miller, 'Introduction: Land and People', p. 20.

wool), graze more cattle, or indulge in new forms of farming, displaying those changed attitudes towards the exploitation of land that are discussed more fully below.[88] Did he do so at someone else's expense? It has been forcefully argued that individual enterprise could only lead to the disintegration of village communities which had, before the plague, acted together to regulate their affairs, social, legal and agrarian, since in common-field farming there had to be both mutual cooperation and the presentation of a united front against grasping landlords.[89] Such community of interest and action is not immediately obvious everywhere before the Black Death, and certainly not in eastern England where smallholders, free and unfree, seem to have been aggressively individualistic in their enterprise.[90] Perhaps peasants who lived in common-field areas in the midlands and south were only catching up with their eastern counterparts. But if one or two tenants now wished to enclose or consolidate their holdings, or graze more cattle and sheep on the common pastures or ignore village bylaws, then the social unity of the village community would be shattered, perhaps the more so when there was no longer any need to oppose an oppressive lord. Various historians have analysed the workings of manorial courts in the fifteenth century and have suggested that the village community, less integrated than formerly, could no longer foster and command the same allegiance it once had: the perception of individual rights and objectives became not primary, but certainly more insistent, at the expense of communal ones.[91]

[88] See, e.g., the Deys of Drakenage and the Baillys of Middleton in the Forest of Arden, A. Watkins, 'Cattle Grazing in the Forest of Arden in the Later Middle Ages', *Agricultural History Review* 37 (1989), 12-25, pp. 18-19; for sheep raising in the south see E. Miller, 'The Southern Counties', *The Agrarian History of England and Wales*, III, 703-22, pp. 720-21 and for pastoral farming generally in the north, Pollard, *North-Eastern England during the Wars of the Roses*, pp. 34-37, 58-60, 63-70.

[89] Z. Razi, 'Family, Land and the Village Community in Later Medieval England', *Past and Present* 93 (1981), 3-36, discusses the 'Toronto School' thesis and argues that village solidarity still existed at Halesowen after the plague; more recently E. Clark, 'Social Welfare and Mutual Aid in the Medieval Countryside', *Journal of British Studies* 33 (1994), 381-406, and C. Dyer, 'The English Medieval Village Community and its Decline', *ibid.*, 407-29, have also stressed the continued sense of community and communal action, although much of their discussion concerns the 14th rather than the 15th century.

[90] B. M. S. Campbell, 'Agricultural Progress in Medieval England: some Evidence from Eastern Norfolk', *Economic History Review*, 2nd series, 36 (1983), 26-46, pp. 39-41.

[91] S. Olson, 'Jurors of the Village Court: Local Leadership before and after the Black Death in Ellington, Huntingdonshire', *Journal of British Studies* 30 (1991), 237-56, pp. 255-56; B. Hanawalt, *The Ties that Bound: Peasant Families*

This community of interest or village solidarity needs to be viewed sceptically both before and after the Black Death. In any case, the end of community did not necessarily mean the end of cooperation. It continued to exist at informal levels. Peasants had always worked for each other, and continued to do so throughout the fifteenth century, particularly when money became 'tight' and labour was bartered for goods or other services.[92] This mutual relationship, and particularly that between cottagers and middling tenants, may have broken down in the fifteenth century as general prosperity increased and the labour market became more responsive to demand, but villagers still had to live and work together in relatively small communities. Moreover, in the peculiar circumstances of the fifteenth century, this loss of formal communal identity and action probably scarcely mattered. There was more than enough land for all, with holdings lying vacant and villages at worst becoming totally depopulated, at best shrinking in size, and wage labour offering an attractive alternative. In a county such as Essex the rural economy could not have survived without it, although that may well be an extreme example.[93] Previously landless men were able to take up the vacant tenements, so diminishing the labour supply further and helping to enhance wages which could now provide a family with a more than adequate living. Penn and Dyer have calculated that a wage labourer could earn as much as £4 *per annum*, against an annual expenditure of £2 on food and other essentials, leaving a surplus and disposable income far higher than in the thirteenth century (when such disposable incomes may not have existed at all). Wage labour also offered mobility in two other senses, the freedom to move around and the freedom to work only when one wished to do so. This seems to have been a powerful attraction in some cases, although it should not perhaps be exaggerated.[94]

What we should also expect to see in line with sufficient or increased holdings and ample wages is a rise in the standard of living. Measuring standards of living is a notoriously inexact science, and one particularly difficult to apply to the late middle ages. The evidence is sparse and often highly subjective. Our information on buildings and housing is often drawn from what has survived, which may or may not be typical. Changes in peasant diet are sometimes measured by changes in the food allowances given to harvest workers, where white bread replaced that made from barley, strong ale substituted for water or small ale, fresh fish took the place of salted, and there were more allowances of fresh meat, cheese and dairy

  in Medieval England (New York, 1986), pp. 266-67.
[92] Dyer, *Standards of Living*, pp. 184-85; Dyer, 'The Consumer and the Market in the Later Middle Ages'; and see above, pp. 40-43.
[93] Poos, *A Rural Society*, p. 23 and chapter 9, pp. 183-228, *passim*.
[94] Penn and Dyer, 'Wages and Earnings in Late Medieval England', p. 373; Dyer, *Standards of Living*, pp. 223-24.

products. But harvest workers were heavy manual labourers, and were much in demand at a critical point in the farming cycle. Potential employers tried to lure them with decent food allowances and their diet was probably atypical.[95] Nevertheless, except in years of severe crop failures, as in the north in 1438-40, there was sufficient food for everyone, even the poorer elements in society. Surpluses could also be offered for sale, to supply a market for agricultural produce which still existed and to provide disposable incomes over and above anything that might be earned by wage labour. The evidence of sales and purchases from cases of debt and of personal possessions listed in a limited number of wills suggests that peasants had become consumers. They now had the opportunity to buy cheaper varieties of cloth, either home-produced or imported, and inexpensive manufactured goods again either manufactured at home (although, in the case of metalwares, often made from iron imported from the Basque areas of Spain) or brought in from the Rhineland or the Low Countries.[96]

A rising material standard of living then, as discussed by Professor Dyer, seems likely, although one would have to ask, 'compared with what?' and acknowledge that anything would have been an improvement on the thirteenth century. There may also have been an increased perception of wellbeing, resulting from the lifting of the oppressive weight of lordship, and the ability to enjoy wages and leisure time, the social and physical mobility which was so dependent upon a reduced population. But caution again needs to be exercised. It is far too easy to make general judgements of improved standards of living both in terms of space and of time. There was much regional variation within England (the shift of people and wealth from the midlands to the south east and south west is well known), but what is now clear is that there could be very different responses to the crisis caused by the demographic downturn within regions themselves. In relatively prosperous Berkshire it was possible for the village of Coleshill to be completely depopulated between 1395 and 1424 whilst surrounding villages survived; life can scarcely have been comfortable for those living on the verge of desertion or in villages in the throes of decline in any county. Conversely, one might have expected there to be sustained decline on the poor soils of the Brecklands in Norfolk, a 'marginal' economy if ever

[95] C. Dyer, 'Changes in Diet in the Late Middle Ages: the Case of Harvest Workers', *Agricultural History Review* 36 (1988), 21-37, pp. 22-24; Dyer, *Standards of Living*, pp. 151-60 and esp. p. 159.

[96] Dyer, *Standards of Living*, pp. 169-77; W. Childs, 'England's Iron Trade in the Fifteenth Century', *Economic History Review*, 2nd series, 34 (1981), 25-47, esp. pp. 42-44; the nature of England's import trade still needs proper analysis but see J. L. Bolton, 'Alien Merchants in England in the Reign of Henry VI, 1422-61', University of Oxford B.Litt. thesis (1971), esp. Tables 10 and 12, pp. 305-27, 339-46.

there was one. Not so: diversification and specialisation in wool, in barley for malting, and, not least, in rabbit-keeping, flexible cropping arrangements coupled with the intensive use of animal manure, and trade through a network of small markets and towns to markets further afield, and particularly to Norwich, all helped to maintain the prosperity of the Brecklands and a high *per capita* income in the fifteenth century. The diverging fortunes of northern and southern England have already been discussed; and even within the north east considerable differences have been noted between the fortunes of the arable and the upland pasture areas, the former suffering badly from the falling demand for cereal products, the latter holding their own up to the 1430s at least, given the increased demand for meat and the extension of cattle rearing.[97]

More such regional studies are badly needed, since those already undertaken do show that the response to changing circumstances varied from region to region and within regions. They also collectively suggest that if there was a period of stagnation in the late medieval economy, which was bound to have affected peasant society, then it came in the middle decades of the fifteenth century, perhaps between the late 1440s and the mid-1460s. This argument will be pursued further in relation to towns, but even here the importance of regional variation can be seen. Within Kent and Sussex those living in the Wealden areas clearly suffered less than those in other parts of these counties. Low assart rents at $2d.$ or $4d.$ an acre were easier to meet than the $12d.$ paid on the Sussex Downlands. Cattle and pigs were kept, not sheep, and so incomes were not as badly affected by the collapse in the wool trade, and there were opportunities for non-agrarian employment in the textile and leather industries.[98] Even allowing for this mid-century depression and for a considerable degree of regional variation, the weight of evidence nevertheless seems to support the argument for peasant well-being, and certainly in the centre and the south of England where the majority of the population lived. But it also suggests that this well-being only lasted as long as demographic stagnation persisted. High wages, low prices and favourable tenancies could not be sustained when the population recovery began in the sixteenth century, simply because the structural changes which had occurred did not work to

[97] Faith, 'Berkshire: the Fourteenth and Fifteenth Centuries', pp. 117, 152-54; Dyer, *Standards of Living*, p. 277; M. Bailey, 'The Concept of the Margin in the Medieval English Economy', *Economic History Review*, 2nd series, 42 (1989), 1-17, p. 14; *idem, A Marginal Economy? East Anglian Breckland in the Later Middle Ages* (Cambridge, 1989), chapter 5, *passim*, and Conclusion, *passim*; Pollard, 'The North Eastern Economy and the Agrarian Crisis of 1438-40', pp. 88-92, 103.

[98] Mate, 'Economic and Social Roots of Popular Rebellion', p. 663; *idem*, 'Kent and Sussex', *The Agrarian History of England and Wales*, III, 680-703, pp. 680-81.

the long-term advantage of the peasantry as a whole. Villeinage had disappeared, with only vestigial traces remaining in some areas,[99] and by and large peasants would not any longer be subject to direct exploitation by lords of their labour and the capital equipment which that condition entailed. That worked, at least temporarily, to their advantage. What did not was the irreversible (and plague-induced) break in the bond between land and family which had given security and continuity of tenure from generation to generation over much of England. The new forms of tenure that had replaced villeinage could all be challenged if and when landlords wished to expropriate peasants to engross and enclose their holdings to take advantage of the new commercial opportunities offered in the early modern period.[100] Nor was there any certainty that peasant families that had prospered in the fifteenth century would survive and continue to do so in the sixteenth. The Black Death produced the demographic conditions which militated against that. It is perhaps best to see peasant society in the fifteenth century as living in quiet and prosperous estate yet also in the midst of imperceptible but radical change which would lead to a sharp differentiation between those with land and the mass of landless wage labourers. A significant realignment was clearly taking place within the ranks of the peasantry itself.

The Gentry and 'Capitalism'

The same might also be said of the gentry, the socio-economic group with whom the future is always thought to lie. In the last decade there has been a plethora of studies of local county communities, especially in the midlands, and of families such as the Pastons and the Townshends in Norfolk, along with intense and wide-ranging debates about the nature and

[99] In Berkshire, for example: Faith, 'Berkshire: the Fourteenth and Fifteenth Centuries', pp. 174-76; and in Warwickshire: Field, 'Migration in the Later Middle Ages: the Case of the Hampton Lovett Villeins', pp. 31-32. For a determined attempt by an ecclesiastical landlord, the prior of Spalding, to keep track of his unfree tenants, see M. Bailey, 'Blowing up Bubbles: Some New Demographic Evidence for the Fifteenth Century?', *Journal of Medieval History* 15 (1989), 347-58, pp. 349-53. At Witney (Oxfordshire) in the late 16th and early 17th centuries, free tenants of customary land in the tithings still had to seek licence from the bishop of Winchester to sue or be sued in the royal courts at Westminster in cases regarding that land: Oxfordshire County Record Office, Witney Manor Court Book, Tithings of Hailey, Crawley and Curbridge, 1588-1611, Misc. Je., ff. 35r, 46v.

[100] Hence the renewal of interest in heritable tenures offering some sort of protection against speculators: Faith, 'Berkshire: the Fourteenth and Fifteenth Centuries', pp. 120-21, 175-77; for the persistence of customary tenures, see Mate, 'The East Sussex Land Market and Agrarian Class Structure', pp. 60-61.

origins of bastard feudalism, on the level of gentry involvement in violence and their role in the politics of the Wars of the Roses.[101] Yet there remains no entirely satisfactory answer to the basic question, 'Who were the gentry?' All those who considered themselves 'gentlemen', a term increasingly used in the fifteenth century? The knights and esquires only? What of the differences between the greater and lesser knights, between old and new families, between county and parish gentry, those whose influence, political, economic and social, was important at a county and perhaps at a national level, those who were important chiefly within their own sphere of influence, the parish, the locality? These are not rhetorical questions, but nor are they susceptible to simple answers. If all ranks between gentlemen and greater knights were to be treated as 'the gentry', then in Leicestershire, for example, at one end of the scale there would have been men with annual incomes of between £5 and £6 *per annum*, little more than that of a prosperous yeoman, at the other knightly families with incomes of over £100 *per annum*. In Nottinghamshire Payling reckons that in 1436, by this definition, the gentry constituted a group of 143 families in all, but wealth was unevenly distributed. The gentry resident in the county controlled something like 54.2% of taxable wealth in 1412, compared with 17.5% for the baronage, but 12 gentry families alone controlled 21.2% of total landed wealth.[102] The income tax of 1412 was levied on all those with incomes of £20 *per annum*. In the most recent general analysis of that tax Professor Bean accepts this as the base level of wealth for the gentry; but that would exclude all those with lower incomes who still thought of themselves as part of that social group. So, how can modern historians define the class when later-medieval social perceptions seem to defy economic realities? Even so, Professor Bean's analysis does provide some interesting figures. The distribution of incomes of all lay landowners in Bedfordshire, Berkshire, Essex, Nottinghamshire, Sussex and Wiltshire in

---

101 C. Carpenter, *Locality and Polity: a Study of Warwickshire Landed Society 1401-99* (Cambridge, 1992); E. Acheson, *A Gentry Community. Leicestershire in the Fifteenth Century c.1422-c.1485* (Cambridge, 1992); S. J. Payling, *Political Society in Lancastrian England. The Greater Gentry of Nottinghamshire* (Oxford, 1991); Moreton, *The Townshends and Their World*; C. F. Richmond, *The Paston Family in the Fifteenth Century: the First Phase* (Cambridge, 1990); C. E. Moreton, 'A Social Gulf? The Upper and Lower Gentry of Medieval England', *Journal of Medieval History* 17 (1991), 255-62; S. Waugh, 'Tenure to Contract: Lordship and Clientage in Thirteenth-Century England', *English Historical Review* 101 (1986), 811-39; P. R. Coss, 'Bastard Feudalism Revised', *Past and Present* 125 (1989), 27-64; D. A. Carpenter, P. R. Coss and D. Crouch, 'Debate: Bastard Feudalism Revised', *Past and Present* 131 (1991), 165-203; Pollard, *North-Eastern England during the Wars of the Roses*, pp. 217-405.
102 Acheson, *A Gentry Community*, pp. 29-44; Payling, *Political Society in Lancastrian England*, pp. 3-8, 11-18.

1412 is laid out in Table 1, where the figure stands for the number of families in each income group.

These figures include the lay nobility; but even allowing for this, they

Table 1: Incomes of Lay Landowners in 1412

County	£5-19	£20-39	£40-99	£100-199	£200-299	£300-399	£400+	No of families
Bedfordshire	34	33	10	1	0	0	0	78
Berkshire	41	32	9	0	0	0	0	82
Essex	24	106	56	4	1	2	0	193
Nottinghamshire	38	57	19	0	0	0	0	114
Sussex	20	52	24	10	1	0	1	108
Wiltshire	91	77	36	6	1	0	0	211

demonstrate that, accepting the broadest possible definition of the gentry, we are talking about a social group with a very wide range of incomes indeed; that in any county the majority lay in the £5-£40 income bracket; and that in any county, even allowing for wide variations in geographical size and potential wealth, the overall number of gentry families was small. Using the multiplier already used for the peasantry, three, then in Bedfordshire at the one end of the scale, gentry society amounted to some 234 souls, and at the other end, in Wiltshire, 633. By comparison, the population of Berkshire and Sussex in 1524-25 has been estimated at 35,590 and 60,000 respectively. The gentry therefore formed a very small group in local society indeed, but they controlled a very substantial proportion of the landed wealth.[103]

General pronouncements on the fortunes of this class in an age of plague are no more possible than they are for the peasantry. To assume that they all prospered, that all were thrusting proto-capitalists, actively engaged in the land market, investing in and experimenting with new forms of farming, rebuilding their manor houses, extensively endowing their parish churches and founding chantries and almshouses, would be unrealistic and certainly not supported by the evidence.[104] Yet, as with the peasantry, what

[103] The 1412 land tax was levied on all those with freehold land, fees and annuities worth £20 *per annum*, but for certain counties the commissioners returned assessments for all those with incomes of £5 *per annum* or above; J. M. W. Bean, 'Landlords' in *The Agrarian History of England and Wales*, III, 526-86, pp. 529-32, especially Table 6.2. The actual grant, made in the parliament of 1411, drew no social distinctions, simply referring to 'each man or woman of whatsoever estate or condition': *Rotuli Parliamentorum*, III, p. 648. J. Cornwall, 'English Population in the Early Sixteenth Century', *Economic History Review*, 2nd series, 23 (1970), 32-44, p. 39.

[104] C. Carpenter, 'The Religion of the Gentry in Fifteenth-Century England', in *England in the Fifteenth Century: Proceedings of the 1986 Harlaxton Symposium*, ed.

the Black Death brought was mobility, social and economic. The demographic consequences of plague for the gentry – the failure of male heirs, the transmission of lands through the female line – meant that this could not be a closed caste. Some ancient families did survive, but much land came on to the market, either for purchase or for acquisition through marriage. As Dr Payling has shown, the motives for acquisition of land by such means were often as much social as economic, as merchants, lawyers, administrators, gentlemen-bureaucrats and rich clothiers sought the social standing that only land could bring. The availability of heiresses also allowed established families with land to expand their estates, and the demographic circumstances of the late middle ages thus provided a stimulus to upward social mobility, both into and within landed society, so contributing significantly to the emergence of the gentry as a 'class'. Indeed, argues Dr Payling, in this respect it might well be compared to the great expansion of the land market in the wake of the Dissolution of the Monasteries. This is a compelling argument and perhaps the major contribution in recent years to discussions about the plague as an agent of social change. [105]

It also brought economic change and new attitudes to the exploitation of estates. It is easy to list the achievements of the gentry and the way in which they took the opportunities offered to them to experiment with new forms of agriculture, with leys farming and other forms of intensive husbandry, and to increase flocks and herds, as much for the meat as for the wool and hides they produced. There is now abundant evidence of all these developments, and a sufficient number of local studies to show us that, as with the peasantry, fortunes varied significantly from region to region depending, often, on access to markets.[106] But what matters is mobility in the sense of changed attitudes to the exploitation of estates amongst a

D. Williams (Woodbridge, 1987), 53-74; C. F. Richmond, 'Religion and the Fifteenth-Century English Gentleman', in *The Church, Politics and Patronage in the Fifteenth Century*, ed. B. Dobson (Gloucester, 1984), 192-208; E. Duffy, *The Stripping of the Altars* (New Haven and London, 1992), pp. 121-33; Mate, 'The East Sussex Land Market and Agrarian Class Structure', p. 49. For farming, see below, p. 61.

[105] Payling, 'Social Mobility, Demographic Change, and Landed Society in Late Medieval England', pp. 51-71, *passim; idem, Political Society in Lancastrian England*, pp. 67-70.

[106] These issues, and farming techniques generally, are now discussed in full, region by region, in Chapter 3, 'Farming Practice and Techniques' (various authors), and Chapter 4, 'Marketing the Produce of the Countryside' (by D. L. Farmer), both in *The Agrarian History of England and Wales*, III, 175-323, 324-430. Leys farming or 'convertible husbandry' is specifically discussed by Bolton, *The Medieval English Economy*, pp. 243-45. For a more sceptical view of gentry enterprise, and of Brenner's thesis generally, see Mate, 'The East Sussex Land Market and Agrarian Class Structure', pp. 46-65.

relatively small social group that controlled directly so much of landed wealth. Here the critical question being asked is whether social and economic conditions after the Black Death allowed the emergence of the capitalist.

To arrive at a definition of capitalism, and thus of a capitalist, is almost as difficult as arriving at a definition of feudalism. There are as many opinions as there are historians, and it would be wrong to think, for example, that there were no capitalists amongst the merchants and gentry of the thirteenth century. But Professor Dyer's argument would be that, in English agrarian society, weakened lordship and cheap land provided the environment for the engrossing of holdings and that the class best able to exploit this situation was the numerous body of yeomen, the farmers and clothiers produced by the peculiar combination of low population, falling landlord incomes and the expanding rural cloth industry after 1348-49 and especially after 1400. There was land to be had, demesnes to be leased from greater landlords and sometimes from wealthier gentry who were not interested in cultivating their estates themselves. This offered the opportunity to experiment and to produce for the market, but that market had to be judged most carefully. Simply producing grain in vast quantities when demand had fallen was pointless. New specialisms were important, and especially cattle raising and dairying in certain areas, but in all cases the size of the labour force had to be judged carefully, because of costs. There also had to be investment, in new farm buildings, in stock and in hedges and enclosures, and capital would be expected to reproduce itself to allow for further investment in the expansionist days of the sixteenth century.[107]

For Professor Dyer, those who benefited from what were structural changes in both attitude and opportunity came from the top ranks of the peasantry and from the lower, rather than the upper, ranks of the gentry. The latter, he argues, ran their estates to provide for well-fed households and had sources of income other than from the sale of agricultural produce and therefore less incentive to farm for the market. That remains to be seen, but the point that Professor Dyer is stressing is the mind-shift needed here to think in terms of profit, organisation and costs – to think, in short, as 'capitalists'. For him this resulted from the opportunities offered by the plague for the enterprising to acquire and engross land and to organise production most efficiently in the face of market recession.

This argument, however, raises as many questions as it solves. Can we be certain that it was mainly the yeomen, some 5,000 families, holding as much as a fifth of the land in lowland England towards the end of the

[107] Dyer, 'Were there any Capitalists in Fifteenth-Century England?', pp. 1-21, first discusses definitions of capitalism before searching for capitalists in what he himself describes as a controversial article. It is required reading.

fifteenth century, who took advantage of the opportunities offered by the demographic crisis? Why exclude the gentry, and especially the new members of the gentry such as the Townshends and Pastons in late fifteenth-century Norfolk, both risen from the ranks of the lawyers and both farming extensively for the market?[108] The demographic argument must also work against Professor Dyer. His prime example, the Heritage family of south Warwickshire, thrived not least because they had heirs; but not all did. The notion of a relentlessly improving capitalist yeoman class should be tempered by the harsh reality of late medieval life: that many of the families would survive for only a few generations, and that their enterprise would die with them. Nonetheless, at the heart of Dyer's thesis lies the idea of structural change in rural society caused by plague and, critically, change which allowed larger units of production to emerge in the sixteenth century. The Black Death must therefore be seen as the essential precursor of the enclosure movement of the sixteenth and seventeenth centuries.

It is this idea of structural change which is central to current interpretations of the consequences for rural society of the demographic crisis of the late middle ages. If we can grasp it, then it allows us to move away from endless and sometimes fruitless discussions as to whether one group in society became poorer and another richer, or whether there was depression in one region and 'success' (whatever that might mean) in another (however important that might be in the immediate circumstances of the fifteenth century), to considerations of much more complex changes. Plague led to social and economic mobility, to a break in the family–land relationship at all levels, peasantry and gentry. That brought land on to the market, which in its turn opened the way for those with enterprise to engross and reorganise their holdings and to experiment with new methods of farming – and thus to the emergence of capitalist attitudes. The change in the nature of the family, from functionally extended to nuclear, the stress on individualism perhaps caused by the sense of the impermanence of life, also helped to promote structural change which offered the opportunities for those who were fortunate enough to survive and to have heirs, and who also had the necessary drive, to prosper. Plague is not seen as a dead hand (and no pun is intended) but as a positive force for the social and economic change which laid the foundations of early modern England.

---

[108] Moreton, *The Townshends and their World*, pp. 115-77, *passim*; Britnell, 'The Pastons and their Norfolk', pp. 132-44; Richmond, *The Paston Family in the Fifteenth Century*, pp. 23-63, *passim*; Acheson, *A Gentry Community*, pp. 45-76, *passim*.

The Towns: Prosperity or Decline?

It is high time that a similar approach was adopted to the study of urban history in this period. There has for too long been a seemingly endless debate about prosperity or decline, tempered recently by the partial revision that perhaps there was general urban prosperity up to about 1420 or 1430, followed by a period of stagnation, and then limited recovery for some towns but prolonged depression for others.[109] The current theoretical model, owing not a little to Dr Bridbury's original arguments, runs thus: that the division between town and countryside has been too artificially drawn by modern historians; and that if the countryside prospered, then there would have been continuing demand for the goods and services which towns, as centres where trade and industry were at their most efficient, could provide. This situation obtained up to about 1420 but the cumulative effects of depopulation, shortage of money and, in the north, famine, brought great difficulties in the mid-century to country and town alike. When in the last decades of the fifteenth century recovery came, it was essentially regional in nature, with York never regaining its former industrial and commercial pre-eminence as the cloth industry moved to the new towns in the West Riding – Halifax, Leeds, Wakefield – and its overseas trade through Hull almost vanished. In southern and eastern England, Salisbury, Bury St Edmunds, Norwich and above all London flourished and there emerged a series of new towns such as Lavenham whose fortunes were linked with those of the rural cloth industry.[110]

---

[109] The debate on late medieval towns has produced a vast literature which has been judiciously considered by Palliser, 'Urban Decay Revisited' and A. Dyer, *Decline and Growth in English Towns 1400-1640* (London, 1991), the latter containing an excellent bibliography. Anyone not acquainted with the controversies should read these two works first.

[110] See, e.g., Britnell, *Growth and Decline in Colchester*, pp. 262-64; Pollard, *North-Eastern England during the Wars of the Roses*, pp. 71-74; *idem*, 'The North Eastern Economy and the Agrarian Crisis of 1438-40', pp. 102-03; P. J. P. Goldberg, *Women, Work, and Life Cycle in a Medieval Economy, c.1300-1520* (Oxford, 1992), pp. 39-81, *passim*; Kermode, 'Merchants, Overseas Trade and Urban Decline', pp. 52-69; S. Rigby, 'Urban Decline in the Later Middle Ages: the Reliability of the Non-Statistical Evidence', *Urban History Yearbook*, 1984, pp. 45-57, *passim*, for prosperity and decline in Grimsby; M. K. Dale, 'The City of Salisbury' in *Victoria County History of Wiltshire*, VI, ed. E. Critall (London, 1962), 69-198, pp. 124-29; D. R. Carr, 'The Problem of Urban Patriciates: Office Holders in Fifteenth-Century Salisbury', *Wiltshire Archaeological and Natural History Magazine* 83 (1990), 118-35, p. 135; Gottfried, *Bury St Edmunds and the Urban Crisis*, pp. 73-130, which also deals with Lavenham, Long Melford and other Suffolk cloth 'towns'; J. Pound, *Tudor and Stuart Norwich* (Chichester, 1988), pp. 31-38, especially Table 4.1; C. Phythian-Adams, *Desolation of a City: Coventry and the Urban Crisis of the Late Middle Ages* (Cambridge, 1979), pp. 31-67. There is as yet no general study of

Population decline of itself is seen as a poor indicator of urban economic performance. All towns needed in-migration to maintain their populations but whilst those in decline, such as York, Colchester and Coventry, failed to attract the necessary immigrants, others successfully managed to maintain their populations at levels commensurate with the general demographic decline. If there were vacant sites and empty buildings within such towns, then that was only to be expected in an economy where deserted villages did not necessarily mean agricultural depression. Consequently, even allowing for regional variation, with decline in some areas being balanced by vitality and the growth of new towns in others, urban wealth constituted a greater share of national wealth in 1524 than it had in 1334.[111] Towns were emphatically not in general decline. They still had a vital role to play as commercial, industrial and distributive centres, serving international markets for cloth and local demand from a wealthier rural population for a whole variety of industrial and consumer goods.

Such a model is not of course acceptable to those who point to the misfortunes of Coventry, York, Newcastle, Scarborough, Lincoln, Grimsby, and Gloucester, to the disappearance of over half the smaller market towns and villages in the west midlands and of nearly 60% of those in Lincolnshire, or to the decay of Towcester (Northamptonshire) or Abbots Bromley (Staffordshire).[112] If trade and industry collapsed, if the urban rents on which so many merchants and others depended as sources of income

---

London's role in the late medieval economy, but some indications of the 'pull' of the capital can be found in: D. Keene, 'Medieval London and its Region', *London Journal* 14 (1989), 99-111, pp. 105-07; Dyer, 'The Consumer and the Market in the Later Middle Ages', pp. 308-09; Pollard, *North-Eastern England during the Wars of the Roses*, pp. 73, 77; Kermode, 'Overseas Trade and Urban Decline', pp. 51, 59-60, 69-70; Holt, 'Gloucester in the Century after the Black Death', p. 152; R. Hilton, 'Medieval Market Towns and Simple Commodity Production', *Past and Present* 109 (1985), 3-23, p. 13; Palliser, 'Urban Decay Revisited', p. 12; Poos, *A Rural Society*, p. 43.

[111] The debate on this issue, which in some ways may be characterised as Bridbury v. Rigby, is admirably summarised by Palliser, 'Urban Decay Revisited', pp. 8-13, and by Dyer, *Decline and Growth in English Towns*, pp. 37-50, which also considers problems of interpreting evidence of declining population and decayed buildings.

[112] See above, n. 110 and F. W. Hill, *Medieval Lincoln*, new ed. (Stamford, 1990), pp. 269-88; S. Rigby, '"Sore Decay" and "Fair Dwellings": Boston and Urban Decline in the Later Middle Ages', *Midland History* 10 (1985), 45-60, p. 58; Hilton, 'Medieval Market Towns and Simple Commodity Production', p. 10; Holt, 'Gloucester in the Century after the Black Death', pp. 157-59; Britnell, *Commercialisation of English Society*, pp. 155-61; P. Goodfellow, 'Medieval Markets in Northamptonshire', *Northamptonshire Past and Present* 7 (1987-8), 301-23, pp. 315-17; T. R. Salter, 'Urban Hierarchy in Medieval Staffordshire', *Journal of Historical Geography* 11 (1985), 115-37, pp. 124-25.

declined and profits shrank, then the amount of credit which townsmen could offer their rural customers would also contract and that in itself would contribute further to economic decline – or so it is argued.[113] And, since economic historians love nothing more than to challenge each other's interpretation of statistical material, there has been profound disagreement over comparisons made between the 1334 and 1524 tax returns, 200 years apart and levied on fundamentally different bases of assessment.[114] Decline still remains the order of the day, and that decline is used as a measure for rural decline, since town and countryside are held to be inseparable.

The Role of the Market Towns

These two theses seem completely irreconcilable, and much time and effort has been expended in proving that this is so. But the endless arguments may well have missed the point. It is quite possible that the demand from a countryside made relatively more prosperous by the consequences of plague could be met from within its own resources or by calling on the goods and services provided by a range of smaller market towns. The idea that town and countryside were inseparable itself needs to be challenged. More than one recent study has noted that larger towns themselves consumed most of what they produced; that merchants may have invested as much in urban as in rural property, so limiting the transfer of wealth to the countryside; and, most importantly, that the countryside might well have been able to provide for its own needs from within its own resources and by using the services of different types of town from those which have so far been studied in any depth. 'It could be argued', says Dr Rigby, 'that the prosperity of small market centres and industrial centres should be set against the decay of larger urban centres which were well placed to advertise their woes... Although small market towns made up the bulk of England's urban centres, historians have only recently started to give them the attention they deserve, and they have played little part in the debate on urban decline.' Here he echoes Hilton's arguments, that to see the apparent smallness of the urban sector as a proper measure of the commercialisation of society is misleading because in doing so we ignore the importance of the local market town, where for the most part small producers sold their goods for money in order to buy other products for consumption. Regional capitals and county boroughs stood at the head of the urban hierarchy in England, at the apex of exchange and society, but it was the very large number of lesser market centres that provided the

[113] Kermode, 'Merchants, Overseas Trade and Urban Decline', pp. 63-69.

[114] See above, n. 111 and S. H. Rigby, 'Later Medieval Urban Prosperity: the Evidence of the Lay Subsidies'; A. R. Bridbury, 'Dr Rigby's Comment: a Reply'; and J. F. Hadwin, 'From Dissonance to Harmony in Late Medieval Towns', all in *Economic History Review*, 2nd series, 39 (1986), 411-26.

primary base. Indeed, it was the strong backbone of small towns which distinguished medieval England from other European countries.[115] In addition, if we look simply at the trade passing through towns we will be deceiving ourselves as to its total volume. A great deal of exchange bypassed markets. It was conducted within the countryside itself, often in villages and often between individuals in the form of barter of goods for services. Equally, we probably underestimate how much was produced within the late-medieval countryside and the role of itinerant traders in supplying local demand. Cloth was (and always had been) made in vast quantities all across rural England and almost every village had its own tailor to make it up into the basic clothing which was all most of its inhabitants either required or could afford. Wooden products and ironware were manufactured locally. Tables, stools, benches and chairs, bowls and platters, tools, locks, bolts and nails were produced to meet the needs of rural dwellers, as were all manner of leather goods (especially boots and shoes) and pottery. Butchers and fishmongers moved from village to village, from market day to market day, selling the meat and fish that helped improve the basic diet. If demographic decline brought greater wealth and improved standards of living to rural dwellers generally and structural change brought more wealth to individual families, then the demand generated by such wealth may well have been met by rural craftsmen and traders and by the goods and services provided by a whole series of small market towns.[116]

---

[115]   Rigby, '"Sore Decay" and "Fair Dwellings"', p. 57; Dyer, 'The Consumer and the Market in the Later Middle Ages', p. 324; Hilton, 'Medieval Market Towns and Simple Commodity Production', p. 4; D. Postles, 'An English Small Town in the Later Middle Ages: Loughborough', *Urban History* 19 (1992), 7-29, pp. 7-8. The whole question of mercantile investment in urban property, either directly or indirectly through guilds and fraternities, is in urgent need of investigation, but see: Kermode, 'Merchants, Overseas Trade and Urban Decline', pp. 67-68; C. M. Barron, 'Richard Whittington: the Man behind the Myth', in *Studies in London History presented to P. E. Jones*, ed. A. E. J. Hollandaer and W. Kellaway (London, 1969), 197-248, pp. 221-27; J. C. L. Stahlschmidt, 'Lay Subsidy [for London] temp. Henry IV', *Archaeological Journal* 44 (1887), 56-82, *passim*; Thrupp, *Merchant Class of Medieval London*, pp. 118-30; Holt, 'Gloucester in the Century after the Black Death', pp. 158-59; A. Butcher, 'Rent and the Urban Economy: Oxford and Canterbury in the Later Middle Ages', *Southern History* 1 (1979), 11-43, p. 16; Dyer, *Standards of Living*, pp. 204-05; H. Swanson, *Medieval Artisans. An Urban Class in Late Medieval England* (Oxford, 1989), pp. 160-61; and for institutional property investment, Phythian-Adams, *Desolation of a City*, pp. 64-67 and R. H. Hilton, 'Some Problems of Urban Real Property in the Middle Ages' in his *Class Conflict and the Crisis of Feudalism* (London, 1990), 92-101, pp. 99-101.

[116]   'Informal exchange' is discussed by Dyer in 'The Consumer and the Market in the Later Middle Ages', pp. 319, 321-24, and in 'The Hidden Trade of the

This symbiotic relationship between small towns and the countryside is now under thorough investigation. Some of the seigneurial boroughs and chartered markets created during the expansionist days of the thirteenth century did sink back into oblivion, leading to an overall contraction in the number of towns but one in line with the general decline in the population. This was certainly the case in Staffordshire where Kinver, Newborough, Betley, Rocester and Church Eaton returned to village status. But this still left a county without any one dominant town well served by a range of small urban centres: Stafford itself, Tamworth, Lichfield, Newcastle-under-Lyme, Uttoxeter, Burton-on-Trent, Wolverhampton and Walsall, all of them to thrive in the early modern period.[117] Other local studies show us why. Shipston-on-Stour, with a population of 300 or more on the eve of the Black Death, was one of the many small towns that flourished without ever being a borough in the formal sense of being granted a specific charter of urban privileges. Its role was to provide a range of relatively cheap goods and services to the local peasants, clergy and gentry who generated a large and continuous local demand. It stood at the centre of a well defined hinterland and most of its trading contacts lay within a radius of no further than eight miles from the town. The peasants from the Felden area of Worcestershire exchanged their agricultural produce for other foodstuffs, clothing, farming equipment and household utensils, and there were at least 30 gentry and clergy households to use its services. The district as a whole needed to exchange its grain, especially wheat, for the wood and constructional timber it lacked, whilst more sophisticated tastes could be satisfied by goods which came through links to a network of nearby larger markets – Banbury, Chipping Campden, Chipping Norton and Stratford-upon-Avon. Shipston thrived. Whether it suffered depopulation in the mid-fifteenth century remains largely unknown, but by its close both trade

Middle Ages: Evidence from the West Midlands', *Journal of Historical Geography* 18 (1992), 141-57, pp. 149-51; P. Stamper, 'Woods and Parks' in *The Countryside of Medieval England*, ed. Astill and Grant, 129-48, pp. 135-40; J. Langdon, 'Agricultural Equipment', *ibid.*, 86-107, but especially p. 103 which stresses that medieval husbandmen made many of their own tools; J. Birrell, 'Peasant Craftsmen in the Medieval Forest', *Agricultural History Review* 17 (1969), 91-107, considers the 13th-century evidence and A. Watkins, 'The Woodland Economy of the Forest of Arden in the Later Middle Ages', *Midland History* 18 (1993), 19-36, p. 25, the 15th. Dyer shows the extent of peasant possessions, many of which would have been supplied by local craftsmen and artisans: *Standards of Living*, pp. 172-77. For tinkers and other itinerant traders, Dyer, 'The Consumer and the Market in the Later Middle Ages', pp. 321-22 and *idem*, *Standards of Living*, pp. 156-57, 172-75, 176-77; and for 17th-century comparisons, M. Spufford, *The Great Reclothing of Rural England: Petty Chapmen and their Wares in the Seventeenth Century* (London, 1984), pp. 1-22 and *passim*.

[117] Salter, 'Urban Hierarchy in Medieval Staffordshire', pp. 124-26.

and the property market seem to have been buoyant.[118]

In this area of the west midlands the countryside was servicing its own needs. The same was true in north-central Essex where the diversified and commercialised nature of the economy cannot be ascribed to the tentacles of market forces emanating from the nearest large town, Colchester, or from the capital, London. It was self-generating, and demand was served by a series of small market towns – Thaxted, Braintree, Bocking – and a broad range of middle sized communities with between 150 and 250 inhabitants, quite capable of supplying a whole range of basic goods necessary to and sought by peasant society. Access to a variety of goods and services would not therefore have required a very long journey for dwellers in the late medieval Essex countryside. Here and elsewhere the economies of most small towns were bound up with the spending of consumers of modest means, the peasants and gentlemen, yeomen and esquires, who formed the vast majority of consumers.[119] Perhaps we spend too much time looking at the purchasing power of elites and ignore the fact that collectively it was that of the lower orders which was more important, and that most of it was exercised in small market centres which may well have benefited very considerably from the demographic and structural changes of the fifteenth century.[120]

As long ago as 1974 Professor Everitt warned us that we ought to look not at the greater but at the primary centres, the Banburys of the late medieval and early modern world, if we wished to grasp the real urban strength of England. His warning is now being heeded, but until research in this field has progressed further, and until the role of itinerant traders and the 'pull' of London have been further and fully investigated, we need to reserve our judgment on the effects of the Black Death on the urban economy. London remains the great unknown. It may be that constant migration to the capital affected population recovery in other towns, whilst the concentration of wealth there (with 60% at least of all English imports and exports flowing through London and its outports) may have had equally deleterious effects on some towns but beneficial consequences for small 'satellite' towns such as Henley-on-Thames, Ware, Kingston, Brentford, Enfield, Romford and Tottenham. We need also to know more about regional variations, since the rise of Exeter and other south-western

---

[118]   C. Dyer, 'Small Town Conflict in the Later Middle Ages: Events at Shipston-on-Stour', *Urban History* 19 (1992), 183-210, pp. 190-92, 210.

[119]   Poos, *A Rural Society*, pp. 34-41.

[120]   This point is powerfully made by Postles in his recent study of Loughborough (Leics.) where he argues that non-agrarian activity within the town continued to develop because, rather than in spite of, the town's relationship with the surrounding countryside, its 'pays': 'An English Small Town in the Later Middle Ages: Loughborough', pp. 28-29; Dyer, 'The Hidden Trade of the Middle Ages', p. 153.

towns can be contrasted with the stagnation and decline in the north east. But there is an increasing volume of evidence to suggest that the strength of the primary towns, in response to the consequences of demographic change, was the main urban legacy of the fifteenth century to the early modern period. The jury is out: the verdict could be very interesting.[121]

The Status of Women: Economic Independence and Marriage
There remains the most fascinating of the current debates, that concerning the extent to which demographic change affected the status of women in society. This has been one of the most interesting and fruitful areas for recent research; but, like all investigations into the social, economic, political and legal standing of medieval women, it has been bedevilled by the problem of the evidence. Given the inferior legal status of women, subordinate as they were at nearly all times to men, contemporary records concentrate on male householders, male tenants, male guild members. Women do appear in their own right, but usually in default of a man to stand in their stead. The problems raised by the skewed nature of the evidence are general, but particularly acute for medievalists; and yet to ignore the history of at least half the population would seem absurd, tentative though any conclusions drawn from such evidence must be.[122] The purpose here, however, will be to consider the fortunes of the majority, the wives, widows, and unmarried daughters who played such an important role in the workforce, and not those of that small minority, the gentlewomen, on whom far too much attention has sometimes been focused. Three related questions need to be addressed. First, did the demographic changes caused by the plague bring new employment opportunities for women in both town and countryside which allowed them a greater degree of personal independence? Then, did this affect nuptiality, and lead to a society where life-cycle servanthood meant both later and companionate marriage, with a rough equality of age between man and wife, to women having a greater choice in their marriage partner, and to a

[121] A. Everitt, 'The Banburys of England', *Urban History Yearbook* 1 (1974), 28-38, pp. 35-36; Bridbury, *Economic Growth*, pp. 79, 81; McIntosh, *Autonomy and Community*, pp. 144, 153-54, 157, 229, 230-31: D. Moss, 'The Economic Development of a Middlesex Village [Tottenham]', *Agricultural History Review* 28 (1980), 104-14, pp. 108ff; Keene, 'Medieval London and its Region', pp. 104-05; Bolton, *The Medieval English Economy*, pp. 253-55, 302; E. M. Carus-Wilson, *The Expansion of Exeter at the Close of the Middle Ages* (Exeter, 1963), *passim*; W. R. Childs, 'Devon's Overseas Trade in the Late Middle Ages', in *The New Maritime History of Devon, I, From Early Times to the Late Eighteenth Century*, ed. M. Duffy (London, 1992), 79-89, pp. 79, 88; Dyer, *Decline and Growth in English Towns 1400-1640*, p. 72.
[122] Problems of evidence are discussed by Goldberg, *Women, Work and Life Cycle*, pp. 26-38.

high proportion of women not marrying at all? Lastly, and as before, did this result in structural change both to marriage patterns and to the nature of the family, and to a regime which 'distinguished England culturally from other more southerly regions of medieval Europe and brought English society of the later Middle Ages much closer to that of the early modern period'?[123]

Some of the evidence has already been rehearsed, but it now needs to be reconsidered in a different context.[124] Before doing so, one point must be made quite clear: that at all times, before and after the Black Death, women played a major role in the workforce. They laboured in the fields, alongside men, performing all but the heaviest tasks. In pastoral areas, dairying was given over to women, and everywhere, in town and country alike, they brewed and sold ale, washed, combed and carded wool and spun it to provide yarn for the weavers. They were general dealers, hucksters, buying and selling petty merchandise; they helped their husbands sell retail; and they kept house and brought up children. Any change brought by the plague was therefore, in the first instance, of degree rather than kind, and consequent upon shortages of male labour. Women had a greater part to play in the workforce, but not necessarily a new role or roles. Their status may have been enhanced by the plague: whether it was changed is another matter.[125]

The first indications of enhanced opportunities can be seen in the indictments brought under the Statute of Labourers in the half-century or so after 1348. Some care has to be exercised with the evidence, since it is possible that male jurors presented female offenders in order to maintain traditional wage differentials and to ensure that women were paid less for doing men's work. Women might therefore have appeared before the

[123] H. J. Hajnal, 'European Marriage Patterns in Perspective' in *Population in History: Essays in Historical Demography*, ed. D. V. Glass and D. E. C. Eversley (London, 1965), 101-46, *passim*; R. M. Smith, 'Hypothèses sur la nuptialité en Angleterre aux xiiie – xive siècles', *Annales: économies, sociétés, civilisations* 38 (1983), 107-36, *passim; idem*, 'Geographical Diversity in Resort to Marriage in Late Medieval Europe: Work, Reputation and Unmarried Females in the Household Formation Systems of Northern and Southern Europe' in *Woman is a Worthy Wight. Women in English Society c.1200-1500*, ed. P. J. P. Goldberg (Stroud, 1992), 16-59, pp. 17-27 for a discussion of Hajnal's theories and subsequent critiques; pp. 27-46 for contrasts between northern and southern Europe; Goldberg, *Women, Work, and Life Cycle*, p. 20 and pp. 333-45 for comparisons between Yorkshire and Tuscany.

[124] See above, pp. 34-40.

[125] S. A. C. Penn, 'Female Wage-Earners in Late Fourteenth-Century England', *Agricultural History Review* 35 (1987), 1-14, pp. 1-3; R. Hilton, 'Lords, Burgesses and Hucksters', *Past and Present* 97 (1982), 3-15, p. 11; J. M. Bennett, *Women in the Medieval Countryside: Gender and Household in Brigstock before the Plague* (New York, 1986), pp. 82-84, 115-29, 160-62.

justices disproportionately to their total numbers in the workforce, having been singled out for special treatment. It is also difficult to make comparative judgements of a greater or lesser role when the pre-plague evidence is so limited. Indeed, the most interesting feature of Penn's recent study is not so much what it shows about female participation in the workforce as about the physical and social mobility of women after the plague. They worked alongside men in the countryside, in harvest gangs, and were often paid the same wages. They moved from village to village in search of employment, as wage labourers solely responsible for their own well-being. The independent female worker was rapidly appearing in peasant society, as well as in the towns, and the simple, physical shortage of male labour was bringing for some women at least greater mobility and greater opportunities for employment within a traditional, female occupational framework.[126]

The consequences of this demand for female labour seem to have been quite profound, particularly within towns, where it resulted in an imbalance in sex ratios as young women in-migrated in search of employment. There may well have been less need for female labour within the countryside, although paradoxically more need for live-in servants, male and female, on yearly contracts. Agrarian service in early modern England reached its maximum extent in periods of labour shortage, as in the late seventeenth and early eighteenth centuries, when there was a move away from grain to pastoral farming, and for clear financial reasons. As wages rose and prices fell, farmers needed to control costs by employing reliable full-time labour on annual contracts, especially if they were running more livestock.[127] These were precisely the conditions that obtained in the late fourteenth and fifteenth centuries and they seem to have generated the same response. In Rutland in 1377, 20% of households contained servants. Comparable proportions were to be found in Gloucestershire and Leicestershire, although in the West Riding of Yorkshire it was much lower, at about 10%. But there does seem to have been extensive female migration to towns, and here the extent of servanthood in general is quite striking: 20-30% of the urban population over the age of 14 in York, and 19% of all taxpayers (not the total population) in Worcester, suggesting a much higher proportion of servant labour in towns, perhaps on average 20% of the population compared with 10% in the countryside.[128] A high

[126] Penn, 'Female Wage-Earners in Fourteenth-Century England', pp. 8-14.
[127] Smith, 'Human Resources', p. 210, citing A. Kussmaul, *Servants in Husbandry in Early Modern England* (Cambridge, 1981), pp. 97-119.
[128] Smith, 'Human Resources', p. 210; Miller, 'Introduction: Land and People', p. 11; Goldberg, 'Female Labour, Service and Marriage in the Late Medieval Urban North', p. 21; Poos, *A Rural Society*, pp. 181-82, 183-206, 223. Poos suggests that in rural Essex women made up one-third of the labour force, *ibid*, p. 217; C. Barron, 'The Fourteenth-Century Poll Tax Returns for

proportion of such servants were women, but it must be remembered that they were only part of the female labour force. The two most comprehensive studies of women and work are those by Goldberg and Swanson, based mainly but not exclusively on evidence from York and Yorkshire. They show that women were to be found in virtually all occupations as independent traders and manufacturers, with the greatest concentrations, as might be expected, in the victualling, textile, cloth and service sectors of the economy: women appear as ale wives, spinsters, hucksters, shepsters (dress makers), lavenders (laundresses), nurses, and to a lesser extent in the metalworking trades, as nail and pin makers, goldsmiths and even as blacksmiths and armourers. There were few to be found in trades and industries which required access to capital, which women so clearly lacked, except as widows, where they may have taken over the husbands' businesses as tanners, butchers, haberdashers or drapers. But almost everywhere else their activities expanded along traditional lines or they filled niches left by a shortage of labour. Whilst there was always a need for female labour in towns, it is quite clear that this was much more the case after the Black Death: in London, Lacey argues that the economy would scarcely have functioned without it.[129]

The critical question, however, concerns female servanthood, and here a definition of terms is vital. Service was not the domestic and non-productive function that it later became. There were servants to be found in non-productive households, performing purely domestic duties, and it is likely that in other households servants combined such duties with their other employment. Nor were servants entirely female. At Kibworth, of the 31 servants in the poll tax lists, 13 were eldest sons, either boys of little more than 14 years or men in their mid-twenties returning after an absence

Worcester', *Midland History* 14 (1989), 1-29, pp. 7-8; Kowaleski, 'The History of Urban Families in Medieval England', p. 53; Hilton, 'Medieval Market Towns and Simple Commodity Production', p. 9.

[129] Goldberg, *Women, Work, and Life Cycle*, pp. 104-37, *passim*, for York, pp. 137-49 for Yorkshire; *idem*, 'Female Labour, Service, and Marriage in the Late Medieval Urban North', pp. 28-36; *idem*, '"For Better, For Worse": Marriage and Economic Opportunity for Women in Town and Country', in *Woman is a Worthy Wight*, ed. Goldberg, 108-25, *passim*; Swanson, *Medieval Artisans*, pp. 19, 21, 23, 30, 35-36, 51, 58, 60, 68, 71, 72, 74, 80, 81; K. Lacey, 'Women and Work in Fourteenth and Fifteenth Century London' in *Women and Work in Pre-Industrial England*, ed. L. Charles and L. Duffin (London, 1985), 24-82, pp. 45-58; M. K. Dale, 'The London Silkwomen of the Fifteenth Century', *Economic History Review*, 1st series, 4 (1933), 324-35 *passim*; D. Hutton, 'Women in Fourteenth Century Shrewsbury', in *Women and Work in Pre-Industrial England*, ed. Charles and Duffin, 83-99, pp. 88-98; H. Graham, '"A Woman's Work...": Labour and Gender in the Late Medieval Countryside', in *Woman is a Worthy Wight*, ed. Goldberg, 126-48, discusses female occupations in the village of Alrewas (Staffs.), 1325-75.

of some years and possibly in the expectation of succeeding to their father's holding.[130] In towns formal apprenticeships provided cheap labour and although young women were trained alongside young men, they were excluded from apprenticeship structures. Female servants, on yearly contracts and usually moving from one household to another at the end of the year, provided cheap but more importantly certain labour. They were paid mainly in bed and board and they had to remain celibate, since that was a condition of servanthood.[131] Because of the shortage of male labour it is now strongly suggested that servanthood became part of the female life cycle in the late fourteenth and fifteenth centuries (hence the term, life-cycle servanthood) with the main demand coming from towns, which attracted migrants from the surrounding rural areas. The age of entry to servanthood seems to have been about 12 for young girls, and they stayed in service until their mid-twenties, only marrying when they finally left service altogether.[132] Marriage, it is argued, became companionate, that is between partners of roughly equal ages, with the man perhaps only one or two years older than the woman, and the woman may also have had a greater choice of her partner. Such wages as she earned may have gone towards the dowry which she, rather than her father, would have controlled, and she could afford to survey the field of such eligible young men as there were. As a result of life-cycle servanthood, teenage marriage was not therefore the norm, whilst a surprisingly high proportion of women seem to have chosen not to marry at all. Childbirth was always dangerous in the middle ages, but plague does seem to have struck particularly at the very young; and fear of bringing children into a society where death rates were so high may have led to a turning away from marriage in an age when women could work to support themselves.[133]

It is this combination of plague-induced circumstances which has led to the arguments about the emergence of a 'European' or 'North-Western European' marriage pattern in late fourteenth- and fifteenth-century England. It was Hajnal who first began the debate by suggesting, perhaps confusingly, that a non-European pattern obtained in England with early marriage and therefore more children of the marriage. In this he was

[130] Goldberg, *Women, Work, and Life Cycle*, pp. 188, 193; Howell, *Land, Family and Inheritance*, pp. 224-25.
[131] Swanson, *Medieval Artisans*, pp. 115-16; Smith, 'Human Resources', p. 210.
[132] Poos, *A Rural Society*, pp. 147, 187; Goldberg, 'Female Labour, Service and Marriage in the Late Medieval Urban North', p. 23.
[133] Goldberg, *Women, Work and Life Cycle*, pp. 269-70, 276; *idem*, 'Mortality and Economic Change in the Diocese of York', pp. 50-51; Poos, *A Rural Society*, pp. 156-59; Smith, 'Human Resources', p. 210; Gottfried, *Black Death*, p. 160 and n. 78; the work of P. Ariès in *Centuries of Childhood. A Social History of the Family*, trans. T. Baldick (London, 1962), is discussed critically by S. Shahar, *Childhood in the Middle Ages* (London, 1992), pp. 1-4.

followed by Razi in his study of Halesowen. Hajnal contrasted this with the later and companionate marriage which he held was found widely elsewhere within Europe, and although he later accepted that life-cycle female servanthood was a feature of later medieval English society, his whole thesis has been challenged, most significantly by Smith, Poos and Goldberg. They argue that female servanthood and other work opportunities, most notably in towns but also in the increasing pastoral sector of the rural economy, underlay a late marrying regime comparable to what is called the West European model which other historians had seen as emerging in England only in the early modern period.[134] The demographic consequences of this plague-induced regime (fewer children and smaller nuclear families) have already been discussed; but there were also quite important social repercussions, in the sense of greater freedom of choice for women of where and how they lived and worked and of whom they married, if they married at all.[135] Even in widowhood, women in peasant society seem to have been much better off than they had been in the thirteenth century. There was no longer the intense pressure on them to remarry, to provide a holding for a landless male; and Smith suggests that because of the value of their labour, husbands were more inclined to settle land on their wives in their lifetime, through joint tenancies, leaving widows with greater freedom to do as they willed with the holding after their husbands' death. He also adds a more cautionary note that landholding widows were not necessarily in the advantageous position often supposed. Sons and daughters migrated, leaving them to work the holding with expensive hired labour, and his tentative suggestion is that it was better to be a wife than a widow in the fifteenth century.[136]

Nonetheless, discounting all notions of a 'golden age for women', since such wondrous epochs never seem to have existed, the late fourteenth and at least the first half of the fifteenth century do seem to have been a period of limited opportunities firmly grasped. Yet the most important question is the third of those originally asked: did plague cause structural, permanent changes, or were these improved circumstances entirely dependent upon a diminished population, to vanish when demographic recovery began? As far as employment opportunities are concerned, they seem to have lasted little beyond that point. Goldberg sees the problem in terms of both the recovery

---

[134] The best general discussions of these issues are Goldberg, *Women, Work, and Life Cycle*, pp. 204-32 and Poos, *A Rural Society*, pp. 133-58, *passim*; Hajnal, 'European Marriage Patterns in Perspective', pp. 116-20; Smith, 'Hypothèses sur la nuptialité', pp. 107-09, 130-31.

[135] Goldberg, 'Female Labour, Service, and Marriage in the Late Medieval Urban North', p. 27; Kowaleski, 'The History of Urban Families', pp. 54-55.

[136] R. M. Smith, 'Coping with Uncertainty: Women's Tenure of Customary Land in England, *c.*1370-1430' in *Enterprise and Individuals*, ed. Kermode, 43-67, pp. 47-49, 61-63.

and of the recession which bit deeply into York's economy after the middle decades of the fifteenth century. Then, 'as in the era of the Industrial Revolution, men, fearful for their position in an increasingly precarious labour market, forced women into marginal and exclusively female trades'. So, by the late fifteenth century, women were being excluded from all craft industries and there was an increasing polarisation between the large female groups associated with the more prosperous mercantile households and the male servant groups attached to artisan households. Female service was becoming largely domestic and non-productive, and low-status in terms of occupation.[137]

Whether conditions in York, the capital of a region in deep recession, were typical of those to be found elsewhere can only be tested by further local studies (as Goldberg is the first to admit), particularly since the consequences of plague in this context do seem to have been markedly different from those in other areas of Europe, and most notably from those in the Mediterranean world.[138] Yet the important point to note is that there had been no structural change in occupational status which would have sustained the advantages women had gained beyond the end of demographic decline. In a male-dominated society, they had failed to gain access both to ruling elites in guild and town government and to sources of capital which would have allowed them to become fully independent traders or manufacturers. Few women were admitted to the franchise of any town, few attained any role in guild government and only in London was there a separate female guild, that of the silkwomen, very much a minority occupation at the luxury end of the market. Most female employment was also discontinuous. Exempt as they were from the clause in the Statute of Labourers confining workers to a single trade, women took up a variety of occupations, moving from one to another at the end of the year. They may have acquired a variety of skills in the process but they lacked the formal training in one occupation and thus the work identity of their male counterparts; and without access to capital (since the law worked in the favour of transfer of assets to the man) and to the political power that their economic status perhaps demanded, they were unable to preserve their hard-won advantages into the sixteenth century.[139]

In terms of female employment, then, there had been no substantial change, but the same cannot be said of marriage and the family. A North-West European marriage pattern, quite distinct from that which obtained in Southern Europe, does seem to have been established, or rather

[137]   Goldberg, 'Female Labour, Service, and Marriage in the Late Medieval Urban North', pp. 35-36; *idem, Women, Work, and Life Cycle*, pp. 16-17.

[138]   Goldberg, *Women, Work, and Life Cycle*, pp. 333-45.

[139]   Goldberg, *Women, Work, and Life Cycle*, pp. 334-36; Swanson, *Medieval Artisans*, pp. 107, 110, 116, 160-61; Lacey, 'Women and Work in Fourteenth and Fifteenth Century London', p. 25.

to have established itself, as a result of demographic change, characterised by life-cycle servanthood, later marriage, fewer children of the marriage, the nuclear rather than the extended family, and more men and women remaining unmarried. These are held to be the characteristics of the family in early modern England, and the emergence of such a family structure is thought to have been essential to the growth of individualism and enterprise, and to the transition from feudalism to capitalism.

CONCLUSIONS

In the relentless search for general explanations of the transition from the medieval to the early modern, pre-industrial economy, with its wage labour market of sizeable proportions, its mobile population and children who were expected to 'leave home, accumulate their own wealth, choose their own marriage partners and occupy their own economic niche',[140] and with landlords able to dispossess a peasantry that had failed to gain security of tenure in its holdings in order to engross and enclose and create farms suitable for commodity production, historians have perhaps sought to construct too rigid general models and impose them arbitrarily on English society as a whole. If Brenner, on the one hand, argues that everything hinged on the failure of the peasantry to consolidate the degree of proprietorship that protected their French counterparts from seigneurial exploitation, leading ultimately to their separation from the means of production and so, ultimately, to the creation of a large labour force and farms which could supply foodstuffs for workers in town and countryside, then others see the collapse, not the maintenance, of lordship and the weakening of the traditional social domination by lords as creating the liberated peasantry that formed the basis of the free wage workers in England.[141] But the difficulty is that these are theories of general change and allow little room for what all recent studies have revealed: the diversity of the regional responses, urban and rural, to changing conditions in the later middle ages. Poos's Essex, as he would be the first to admit, seems to bear little resemblance to Mate's east Sussex or to Pollard's north-eastern counties, and the decline of Phythian-Adams's Coventry has to be matched against the vitality of Postles's Loughborough. These regional studies have perhaps taught us two vital things. Firstly, to bring us back to the start of this essay, that notions of general prosperity or decline should be abandoned in favour of much more subtle pictures of varying fortunes and of changes that were to benefit some and disadvantage others. Secondly,

---

[140] Poos, *A Rural Society*, p. 291, citing R. S. Schofield, 'Family Structure, Demographic Behaviour, and Economic Growth' in *Famine, Disease, and the Social Order in Early Modern Society*, ed. J. Walter and R. Schofield (Cambridge, 1989), 279-304, p. 285.

[141] These arguments are summarised best by Dyer, 'Were There any Capitalists in Fifteenth-Century England?', pp. 8-9.

and most importantly, underlying them all seems to be the idea that plague, at its most persistent and virulent in the late fourteenth and fifteenth centuries, brought the structural changes which were the essential precursors of early modern England. For plague remains central to the whole debate. If the outcome of the crisis of the early fourteenth century was simply a return to the *status quo ante*, then the same cannot be said of the consequences of the Black Death. English society in 1500 was not as it had been in 1350. Change was slow and subtle, and would not have been understood by contemporaries in terms of a transition from feudalism to capitalism – both essentially modern constructs artificially imposed upon the middle ages. But changes there were, and for most of them the Black Death can be held directly or indirectly responsible: what would result from them in the sixteenth and seventeenth centuries is perhaps entirely another matter.

The English Church and English Religion after the Black Death

CHRISTOPHER HARPER-BILL

Introduction

To most people, looking back into the past, the history of the Church during the Middle Ages in England appears one continuous and stately progress. It is much nearer the truth to say that in 1351 the whole ecclesiastical system was wholly disorganised, or indeed more than half ruined, and everything had to be built up anew.... In time the religious sense and feeling revived, but in many respects it took a new tone, and its manifestations ran in new channels. If the change is to be described in brief, I should say that the religion of Englishmen, as it now manifested itself on the recovery of religion, and as it existed from that time to the Reformation, was characterised by a devotional and more self-reflective cast than previously.

Cardinal Gasquet[1]

I am not aware that any evil custom has ever been shown to have first started from this plague, or any good custom to have been killed by it... Where the shock found discipline already lax, it loosened the bonds still further; where the economic crisis fell upon houses that were already in debt, it dragged them into still deeper embarrassments.

G. G. Coulton[2]

These are the considered judgements of two of the foremost medievalists of an earlier generation, distinguished advocates respectively of the Roman Catholic and Protestant interpretations of the history of the pre-Reformation church. It will be the object of this essay to demonstrate that they were both right. The initial impact of the Black Death was catastrophic. It is surely inconceivable that the onslaught which in 1348-49 carried off one third of the people and 40% of the clergy should not have had an enormous impact on the religious belief and practice of the English people. In the longer term, however, the institutional Church coped remarkably well with this, as with other crises of the late fourteenth century, and emerged three generations later as a reinvigorated body – although it is doubtful whether the increase in introspective piety attributed by Gasquet to the aftermath of the plague can, in fact, be adjudged to be solely, or even primarily, a consequence of endemic pestilence.

---

[1] F. A. Gasquet, *The Great Pestilence (A.D. 1348-9)* (London, 1893), p. xvi.
[2] G. G. Coulton, *Five Centuries of Religion*, 4 vols (Cambridge, 1923-50), II, pp. 392, 396.

THE BLACK DEATH

On 24 October 1348 the bishop of Winchester ordered the clergy of his diocese to organise in their churches services and processions designed especially to pray for relief from the ravages of the plague which had just hit England.[3] In the next seventy years such penitential exercises were frequently ordered by English prelates in an effort to avert God's anger at the sins of the people. Contrition in England was organised by the ecclesiastical hierarchy, and was regimented rather than hysterical. A more rounded view of the evils of the times was, however, presented by Archbishop Thomas Arundel in September 1413, when he ordered that such religious observances should be implemented to pray not only for relief from the pestilence, but also for peace and for the eradication of sedition, schism and heresy.[4] The archbishop saw the recurrent outbreaks of plague as only one of the many evils by which the kingdom had been afflicted during his lifetime. There has been a tendency for modern historians, economic, ecclesiastical or political specialists, to view the social disruption, the political crises and the religious malaise of the late fourteenth century as separate phenomena, but contemporaries – the poetic genius who was the author of *Piers Plowman* as much as the archbishop of Canterbury – perceived one general crisis of manners and morals at every level of society.[5] The Lenten sermons of Archbishop Fitzralph of Armagh, one of the foremost preachers of the age, reveal his preoccupation with social and political shortcomings as much as with the impact of the plague.[6] They are characteristic of late fourteenth-century orthodox sermon literature, which in some ways foreshadows the pessimism of John Wyclif and the academic Lollards. Between the mid-fourteenth and the mid-fifteenth centuries, the Church in England, and indeed throughout Latin Christendom, suffered a prolonged series of crises. There were many extremely important developments in the history of the Church and of popular religion in the 180 years between the Black Death and the English Reformation, but it is extremely difficult with any confidence to ascribe any of these to the effects of pestilence alone.

[3]   *The Register of William Edington, Bishop of Winchester 1346-66*, ed. S. F. Hockey, 2 vols, Hampshire Record Series, 7-8 (Winchester, 1986-87), II, p. 24, no. 166; translated in full in Gasquet, *Great Pestilence*, pp. 107-09.

[4]   *The Register of Bishop Philip Repingdon, 1405-19*, ed. M. Archer, 3 vols, Lincoln Record Society, 57-58, 74 (Lincoln, 1963-82), II, pp. 362-63.

[5]   J. Coleman, *English Literature in History, 1350-1400: Medieval Readers and Writers* (London, 1981), p. 60. For the most accessible modernised version of *Piers Plowman*, see *Piers the Ploughman*, ed. J. F. Goodridge (Harmondsworth, 1959, rev. ed. 1966); for a recent discussion, see F. R. H. Du Boulay, *The England of Piers Plowman: William Langland and his Vision of the Fourteenth Century* (Woodbridge, 1991).

[6]   K. Walsh, *A Fourteenth-Century Scholar and Primate: Richard Fitzralph in Oxford, Avignon and Armagh* (Oxford, 1981), pp. 287-89.

There was much more to the shift of mental climate in the fourteenth century than purely economic factors arising either from the general downturn before 1348 or the demographic disaster of the Black Death. The buoyant confidence which had been so characteristic of the Latin Christianity of the expansionist western European society of the previous two hundred years was shattered by a series of disasters. The fall of Acre in 1291 marked the end of the crusading states of Outremer. For a century the die had been cast, and only a foothold maintained in the Near East. Yet the crusading ideal had been at the centre of the Christian life even for those who never ventured beyond their own locality, an ideal furthered by preaching, appeals and taxation. Henceforth holy war was to be defensive, designed to stem Islamic incursions into the West. Neither the preaching nor the taxation ceased, although in England the crown creamed off much of the profit without making any positive contribution to the defence of Latin Christendom.[7] The triumphalism of a previous age had, however, long ago evaporated.

Then, in 1337, the simmering hostility between the kings of France and England exploded into open confrontation. Most of the other powers of fourteenth-century Europe were drawn into the endemic conflict which has become known as the Hundred Years War. The Church in France suffered most obviously from the indiscriminate looting of English armies and of the free companies who profited most from the war, but in England too the clerical order came under considerable pressure, constantly subjected to royal demands for taxation and to orchestrated campaigns for wholesale disendowment to further the war effort: in this at least John Wyclif was merely a mouthpiece for views held by a considerable proportion of the politically influential classes who remained religiously orthodox.[8]

At the same time as western Europe was hit by economic downturn, endemic disease and perennial warfare, it also suffered a series of crises of ecclesiastical authority. The arrest at Anagni in 1303 of the aged Pope Boniface VIII by the agents of the French king has conventionally been regarded as a watershed in the history of the Catholic Church.[9] It has been seen as a signal to the other rulers of western Europe, and to the Church's hierarchy, that the uncharacteristic period of religious unity under papal leadership, established in the late eleventh century, often disputed but never overthrown, had at last been undermined. It is doubtful whether,

---

[7] C. Tyerman, *England and the Crusades, 1095-1588* (Chicago, Illinois, 1988), pp. 229-58, esp. pp. 252-58.

[8] For this issue, see M. Wilks, 'Royal Patronage and Anti-Papalism from Ockham to Wyclif', in *From Ockham to Wyclif*, ed. A. Hudson and M. Wilks, Studies in Church History, Subsidia, 5 (Oxford, 1987), pp. 135-63.

[9] For the most recent and concise general account of papal history in this period, see J. H. Lynch, *The Medieval Church: a Brief History* (London, 1992), pp. 313-35.

despite King Edward I's own conflict with Boniface VIII, the dramatic events at Anagni made much impact on the consciousness of the English people in general. The same cannot be said for the removal of the papacy in 1309 to Avignon. Politically and militarily, this was a thoroughly sensible move on the part of Pope Clement V, for the papal states were in chronic disorder and Avignon provided the stable base which Rome had seldom been. From here the popes could mount a campaign to reduce their Italian territories to obedience, and could exercise more effective control over the churches of northern Europe. This, however, was not the popular belief, and in England there was a common perception, orchestrated by the government, that the pope had become the creature of the French king. This resentment was, of course, accentuated by the outbreak of the Hundred Years War. There was no acknowledgement of the papacy's effort to negotiate a peaceful settlement as a preliminary to a new crusade. Rather English soldiers posted bills in France confidently proclaiming that it mattered little that the pope had become French, since Jesus now had become English.[10]

Worse was to come. A major crisis of spiritual authority was prompted by the outbreak in 1378 of the Great Schism within the Western Church. Almost immediately after the return of the Papacy to Rome in that year, a group of French cardinals challenged the legitimacy of the new Italian pope, Urban VI, and elected one of their own number as Clement VII. There had been many papal schisms before, but hitherto it had been reasonably certain who was the rightful pontiff and who the politically motivated usurper. The issue now was not clear cut, and Europe divided in its allegiances along lines predetermined by the alliance of powers on either side in the Hundred Years War. Two English expeditions, to Flanders in 1383 and to Castile in 1386, were blessed by the Roman pope as crusades, with the full panoply of indulgences, because they were directed against the schismatic allies of the French.[11] This is not to say that the schism was welcomed for political reasons or was cynically exploited. Throughout western Europe, including England, there was profound disquiet at an obvious scandal which made a travesty of Christian unity, even within the Latin Church, and much agonised thought was devoted by prelates and academics to the means by which the schism could be ended.[12] Things got worse before they got better. The cardinals from both papal courts who met at Pisa in 1409 hoped to resolve the schism, but succeeded

[10] W. A. Pantin, *The English Church in the Fourteenth Century* (Cambridge, 1955; repr. Notre Dame, Indiana, 1963), p. 82.

[11] M. McKisack, *The Fourteenth Century* (Oxford, 1959), pp. 429-32; P. E. Russell, *The English Intervention in Spain and Portugal in the time of Edward III and Richard II* (Oxford, 1955), pp. 400-48.

[12] M. M. Harvey, *Solutions to the Schism. A Study of Some English Attitudes, 1378 to 1409*, Kirchengeschichtliche Quellen und Studien, 12 (St Ottilien, 1983).

only in electing a third rival pope. It was five years more before the Council of Constance, in whose convocation King Henry V and the German Emperor Sigismund were instrumental, succeeded at last in restoring a single papacy. The vicissitudes of papal history, just as much as the ravages of plague, must be taken into account when considering the history of the English Church and of religion in England in the fourteenth and early fifteenth centuries. It is surely significant that the first notable outbreak of heresy in England coincided with the onset of the Great Schism, and· that religious dissent in England evaporated rapidly once unity was restored in the Church.

Already before the chaotic mortality of the Black Death or the scandal of the papal schism, there had been a fundamental shift in the theological climate of western Christendom.[13] It is not coincidental that the great age of expansion, territorial and economic, in the twelfth and early thirteenth centuries had coincided with an era of exuberant theological optimism, culminating in the great synthesis of humane learning and divine revelation produced by St Thomas Aquinas (d. 1274). For Aquinas, writing in the Paris of St Louis (who was presented as the ideal model of Christian kingship), and contemplating the expansion of Latin Christianity on the frontiers of Europe, it was easy to believe that the divine purpose was comprehensible; that God's purpose was working itself out through the worldly agency of a church and of kings approved by Him; that while human reason must always be subservient to divine grace and revelation, it was in fact possible for the rational man informed by faith to comprehend the nature and the intent of God; that, in short, 'all was for the best in the best of all possible worlds'. Aquinas rationalised the divine. He believed that God is intelligence and reason and that His creation, both the universe and the known world, conforms to His reasonable nature.

It is in no way demonstrable, but it seems highly likely, that the economic and territorial contraction, the military reversals and the misfortunes of the papacy in the early fourteenth century were significant factors in the theological *volte-face* which is associated with the English Franciscan theologian, William of Ockham, who died in 1349. If the western interpretation of the Christian religion was correct, if the Roman Church had conscientiously fulfilled Christ's mandate to St Peter, how could one explain the fact that a reasonable God was allowing the successive crises and disasters which were besetting Latin Christendom? Ockham and his followers, who dominated the theological faculties of the fourteenth and fifteenth centuries, certainly never denied the existence of God or the truth of revealed religion. They did, however, assert strongly

---

[13] For what follows, see the easily comprehensible discussion by F. R. H. Du Boulay, *An Age of Ambition* (London, 1970), pp. 160-78; for far greater detail, D. Knowles, *The Evolution of Medieval Thought* (London, 1962), pp. 291-336.

that no religious truth is demonstrable, but rather must be accepted by the exercise of faith, rather than of reason. God's attributes cannot be delineated by the application of human rationality. All that can be posited of God is His absolute power, which in human terms may be seen as capriciousness. How else could one interpret the reverses which were now besetting His people? While the Ockhamists did not set out to change the religious perceptions of their world, it is certain that their pessimism about the capacity of mankind to comprehend the divine nature and purpose was both a reflection of the declining fortunes of western Europe and also influenced the religious perceptions of those exposed to their views, at however great a remove (such as the audience of mendicant sermons or those confessed by priests influenced, even unconsciously, by the new theology).

The Secular Clergy

The shock of the first onslaught of the plague cannot be better illustrated than by a mandate issued by the bishop of Bath and Wells on 17 January 1349.[14] He observed that the raging pestilence had left many parishes devoid of pastoral care, and that neither for love nor money could priests be found to undertake the ministry of the Church, most especially to visit the terminally sick; many people were dying without the sacrament of penance because they believed that they could only confess to a priest. He ordered all incumbents in his diocese to make known to their congregations that if anyone on their deathbed did not have access to a priest, they should make their confession to a layman, or even to a woman, and such confession would be most beneficial for the remission of their sins. Any lay person who heard such a confession was bound, like a priest, to maintain strict secrecy. The bishop granted forty days' relaxation of penance to those who should go to confess to a priest before they were struck down by fatal illness, and also to priests who encouraged their flocks to do this and who heard their confessions. It was stipulated that any survivors who had confessed to a lay person must repent of the same sins before his parish priest. Nevertheless, in the gravest of emergencies, a Catholic bishop had authorised a practice the advocacy of which half a century later would be regarded as one of the more obnoxious tenets of the Lollard heretics.[15]

Statistics of clerical mortality can be compiled for many areas from the lists of admissions to ecclesiastical livings recorded in bishops' registers, of which England has a series unparalleled in western Europe.[16] One source,

14   *Concilia Magnae Britanniae et Hiberniae*, ed. D. Wilkins, 4 vols (London, 1737), II, pp. 735-36, conveniently translated by Gasquet, *Great Pestilence*, pp. 81-83.
15   A. Hudson, *The Premature Reformation: Wycliffite Texts and Lollard History* (Oxford, 1988), pp. 294-301, esp. p. 298.
16   D. M. Smith, *Guide to Bishops' Registers of England and Wales* (London, 1981).

however, gives a more general indicator for the whole country. The crown presented to livings in the king's own gift and those temporarily in his hands because of the vacancy of a bishopric, the minority of a tenant-in-chief, or because the advowson pertained to one of those alien priories which were in the crown's custody because of the war with France.[17] The average annual number of royal presentations for a few years before 1348 was about a hundred. In 1348 there were 159 such presentations, just over half of these in the months from September to December. Then, from 25 January 1349 to 24 January 1350, the king presented to 849 ecclesiastical livings, over eight times the number for a normal twelve-month period.[18] The figure is certainly inflated because so many ecclesiastical and baronial patrons themselves died in the course of the year, and by the habit of royal clerks of exchanging benefices in order to swell their income; nevertheless, these figures provide some indication of the extent of the crisis at a national level.

In Somerset, one of the first areas to suffer, the average number of institutions each year by the bishop of Bath and Wells was thirty-five. In December 1348 alone there were thirty-two institutions, and in the calendar year 1349 the total was 232, almost a seven-fold increase.[19] In Exeter diocese, covering Devon and Cornwall, the annual average of admissions in the early 1340s was thirty-six; from November 1348 to September 1349, when the plague was apparently abating, the total was 371.[20] For Norfolk and Suffolk, the register of the bishop of Norwich records the average number of institutions in the five years before 1349 as seventy-seven; in 1349, eight hundred parishes lost their incumbents, eighty-three of them twice, ten of them three times.[21] On the other side of the country, in the diocese of Hereford, an annual average of thirteen institutions rose in 1349 to 175, with a further forty-five in 1350; to many of these the bishop himself collated because the normal patron was dead or

---

[17]   These presentations are normally enrolled on the patent rolls, and also appear in bishops' registers.

[18]   Gasquet, *Great Pestilence*, pp. 76-79.

[19]   *Ibid.*, p. 165, which uses figures derived from the then unpublished *Register of Ralph of Shrewsbury, Bishop of Bath and Wells 1329-63*, ed. T. S. Holmes, 2 vols, Somerset Record Society, pp. 9-10 (London, 1896).

[20]   Gasquet, *Great Pestilence*, p. 87, using figures derived from the then unpublished *Register of John de Grandisson, Bishop of Exeter AD 1327-69*, ed. F. C. Hingeston-Randolph, 3 vols (London and Exeter, 1894-9).

[21]   A. Jessopp, 'The Black Death in East Anglia', in his *The Coming of the Friars* (London, 1899), pp. 166-211, especially pp. 200, 214-15. On pp. 220-21 he speculates on the mortality of unbeneficed clergy and estimates a minimum of two thousand clerical deaths in 1349. The register of William Bateman, bishop of Norwich 1344-55, on which Jessopp's figures for incumbents are based, will shortly be published by the Canterbury and York Society, edited by Dr P. Pobst.

had failed to present.[22] In the huge diocese of Lincoln, covering eight counties, Bishop Gynewell instituted in July 1349 alone to 250 vacant livings, whereas only 212 vacancies had occurred in the previous eighteen months.[23] The percentage of deaths of incumbents throughout England during the first attack of the plague in 1348-49 has been estimated at 39% for York diocese, 40% for Coventry and Lichfield, 43% for Hereford, 44% for Worcester, and 48% each for the dioceses of Bath and Wells, Exeter, Norwich and Winchester, giving a national mortality rate for beneficed clergy of approximately 45%.[24] Those who served their cures in person and tended their dying parishioners were naturally more likely than their absentee colleagues to die themselves. A detailed study of Coventry and Lichfield diocese has shown that mortality among rectors (who might be non-resident) was 33%, but that the death rate for vicars, bound by oath to personal residence, was 46%.[25] There is no way of knowing the death rate among the large numbers of parochial and stipendiary chaplains who were hired to serve parishes with non-resident rectors or to provide assistance to resident incumbents in very many larger parishes. It is probably reasonable to assume, however, that in about nine out of every twenty English parishes, the priest who actually ministered to the people died during the first onslaught of the Black Death.

This, of course, was not the end of the matter, for the plague was endemic, and the next major outbreak came in 1361-62. A comprehensive survey of institutions in the large diocese of York indicates that the death rate in these years was much lower, at 6%, though rising again to 13% in the 1369 outbreak.[26] The evidence of a southern register, however, suggests that while clerical mortality was certainly lower than in 1349, the difference is not that great. Whereas in 1349-50 Bishop Edington of Winchester admitted 369 new incumbents, in 1361-62 he instituted only 225; yet this must be set against figures of only thirty-six institutions in 1359-60 and fifty-two in 1363-64.[27] Only by the terrible standards of the first onslaught

[22] Gasquet, *Great Pestilence*, pp. 141-42, using figures drawn from the then unpublished *Registrum Johannis de Trillek, Episcopi Herefordensis, AD MCCCXLIV–MCCCLXI*, ed. J. H. Parry, Canterbury and York Society, 8 (London, 1912).

[23] A. Hamilton Thompson, 'The Registers of John Gynewell, Bishop of Lincoln, for the Years 1349-50', *Archaeological Journal*, 68 (1911), 301-60.

[24] J.-A. H. Moran, 'Clerical Recruitment in the Diocese of York, 1340-1530: Data and Commentary', *Journal of Ecclesiastical History*, 34 (1983), 19-54, p. 26.

[25] R. A. Davies, 'The Effect of the Black Death on the Parish Priests of the Medieval Diocese of Coventry and Lichfield', *Historical Research*, 62 (1989), 85-90.

[26] Moran, 'Clerical Recruitment', p. 33.

[27] *Reg. Edington*, pp. 57-120, 176-239, *passim*; Ormrod, below, p. 152, n. 17.

could the epidemic of 1361-62 be considered anything less than catastrophic.

With such high clerical mortality, so many churches left vacant and so few surviving unbeneficed chaplains who might fill them, there was obviously an urgent need to replenish the ranks of ordained ministers, especially of priests, at a time when the pool of potential recruits was itself greatly diminished. The drastic fall in population did not mean that there were any fewer parish churches to be served, even if the larger parishes could perhaps function with fewer assistant clergy. Moreover, demand for mass priests to celebrate for the souls of the dead had increased greatly. English prelates certainly appreciated the urgency of the situation. Archbishop Zouche of York obtained a papal indult allowing him to hold ordinations on days other than those prescribed by canon law, and his register includes numerous dispensations for the ordination to the priesthood of illegitimate males.[28] In January 1351 Archbishop Fitzralph of Armagh received papal permission to dispense forty illegitimate men and twenty sons of priests or men who had been married (all normally barred from holy orders).[29] In October 1350 the pope allowed the bishop of Norwich to ordain as priests sixty clerks who had passed their twentieth birthdays (the canonical age was twenty-five), since many parishes lacked ministers because of the plague.[30] In the winter of 1349-50 the archdeacon of St David's almost herded young Welshmen over the border for ordination by the bishop of Hereford.[31]

A detailed analysis of the registers of the archbishops of York has revealed that surprisingly large numbers of clergy were ordained during and immediately after the main outbreaks of pestilence in the second half of the fourteenth century.[32] The annual numbers ordained from 1344 to 1346 were 132 secular priests and 306 acolytes. From 1349 to 1351 this rose to an annual average of 402 secular priests and 431 acolytes, with the quite remarkable figures of 683 acolytes ordained in 1349 and 724 priests in 1350. In the period 1356-60 there was a sharp drop to an annual average of sixty-nine priests and eighty-five acolytes, but with the second great outbreak of plague in 1361-62 the annual average rose to 107 priests and 114 acolytes. There was another drop from 1363 to 1368 (an average of sixty-seven priests a year), but in 1368, with another onslaught of the fatal

[28] *Letters from the Northern Registers*, ed. J. Raine, Rolls Series, 61 (London, 1873), pp. 401-02.
[29] Walsh, *Fitzralph*, p. 282.
[30] Norfolk Record Office, Register of William Bateman, fol. 118v.
[31] G. Williams, *The Welsh Church from Conquest to Reformation* (Cardiff, 1962), p. 147. This work provides (pp. 146-75) a truly excellent account of the impact of the Black Death on the Welsh church, which might serve as a model for a similar study of England.
[32] These figures are all taken from Moran, 'Clerical Recruitment'.

disease, the number of acolytes ordained shot up to 239; and from 1369 to 1380, with outbreaks of pestilence recurring in 1369, 1375 and 1378, the annual average rose again to 130 priests and 148 acolytes. So, in the diocese of York, a clerical career remained attractive until the 1370s, the ranks of the clergy were replenished from a greatly reduced population, and compared with the pre-plague period, far more ordinands progressed quickly to the priesthood, whereas hitherto many had remained for long periods, or indeed permanently, as acolytes or subdeacons. By the period from 1392 to 1410, however, when the York lists begin again after a break, ordinations had fallen by 34% compared with the levels of the 1370s and 29% compared with the pre-1348 figures. Until the 1440s these levels remained fairly stable, there was a dip in the 1450s, and then after 1460 there was an extraordinary and steady rise from a low of seventy-five secular priests in 1453 to a peak of 363 in 1508. From the 1450s to 1500 there was a rise in the average annual number of priestly ordinations from ninety-eight to 221, an increase of 124%; even supposing that the population as a whole did begin to grow in the later fifteenth century, this rate of increase clearly cannot be explained in demographic terms.

Although in southern and midland dioceses ordination levels did not hold up so well in the period from 1350 to 1380, the same general trend is discernible. In Coventry and Lichfield diocese, for example, the total number of ordinands from 1300 to 1349 was c.6,000, dropping between 1350 and 1399 to c.4,000; this is proportionate to the decline in population. Although it is notable that levels here did not, as in York, rise sharply during attacks of the plague, Bishop Stretton's register shows the same marked decline from the 1380s, and this continued into the next century, when from 1400 to 1449 there were only c.2,700 ordinands. This rose sharply in the second half of the fifteenth century, with c.5,000 ordinands between 1450 and 1499 and, quite remarkably, 5,300 from 1500 to 1532.[33] In the south, the registers of Wykeham at Winchester and Brantingham at Exeter show again that the great drop in ordinations occurred after 1378.[34] Between 1379 and 1455 the annual number of priests ordained in Exeter diocese was only twenty-five, less than half the average of the period 1308-21; this fall was greater than the percentage decline in population, and the level of ordinations did not rise with the supposed demographic upturn of the early fifteenth century. Since there were 521 parishes in the diocese, in the late fourteenth and early fifteenth centuries there were hardly enough ordinands to fill vacant benefices, let alone to provide parochial and stipendiary chaplains and mass priests. William Wykeham appears

[33] R. N. Swanson, *Church and Society in Late Medieval England* (Oxford, 1989), pp. 32-38.
[34] R. L. Storey, 'Recruitment of English Clergy in the Period of the Conciliar Movement', *Annuarium Historiae Conciliorum*, 7 (1977), 290-313, pp. 294-95.

remarkably percipient, in the face of Wyclif's assertion that there were too many clergy in England, when he gave as one of the reasons for his foundation in 1378 of New College, Oxford, the great reduction in clerical numbers due to the plague and other misfortunes; in fact the decline was only then just about to approach its nadir.[35] By the 1380s in southern England generally there was a two-thirds decline from pre-plague levels of ordination.

The one thing which is obvious from these figures is that the initial impact of the Black Death did not cause a crisis of faith or deter men from entering the priesthood. The York statistics, indeed, indicate the opposite, for it would surely be unduly cynical to believe that those who flocked into orders in the most catastrophic years were motivated only by the astute calculation of career opportunities in the multitudinous vacant benefices, especially as for many priests even the tenure of such an established living brought little more than existence at subsistence level.[36] For many of them, personal salvation, and indeed spiritual service to a community in crisis, must have been the main incentive to enter the clerical order. Likewise, while it is certainly true that shortage of skilled labour had created by the 1380s career opportunities which had not been available before 1348, and while administrative posts previously restricted to clerks were now open to laymen, it is surely no coincidence that the great fall in ordination levels coincided with the outbreak of the Great Schism and a crisis of leadership and confidence throughout the Western Church. It has been suggested, indeed, that this turning away from the priesthood was the negative and apathetic counterpart to the positive and vigorous criticism of ecclesiastical institutions made by the Lollards, and it is certainly interesting that the decline in ordinations, just like the impact of heresy, was less marked in the north of England. Similarly, the great upsurge in ordinations in the 1460s can be explained partly in economic terms – enclosure in the countryside and the urban crisis – but it also occurred at a time when the divisions of Christendom, last openly revealed at the Council of Basle, had been healed, and when the spiritual and liturgical regeneration of the English church inaugurated by King Henry V and his bishops had taken effect and moulded the minds of a new generation, for whom, perhaps, a clerical career once again conferred status rather than invited contempt.[37] Certainly, in any case, the Black Death did not initiate a decline in clerical numbers which continued unabated until the Reformation; the trough postdated the initial onslaught of the pestilence by thirty years, and clerical

---

35   Storey, 'Recruitment', p. 293.
36   P. Heath, *Medieval Clerical Accounts*, Borthwick Papers, 26 (York, 1964).
37   These reasons for the decline and rise in ordination figures are suggested by Storey, 'Recruitment'.

numbers were once again rising markedly seventy years before the breach with Rome.

Contemporary observers, from markedly different viewpoints, were united in their opinion that the plague had brought about a decline in the quality of the secular clergy, and most particularly that it had stimulated greed and the frenzied quest for inflationary rewards. The Rochester chronicler, writing immediately after the first outbreak, noted that 'in this pestilence many chaplains and stipendiary clerics refused to serve, except at excessive salaries'.[38] Forty years later Henry Knighton, the fiercely orthodox canon of Leicester Abbey, looking back at the plague years, observed that 'so great was the scarcity of priests that many churches were left desolate and without divine office ... hardly could a chaplain be got under £10 or ten marks [which he regarded as extortionate] to minister in any church, and where before a chaplain could be had for four or five marks, or two marks with board, so numerous were priests before the plague, now scarce any would accept a vicarage of £20 or twenty marks'. Not only were the clergy profiteering from the aftermath of the pestilence; the quality of their performance had also declined: 'but in a short time there came crowding into orders a multitude of men whose wives had died of plague, of whom many were illiterate, only able to write after a fashion and incapable of understanding what they read'.[39]

This view of a poorly motivated clergy with an eye to the main chance is supported, from a diametrically opposed position, by the criticisms levelled by the Welsh Lollard Walter Brut when in 1390 he was charged before the bishop of Hereford with heresy.[40] He painted a lurid picture of churchmen, from the summit of the hierarchy to the humblest priests, engaged in the unbridled pursuit of financial gain, with scant regard for the sufferings of their flock. The pope granted livings for excessive fees and sold indulgences; bishops charged for ordination; archdeacons levied extortionate fines as punishment for sin rather than imposing salutary penance; monks and friars peddled for cash the spiritual benefits of which they were custodians; parish priests ruthlessly exacted their tithes but all too often neglected their pastoral obligations, emigrating rather to large towns where they could earn handsome fees for the celebration of requiem masses. This theme of 'mede', disproportionate reward, runs through the

---

[38] *Anglia Sacra*, ed. H. Wharton, 2 vols (London, 1691), II, pp. 375-76, cited by Gasquet, *Great Pestilence*, p. 105.

[39] *Chronicon Henrici Knighton*, ed. J. R. Lumby, 2 vols, Rolls Series, 92 (London, 1889-95), II, p. 63. Knighton also thought that the structure of society was threatened by the improved status of villeins resulting from the labour shortage.

[40] *Registrum Johannis Trefnant, Episcopi Herefordensis, AD MCCCLXXXIX–MCCCCIV*, ed. W. W. Capes, Canterbury and York Society, 20 (London, 1916), p. 352, cited by Williams, *Welsh Church*, pp. 158-59.

orthodox but fiercely critical poem, *Piers Plowman*, whose author remarked that:

[handwritten margin note: Poor Clergy or Clergy of Cleris?]

> Parsons and parish priests complained to the bishop
> That their parishes are poor since the pestilence-time,
> Asked for licence and leave to live in London,
> And sing masses there for simony, for silver is sweet.[41]

In other words, in an age when there was greatly increased demand for masses to ease the souls of the dead through the pains of Purgatory, many priests were over-eager to respond to consumer demand, even if this willingness to celebrate for souls led to the neglect of the spiritual cure of their living charges.

In his wider view of religion and society William Langland may have been a voice crying in the wilderness; but in this matter at least he merely reflected the view of the English ecclesiastical hierarchy. A series of constitutions was promulgated with the intention of curbing clerical wage demands; these were the Church's equivalent of the parliamentary Statute of Labourers. Archbishops Islip of Canterbury and Thoresby of York both *[handwritten margin note: Complaints against Clergy.]* imposed maximum wage rates for chaplains, and in 1378 Archbishop Sudbury of Canterbury, although he raised considerably the levels set by his predecessor, delivered an impassioned diatribe against the conduct of the clergy of his province who 'are so tainted with the vice of cupidity that they are not content with reasonable stipends, but demand and receive excessive wages. These greedy and fastidious priests vomit from the excess of their salaries, they run wild and wallow, and some of them, after sating the gluttony of their bellies, break forth into a pit of evils'.[42] Such colourful rhetoric, even when embedded in the legislation of the Church, should be treated with some caution. Throughout the history of the Christian Church, moralists and legislators have used the most lurid vocabulary to attack perceived abuses. If, for example, we had to rely solely on the letters and treatises of St Bernard of Clairvaux, we would hardly judge the twelfth century to be an age of reform, let alone an heroic period in the history of the Church; while in 1511 Dean Colet accused the ranks of the English clergy of greed and peculation at a time when we know from record sources that the great majority of them were struggling to survive at the same level as their peasant parishioners.[43] More specifically, a detailed study of

[41] William Langland, *Will's Vision of Piers Plowman*, trans. E. Talbot Donaldson (London and New York, 1990), p. 3.

[42] For Sudbury's decree, see *English Historical Documents, 1327-1485*, ed. A. R. Myers (London, 1969), pp. 728-29, no. 435; for the legislation as a whole, B. Putnam, 'Wage-Laws for Priests after the Black Death', *American Historical Review*, 21 (1915-16), 12-32.

[43] For amplification, see C. Harper-Bill, 'John Colet's Convocation Sermon and the Pre-Reformation Church in England', *History*, 73 (1988), 191-210. The concept of anticlericalism on the eve of the Reformation has been virtually

London chantries, allegedly the favourite resort of clerical wasters in the late fourteenth century, has indicated that these were not sinecures, but rather involved a great deal of hard work, both religious and secular, often for little remuneration.[44] Recent work on the church in late medieval Bristol, too, has indicated the valuable contribution made to the religious and social life of that city by its numerous unbeneficed clergy.[45]

The income of the beneficed clergy certainly fell in the wake of the Black Death. Those rectors with extensive glebe, who had hitherto exploited it by hiring labour, might be forced by rising wages to lease out the lands of their church on the best terms they could get. Both rectors and vicars were hard hit by the reduction in tithe income, proportionate to the decline in population and in agricultural production, and there was a similar diminution of offerings and fees for marriages, purifications and even (after the initial upsurge) of mortuaries. A list of revenues of a group of churches transferred in 1351 from the patronage of Lewes Priory to the crown, which gives both pre- and post-plague valuations, is clearly indicative of the immediate decline in parochial revenues; but in the wider context it is obvious that the income of most parish churches continued to decline throughout the later middle ages.[46]

The initial impact of the Black Death on poorer livings in the diocese of Rochester was recognised by the bishop in a mandate issued in June 1349. He lamented that some priests and clerks refused to accept vacant benefices because of their impoverishment, while others who held such livings now wanted to abandon them because the death toll had drastically reduced their already meagre income. He instructed that any priest, when so ordered, should undertake parochial responsibilities, but realistically allowed that such rectors and vicars might bring their income up to ten marks a year (hardly an excessive sum) by the celebration of anniversary masses.[47] This provision at least recognised that it was often necessity

demolished by C. Haigh, 'Anticlericalism and the English Reformation', *History*, 68 (1983), 391-407. In Lincolnshire anticlericalism seems more pronounced, and certainly more organised, in the 1290s than after the Black Death: see D. M. Owen, *Church and Society in Medieval Lincolnshire* (Lincoln, 1971), pp. 140-41.

[44] R. M. T. Hill, '"A Chaunterie for Soules": London Chantries in the Reign of Richard II', in *The Reign of Richard II*, ed. F. R. H. Du Boulay and C. M. Barron (London, 1971), pp. 242-55.

[45] C. Burgess, '"For the Increase of Divine Service": Chantries in the Parish in Late Medieval Bristol', *Journal of Ecclesiastical History*, 36 (1985), 46-65.

[46] R. N. Swanson, 'Standard of Livings: Parochial Revenues in Pre-Reformation England', in *Religious Belief and Ecclesiastical Careers in Late Medieval England*, ed. C. Harper-Bill (Woodbridge, 1991), 151-96; for the Lewes churches see pp. 191-94.

[47] Gasquet, *Great Pestilence*, p. 105, citing London, British Library MS Cotton Faustina Bv, fol. 98.

rather than greed that prompted refusal to serve in the parishes. Over sixty years later, in 1412, a petition was addressed to the pope detailing the impoverishment of many vicarages in the diocese of Norwich, which resulted in their remaining unfilled, to the detriment both of religion and hospitality. [Anti-]Pope John XXIII ordered the bishop to augment these vicarages from the revenues of the corporate rectors if he found this to be true.[48] Five such augmentations are recorded in the Norwich registers between 1438 and 1475.[49] In some cases a reasonable standard of living for the incumbent could be achieved only by uniting two churches – a process familiar in the Anglican Church of the twentieth century. In 1352, for example, the patrons and parishioners of Great and Little Collington (Herefordshire) petitioned the bishop to unite the churches, because since the plague the great reduction in population and crops meant that the two parishes scarcely had the resources to support one priest.[50] In 1366 the bishop of Ely united the churches of All Saints and St Giles, Cambridge, since most of the parishioners of All Saints were dead and the survivors now went to other churches.[51] In Norwich diocese twenty-nine unifications of benefices are recorded from 1349 onwards, whereas there had been only four in the early fourteenth century.[52]

One apparent effect of the shortage of clergy in the wake of the Black Death was the enormous increase in the number of exchanges of livings. Incumbents, and especially those with some influence stemming from birth or governmental service, sought to improve their income and to consolidate their ecclesiastical holdings. During Bishop Sudbury's tenure of the see of London (1361-75), exchanges account for 45% of all institutions, and 239 of these 332 transactions involved exchanges for livings outside the diocese.[53] This situation provoked the outraged attack by Archbishop Courtenay in 1391 on those who exchanged their benefices purely for profit, thus committing the sin of simony, and most especially against the 'choppechurches', those agents who in return for their own cut arranged such deals.[54] That the proliferation of exchanges was associated with the

---

[48]   *Calendar of Papal Registers: Papal Letters 1404-15*, p. 311.

[49]   B. Bruce, 'The Episcopal Administration of the Diocese of Norwich in the Later Middle Ages', University of Oxford B. Litt. thesis (1971), p. 219.

[50]   *Reg. Trillek*, pp. 174-76.

[51]   Historical Manuscripts Commission, *Sixth Report*, p. 299, cited by Gasquet, *Great Pestilence*, pp. 134-35.

[52]   Bruce, 'Episcopal Administration of Norwich', pp. 215-17.

[53]   *Registrum Simonis de Sudbiria Diocesis Londoniensis, AD 1362-75*, ed. R. C. Fowler and C. Jenkins, Canterbury and York Society, 34, 38 (Oxford, 1927-38). For exchanges in general, see Swanson, *Church and Society*, pp. 55-56; A. Hamilton Thompson, *The English Clergy and their Organization in the Later Middle Ages* (Oxford, 1947), pp. 107-09.

[54]   *Concilia*, ed. Wilkins, II, pp. 215-17; translated in J. Dahmus, *William*

shortage of clergy caused by the plague is well illustrated by figures for the archdeaconry of Huntingdon.[55] From 1320 to 1362 there were seventy-six exchanges (2.9 *per annum*), from 1363 to 1398 278 (11.1 *per annum*), from 1398 to 1419 184 (8.7 *per annum*), and from 1425 to 1431 nineteen (3.1 *per annum*), decreasing thereafter as the number of ordinands once more began to rise. The damaging effects of such exchanges, however, despite Courtenay's strictures, should not be over-emphasised, because although many parishes had a high turnover of incumbents, those clergy most likely to exchange for profit did not normally themselves serve their cures, and even in parishes which were the preserve of short-term absentees, stability would often be provided by the parochial chaplain.

The appropriation of parish churches has often been regarded as one of the great evils of the late medieval church. By this process part, often the bulk, of parochial revenues was transferred to the use of the corporate rector, usually a monastery, cathedral or collegiate church; the parish was then served normally by a vicar, with security of tenure, but sometimes by an easily removable chaplain.[56] Not only was the income from glebe, tithe and offerings (which should have been expended within the parish, most especially on relief of poverty) diverted to the support of the monastic and clerical elite; there was also a great diminution in the number of livings sufficiently well remunerated to attract well-qualified and learned priests. As with exchanges, however, the real damage to the religious life of English parishes may have been exaggerated. The vast majority of rectories still held by individual clergy had incomes not much greater than the vicarages of appropriated churches, and if indeed the opportunities for suitable graduate employment within the parishes were reduced, those less learned priests who were prepared, for a modest stipend, to undertake the cure of souls and the cultivation of the glebe were probably far more in tune with the religious and social aspirations of their parishioners than some graduates better suited to scholarship and administration.

Certainly after 1349 monastic communities in particular invoked the ravages of the plague as justification for their petitions for the appropriation of churches of which hitherto they had been merely the patrons, presenting to the diocesan suitable candidates from the secular clergy for the office of rector. In 1351, for example, the church of Cotham (Nottinghamshire) was appropriated to the Augustinian canons of Thurgarton on the grounds of their impoverishment by the pestilence, and in 1351 the nuns of Romsey obtained the appropriation of a prebend within their abbey church on the

Courtenay, Archbishop of Canterbury, 1381-96 (University Park, Pennsylvania, 1966), pp. 261-65.

[55] I am indebted for these figures to the Rev. C. A. Weale, who is currently completing a Ph.D. thesis on the clergy of the archdeaconry of Huntingdon, *c.*1100-1540.

[56] For appropriation, see Hamilton Thompson, *English Clergy*, pp. 109-21.

same grounds.[57] Such complaints were sustained for the rest of the century. In 1358 the canons of Shulbred secured the appropriation of Mid Lavant church (Sussex) because of their poverty 'due to the death of many of their servants in the great pestilence of 1350', and in 1394 an enquiry into the justification for the appropriation of Keevil church (Wiltshire) to the Bonshommes of Edington noted that 'the resources of the house are much burdened by plague, and unless a remedy is quickly found the house, which spends more than £50 a year on hospitality, will no longer be able to support the burdens imposed upon it'.[58] In fact, mention of the plague in petitions for the annexation of parochial revenues became after 1350 common form, just as throughout the century northern monasteries cited the devastation caused by Scottish raids and after 1337 religious houses on the south coast pleaded the ravages to their estates perpetrated by the piratical French.[59] Plague and war were certainly both factors in monastic impoverishment. But more accurate, at least in its comprehensiveness, was the petition of the Benedictines of Winchcombe in 1379 for the appropriation of Twyning church (Gloucestershire): among their misfortunes they listed not only the reduction of their rents and services because of the Black Death but also the ceaseless round of hospitality, costly litigation, calamitous gales and the demands of corrodians living within the precincts.[60] In the late fourteenth century the monasteries and other great churches were certainly suffering economic difficulties, and any heart-rending plea was grist to the mill when seeking from pope, bishop or king the annexation of parochial revenues.

The campaign for appropriation, however, was certainly not the result of the plague, however much the latter was used as a justification. Between 1291 and 1535, when calculations can be made from the *Taxatio* of Pope Nicholas IV and the *Valor Ecclesiasticus* of King Henry VIII, the number of appropriated churches in England increased from about 1,500 to roughly 3,300. The first recorded appropriations, however, date from the 1150s; the recorded annual average before 1291 was 10.7 churches, thereafter only 7.3.[61] In the diocese of Norwich, there are numerous instances of

[57] D. M. Robinson, *The Geography of Augustinian Settlement*, British Archaeological Reports, British series 80 (i) (Oxford, 1980), p. 187; *The Edington Cartulary*, ed. J. H. Stevenson, Wiltshire Record Society, 42 (1987), pp. 3-4, no. 11; *The Thurgarton Cartulary*, ed. T. Foulds (Stamford, 1994), pp. xviii, xx, 69, and charters 1, 967, 988-90, 994, 1003 and 1146.

[58] Robinson, *Augustinian Settlement*, p. 187; *Edington Cartulary*, pp. 62-63, no. 219.

[59] R. A. R. Hartridge, *A History of Vicarages in the Middle Ages* (Cambridge, 1930), chapter 7.

[60] G. Haigh, *The History of Winchcome Abbey* (London, 1947), p. 135.

[61] R. N. Swanson, 'Universities, Graduates and Benefices in Late Medieval England', *Past and Present*, 106 (1985), 28-61, pp. 35-38.

appropriation authorised by the bishop from the 1150s to 1214.[62] Between 1326 and 1347 the registers of the same diocese provide details of fifteen appropriations (one every seventeen months) and between 1349 and 1475 of fifty-four appropriations (one every twenty-eight months).[63] It is true that across the country the great majority of post-1291 appropriations occurred during the reign of Edward III (1327-77), but even within this narrower timespan the Black Death was not the decisive factor.[64] There are twenty-two petitions to the papacy for authorisation recorded in the six years before August 1348, eighteen in the six years thereafter; of petitions known to have been granted by the pope, the figures are seventeen for the five years before August 1348 and twenty in the five following years.[65]

The Regular Clergy

Despite every caveat expressed above when discussing monastic designs upon parochial revenues, it is certain that the religious communities of fourteenth-century England did suffer severely from the aftermath of the Black Death. The shock of the first onslaught is encapsulated in an entry in the chronicle of the Yorkshire Cistercian community of Meaux:

> This pestilence so prevailed in our monastery, as in other places, that in the month of August [1349] the abbot himself, twenty-two monks and six lay brethren died; of these, the abbot and five monks were lying unburied on one day, and then the others died, so that when the plague abated, out of fifty monks and lay brethren, only ten monks and no lay brethren were left. Thereafter, the rents and possessions of the monastery began to diminish, especially as the greater part of our tenants in various places died, and the abbot, prior, bursar and other seniors, when they died, left those surviving unacquainted with the property, possessions and common goods of the house.[66]

The Cistercians, as an order, certainly perceived there to be an immediate crisis of numbers. In 1349 the general chapter, legislating for all houses of the white monks throughout Latin Christendom, decreed that, on account of the plague, novices might make their profession before the end of their year's novitiate, and in 1361 it was authorised that a monk might be professed before the age of fifteen: the reception only of mature postulants had been one of the keynotes of the Cistercian reform of the twelfth

---

[62] *English Episcopal Acta, VI: Norwich 1070-1214*, ed. C. Harper-Bill (London, 1991), index, *s.v.* appropriation.

[63] Bruce, 'Episcopal Administration of Norwich', pp. 207-09.

[64] K. L. Wood-Leigh, *Church Life in England under Edward III* (Cambridge, 1934), pp. 127-53, esp. p. 134.

[65] Hartridge, *Vicarages*, p. 108.

[66] *Chronicon Monasterii de Melsa*, ed. E. A. Bond, 3 vols, Rolls Series, 43 (London, 1866-69), III, p. 37, cited by Gasquet, *Great Pestilence*, p. 153.

century.[67] Yet even here, some caution is necessary in attributing such measures to the Black Death alone, since the Franciscan order, which in 1260 had fixed the age of entry at eighteen, had already in 1316 reduced it to fourteen – a measure which provoked complaints from Oxford University and from satirical writers about the enticement of mere boys into the ranks of the greyfriars.[68]

It has been calculated that numbers in the religious houses of England were reduced by about 50% in the immediate aftermath of the first onslaught.[69] St Albans, the premier monastery, lost forty-eight monks, including the abbot, prior and subprior, within a few days at Easter 1349. The Westminster chronicler records the death of the abbot and twenty-six monks. At Cistercian Newenham, in Devon, three monks survived from a community of twenty-six. The Norwich Dominicans were wiped out almost to a man.[70] Across St George's Channel, the Franciscans lost twenty-five friars at Drogheda and twenty at Dublin.[71] Later in the century, in thirteen houses in Wales listed for the clerical poll taxes of 1377-81 there were only seventy-one religious spread thinly among them.[72] In those houses across Britain which were hit most severely, the impact of the Black Death must, in the short term, have been devastating and demoralising, totally destructive both of the liturgical round which was their raison d'être and of the economic structure which sustained their existence in this world. There survive numerous petitions to the pope by religious superiors for the ordination of young monks as priests below the canonical age of twenty-five years. In January 1351, for example, the abbot of Bury St Edmunds obtained permission to have ten monks under twenty-five ordained priests.[73] In 1354 the abbot of Reading sought permission to have thirty monks in their twentieth year so ordained, because so many priest-monks had died in the recent epidemic.[74] Such petitions multiplied after the outbreak of 1361-62; the abbot of Croxton, for example, requested licence to ordain twelve Premonstratensian canons as priests before their twenty-first birthdays since the plague had so disastrously reduced the

---

[67] S. F. Hockey, *Quarr Abbey and its Lands, 1132-1631* (Leicester, 1970), p. 142.

[68] J. Moorman, *A History of the Franciscan Order from its Origins to the Year 1517* (Oxford, 1968), pp. 352-53.

[69] D. Knowles and R. N. Hadcock, *Medieval Religious Houses, England and Wales*, 2nd edn (London, 1971), p. 47.

[70] For these figures, see D. Knowles, *The Religious Orders in England*, 3 vols (Cambridge, 1948-59), II, pp. 10-11.

[71] Walsh, *Fitzralph*, p. 280.

[72] Williams, *Welsh Church*, pp. 152-53 and Appendix B. The lists are incomplete.

[73] C. Ritchie, 'The Black Death at St Edmund's Abbey', *Proceedings of the Suffolk Institute of Archaeology*, 27 (1955), 47-50.

[74] *Calendar of Papal Registers: Petitions, 1342-1419*, p. 282.

number of priests in the monasteries and churches of the order.[75] One beneficial side-effect of this high mortality, however, was that it did allow promising young men to rise at an early age to high office; careers which were accelerated included those of Thomas de la Mare, the most notable of all the abbots of St Albans, and of Simon Langham, abbot of Westminster and later archbishop of Canterbury and cardinal.[76]

In some houses the Black Death made very little immediate impact, in terms of mortality at least. At the primatial cathedral of Christ Church, Canterbury, only four monks died in 1348-49, and there had certainly been worse crises before, as in 1298 when numbers had sunk below thirty during the conflict between king and archbishop. Here there were sixty-five monks in 1330, forty-six in 1376, but by 1451 the community had increased again to eighty-seven.[77] At Gloucester Abbey numbers fell from forty-six in 1339 to thirty-six in 1351, but had risen again to fifty-four in the late 1370s.[78] Gloucester's marked recovery was certainly exceptional, and few of the greater houses ever again achieved the numbers of the 1320s, but the long-term recovery was proportionately not far short of that of the population of England as a whole. By the reign of Henry VII (1485-1509), monastic numbers stood at between two-thirds and three-quarters of the 1320 level – and this despite the development of new forms of religious devotion which attracted both funds and personnel elsewhere.[79] The average complement of the fifty largest Benedictine houses in England has been estimated at fifty in 1200 and thirty in 1500; of Cistercians thirty and eighteen respectively; and of Augustinian canons, ten and seven.[80] Yet if numbers never after the Black Death reached their previous (probably inflated) heights, new recruits in the century and a half before the Reformation were received into communities which were for the most part, by worldly standards at least, flourishing institutions. Most of the greater houses at some time during this period engaged in ambitious building programmes, as both churches and conventual buildings were reconstructed in the new Perpendicular style of Gothic architecture.[81] There were far greater opportunities than before for monks to engage in advanced studies

---

[75] *Calendar of Papal Registers: Papal Letters 1362-1404*, p. 32; for list of superiors making similar petitions, see Knowles, *Religious Orders*, II, 12.

[76] Knowles, II, 39-48, 54-56.

[77] R. A. L. Smith, *Canterbury Cathedral Priory* (Cambridge, 1943), pp. 3-4.

[78] *Victoria County History of Gloucestershire*, II, p. 58.

[79] Knowles and Hadcock, *Medieval Religious Houses*, p. 47 and Appendix II (pp. 485-95).

[80] Knowles, *Religious Orders*, II, 255-62, p. 259; Robinson, *Augustinian Settlement*, pp. 94-95.

[81] C. Platt, *The Abbeys and Priories of Medieval England* (London, 1984), pp. 209-17.

at the monastic colleges established at Oxford and Cambridge.[82] Great houses, such as Durham and Bury St Edmunds, continued to dominate the economic and social life of their regions, and even smaller communities, such as Augustinian Butley in Suffolk, were still the frequent resort, for hospitality as well as for prayer, of the mighty of the land.[83] As was observed by Dom David Knowles, who had a greater appreciation of all aspects of the medieval religious life than any other modern student, 'to the contemporary, as to the monastic historian today, the fourteenth century is a stream scarcely rippled by the pestilence, and it is a century of dignity and even of opulence'.[84]

If the monasteries remained great social and religious centres, it is more difficult to speak with great certainty of the effects of the plague on the monastic economy. At Tavistock in 1351, Abbot Ash declared that due to various misfortunes, including the onslaught of pestilence and piratical attacks on the Scilly Isles, his house was almost bankrupt; yet in 1333 the fear had already been expressed that the monks would be forced to go out begging for their daily bread.[85] At Christ Church, Canterbury, the shrinkage in market profits had begun before the Black Death, which merely accelerated the process: 'the great plague of 1348-9 therefore had no decisive influence on the fortunes of the Christ Church economy'.[86] Ramsey Abbey was in debt to the tune of £2,500 on the eve of the first outbreak, and at Beaulieu the descent into indebtedness had begun by 1341 at the latest.[87] The labour force traditionally provided for the Cistercian abbeys by their lay brethren, a second tier of uneducated monks

---

[82]   See esp. J. Greatrex, 'Monk Students from Norwich Cathedral Priory at Oxford and Cambridge, c.1300 to 1530', *English Historical Review*, 106 (1991), 555-83.

[83]   See, e.g., R. B. Dobson, *Durham Priory, 1400-1450* (Cambridge, 1973); *The Register or Chronicle of Butley Priory, Suffolk, 1510-1535*, ed. A. G. Dickens (Winchester, 1951).

[84]   D. Knowles, 'The English Monasteries in the Later Middle Ages', *History*, 39 (1954), 26-38, p. 31. Against this optimistic view must be set the social origins of late medieval monks and canons: almost all were of lower than gentry class. It has been suggested that this may account for the ease with which Henry VIII was able to dissolve the religious houses: the aristocracy and gentry, unlike those of the 12th century, had no personal vested interest in the preservation of these communities, since none of their kindred resided therein. See R. B. Dobson, 'Recent Prosopographical Research in Late Medieval English History: University Graduates, Durham Monks and York Canons', in *Medieval Lives and the Historian*, ed. N. Bulst and J.-P. Genet (Kalamazoo, Michigan, 1986), pp. 181-200, at p. 190.

[85]   H. P. R. Finberg, *Tavistock Abbey* (Cambridge, 1951), p. 27.

[86]   Smith, *Canterbury Cathedral Priory*, p. 144.

[87]   J. A. Raftis, *The Estates of Ramsey Abbey* (Toronto, 1957), pp. 234, 240, 250; S. F. Hockey, *Beaulieu: King John's Abbey* (Beaulieu, 1976), p. 108.

engaged mainly in agrarian and pastoral work, had declined dramatically in numbers in the first half of the fourteenth century, and again the plague merely accelerated this long-term trend.[88]

On the English estates of the Norman abbey of Bec, scattered across southern and eastern England, developments which were once attributed to the plague are discernible during the half-century or more before 1348.[89] At Wretham (Norfolk) the number of acres sown fell by some 18% between 1303 and 1339, and there was a marked decline in arable acreage too at Blakenham (Suffolk); this is typical of the abandonment of marginal lands on so many estates. On both manors there was before 1348 a drop in the amount of customary services exacted and an increase in wage labour. On the manor of Ogbourne (Wiltshire) villein resistance to labour services culminated in violent resistance in 1327, the same year in which townspeople rose against their monastic landlords at Bury St Edmunds and St Albans. In short, the surviving records of the Bec manors show land going out of cultivation, customary services ebbing away on manors where they had never been strongly enforced and being maintained with difficulty in the face of peasant conspiracy and rebellion where they had long been an integral part of the manorial economy.

Certainly the economy of many religious houses did suffer badly from the Black Death, in the sense that it represented the culmination of a chain of disasters and the beginning of a long period of economic conditions disadvantageous to landlords. Perhaps the most convincing testimony, simply because of the traditional austerity of their order, comes from the two Carthusian communities of Witham and Hinton, which in 1354-55 petitioned the king that because of the deaths of numerous tenants and servants and because of the provisions of the Statute of Labourers, they had been brought to the verge of ruin for the lack of workmen and retainers; they obtained permission to pay above the specified rates, in order to retain a work force.[90] At Cistercian Beaulieu, already hit by the decline of the lay brotherhood, the abbey had to respond to demands for wage rises at a time when the price of wool (its largest source of revenue) fell to its lowest level during the century. The only solution was to break up the granges and lease out the demesne land in suitably sized parcels. This produced an immediate income in entry fines, but long-term decline in revenue. The historian of Beaulieu is convinced that the plague merely precipitated changes which were already threatening.[91] At Tavistock the inflation of wages is illustrated by those of the shepherds: in 1347 they received 3*d.* a

---

[88] R. W. Hays, *The History of the Abbey of Aberconway, 1186-1537* (Cardiff, 1963), p. 102.

[89] M. Morgan, *The English Lands of the Abbey of Bec* (Oxford, 1946), pp. 97-118.

[90] *Calendar of Patent Rolls, 1354-8*, pp. 16-17, 282, cited by Gasquet, *Great Pestilence*, pp. 170-72.

[91] Hockey, *Beaulieu*, pp. 106-07.

week plus 2*s*. annual stipend, as they had in the late thirteenth century; by 1358 this had risen to 4*d*. a week and 8*s*. 6*d*. a year; there was a further increase in 1398, but thereafter the rate remained stable until the dissolution.[92] At Battle the abbey's income had declined by 1383 to between two-thirds and three-quarters of what it had been on the eve of the Black Death. The greatest losses had occurred around the time of the first outbreak, about 20% of monastic income being permanently lost between 1347 and 1351. Debts then contracted still burdened the monks until at least the 1380s, and only a campaign of frugality and retrenchment averted more serious problems. Yet the ravages of French raiders along the south coast were as damaging to the Battle economy as the pestilence, and the same was the case at Cistercian Quarr on the Isle of Wight.[93]

For some houses, subsequent outbreaks of plague were more damaging than the first onslaught. After the 1416 attack in the north of England there were very many wasted and deserted tenements in Durham, and the bursar's accounts for the cathedral priory show a drastic reduction in rents from urban properties. Another outbreak in 1438-39 was probably responsible for most of the difficulties which threatened the monastic economy at Durham in the ensuing years.[94]

The response of most monasteries to the crisis of falling prices, rising wages and shortage of labour was to lease out the demesne and to retreat further from direct exploitation of the land. A good example of such a policy of leasing may be found among the charters of the Augustinian priory of Dodnash in Suffolk, a modest but not impoverished community which is far more typical of English monasticism in the late middle ages than the great foundations.[95] In 1300 the Benedictines, Cistercians and Augustinians still managed and exploited most of their estates, but by 1400 all but a few home farms had been leased out. The long-term result of this shift was to place monastic lands, in all but name, in the hands of prosperous peasants, yeomen and knights whose successors would ultimately be eager, when the chance was offered by the crown, to acquire outright ownership. Economic expediency on the part of the religious gave rise to a dangerous pattern of assumptions.[96]

92 Finberg, *Tavistock Abbey*, p. 144.
93 E. Searle, *Lordship and Community: Battle Abbey and its Banlieu, 1066-1538* (Toronto, 1974), pp. 261-64; Hockey, *Quarr Abbey*, pp. 134-39.
94 Dobson, *Durham Priory*, pp. 45-46, 285.
95 *Dodnash Priory Charters*, ed. C. Harper-Bill, Suffolk Record Society, Suffolk Charters, 15 (forthcoming, 1996), *passim*.
96 Knowles, *Religious Orders*, II, pp. 122-24; for a different emphasis, see J. N. Hare, 'The Monks as Landlords: the Leasing of the Demesnes in Southern England', in *The Church in Pre-Reformation Society: Essays in Honour of F. R. H. Du Boulay*, ed. C. M. Barron and C. Harper-Bill (Woodbridge, 1985), pp. 82-94.

A few great houses did not adopt this course, but attempted to enforce the old pattern of customary services which, as they disappeared elsewhere, were increasingly regarded as servile and humiliating. The resentment was compounded by the habit of ecclesiastical lords 'of treating disobedience as sacrilege' – as when the archbishop of Canterbury in 1390 imposed penance on his men of Wingham for discharging their carrying service furtively rather than openly.[97] On the estates of Christ Church, Canterbury, the monastic officials, rather than leasing out the demesne, sought to exact every labour service due to them, so that the burden on their villeins was heavier in 1390 than in 1314.[98] On the Westminster estates too, there was a concerted policy of maintaining the old villeinage tenure of rents and labour services; 'never sensitive to economic trends, the monks of Westminster were never more heroically indifferent to them than they were in this period [1348-c.1390]'.[99] They could not succeed in the long term, but their efforts certainly helped to alienate their customary tenants, and such policies explain in large measure why ecclesiastical landlords were the victims of especial venom during the rising of 1381.

Collegiate Institutions

Other, non-monastic, religious corporations also suffered badly from the plague. At Exeter cathedral about ten out of twenty-four canons died in 1348-49, and at least five vicars choral and annuellars.[100] The life of the cathedral was not, however, completely disrupted. Offerings continued to be made at the normal level, and the cathedral workmen carried on with maintenance work on the fabric. The real damage was, in fact, longer-term. While vacant prebends were soon filled, it was far more difficult to replenish and maintain the ranks of the lower clergy on whom the liturgical life of the cathedral depended. Not only were there fewer priests available, but they could get better paid work elsewhere, as rectors or vicars in vacant parishes. The number of vicars choral fell from twenty-four to twenty, that of annuellars from twenty-one to twelve. Plans for additional altars in the cathedral had to be abandoned and two chapels ceased to be served by clergy. It was a quarter of a century before the life of the cathedral began to return to normal.

Amongst academic institutions, at the King's Hall in Cambridge sixteen king's scholars died in 1349, and the warden and eight fellows in 1361-62.[101] There is no indication that the college was ever abandoned in

[97] F. R. H. Du Boulay, *The Lordship of Canterbury* (London, 1966), p. 185.
[98] Smith, *Canterbury Cathedral Priory*, pp. 126-27.
[99] B. F. Harvey, *Westminster Abbey and its Estates in the Middle Ages* (Oxford, 1977), p. 245.
[100] N. Orme, *Exeter Cathedral as it was* (Exeter, 1986), p. 117.
[101] A. B. Cobban, *The King's Hall within the University of Cambridge in the Later Middle Ages* (Cambridge, 1969), pp. 220-22.

the fourteenth century, but in the fifteenth, as the plague became increasingly an urban phenomenon, the scholars began during outbreaks to retreat into the countryside. From 1498 to 1526 the King's Hall records indicate the extent to which Cambridge was affected by plague and sweating sickness: in the summer months up to a third of the fellows retreated to the college's rural estates. It is likely that the scholars and students of the English universities suffered less than most sectors of the population, for the living conditions and diet of all but the poorest students was higher than that of the people as a whole.[102] Far more significant, perhaps, were the psychological effects on the academic community. 'The periodic and traumatic advent of plague and other diseases of the fever variety ensured that the university communities could not evade that outlook of morbidity and preoccupation with death which permeated later medieval England, and which is such a notable feature of the literature and art of the age.' That most of the Oxford and Cambridge colleges were chantry foundations, charged with the obligation to celebrate the liturgy for the dead, must have increased this 'funereal climate of thought'.[103] In the immediate context, the decimation of a generation of administrators meant that the universities were required to replenish rapidly the ranks of the governors both of church and state. There was an increase in the late fourteenth century in the number of fellows studying for a second degree in law: 58% of all higher degrees were taken in the legal faculties, mostly in civil law.[104] There was, however, in the longer term an effort to counteract this tendency, and in the fifteenth century colleges were founded at both universities with the specific intention of providing graduates in theology to serve in the parishes: for example, Lincoln College at Oxford, established specifically to combat heresy, and St Catharine's at Cambridge.[105]

Academic colleges were not the only foundations made in the period between the Black Death and the Reformation. It may be that by the mid-fourteenth century the great days of English monasticism were past, that the cloistered religious had ceased to be regarded as the 'athletes' or the 'knights of Christ', and that the mendicants too, who had replaced the monks and canons as the front-line troops of militant Catholicism, had now become the butt of satire, barbed and disillusioned in the case of Langland, more jocular from the pen of Chaucer.[106] This view, however, requires at

[102]   A. B. Cobban, *The Medieval English Universities* (Berkeley and Los Angeles, 1988), p. 411; see also W. J. Courtenay, 'The Effects of the Black Death on English Higher Education', *Speculum*, 55 (1980), 696-714, pp. 697-703.

[103]   Cobban, *Medieval English Universities*, p. 392.

[104]   Coleman, *English Literature in History*, p. 32.

[105]   Cobban, *Medieval English Universities*, pp. 132, 235.

[106]   For the tradition of anti-mendicant literature, see P. R. Szittya, *The Anti-Fraternal Tradition in Medieval Literature* (Princeton, NJ, 1986); but for a rather different view of the friars, see any collection of late medieval wills.

least some qualification in the light of late medieval endowments. Three houses of Carmelite friars were established between 1349 and 1357: at Ludlow, Doncaster and Northallerton.[107] Two large-scale monastic foundations were made in London, probably as a direct result of the shock caused by the plague. The Cistercian community of St Mary Graces was established by Edward III in the shadow of the Tower on the site of a new cemetery excavated in 1348 for plague victims, and on a similar plot the London Charterhouse was founded a few years later by a combination of lay and ecclesiastical initiative.[108] The Carthusians, the most austere of the monastic orders – *nunquam reformata quia nunquam deformata* – enjoyed a renaissance in England in the late middle ages, perhaps because the monks, although rigidly enclosed and imitating the lives of the desert fathers, responded remarkably to the quest of the literate and pious laity for religious texts which adapted the monastic spirituality of the twelfth century to the new environment of familial piety. Before 1343 there were only two charterhouses in England; in that year Beauvale (Nottinghamshire) was established, and between 1371 and 1414 a further six Carthusian monasteries were founded. The last of these was Henry V's charterhouse at Sheen, which at the dissolution had an income of £800 *per annum*, the same as that of the ancient Benedictine abbey of Malmesbury. Associated with it, on the other side of the Thames, the king established a community of Bridgettine nuns with their attendant chaplains, whose income of £1,730 *per annum* was in the same league as the great pre-Conquest foundations of Peterborough and Ramsey.[109]

More significant, perhaps, because infinitely more numerous, were the foundations of colleges of secular priests who, although they were not bound by a monastic rule, nevertheless lived a common life and had as their main function liturgical intercession for the souls of their founders. In the period from 1350 to 1530 over seventy such colleges (excluding hospitals and academic colleges at the universities) were established throughout England.[110] Among these were some richly endowed communities, such as Newark College at Leicester, founded by Henry, duke of Lancaster, in 1353; Fotheringhay in Northamptonshire, the creation of Edmund, duke of York, in 1411; and Ralph, Lord Cromwell's Tattershall College (Lincolnshire) established in 1439. Of Fotheringhay it has been remarked that 'the statutes show that, apart from salaries and

---

[107] Knowles and Hadcock, *Medieval Religious Houses*, pp. 232-38; P. Klein and A. Roe, *The Carmelite Friary, Corve Street, Ludlow* (Birmingham, 1987).

[108] *Stow's Survey of London*, ed. C. L. Kingsford, 2 vols (Oxford, 1908), I, pp. 124-25: II, pp. 81-83; D. Knowles and W. F. Grimes, *Charterhouse* (London, 1954), pp. 1-16.

[109] Knowles, *Religious Orders*, II, pp. 129-38, 175-82.

[110] Knowles and Hadcock, *Medieval Religious Houses*, pp. 411-51 *passim*.

payments, it was almost monastic in character',[111] and it is indeed difficult to perceive any essential difference between the secular colleges and the houses of Augustinian canons, following their infinitely flexible rule, which had proliferated in the twelfth century. Considering the adverse economic conditions which so disadvantaged the landholding classes, and that saturation point for religious foundations had been reached before 1300, the rate of endowment in the late middle ages was in fact quite remarkable.[112]

The Episcopate

What of the leadership provided for the English church in the period of endemic plague which produced 'a pastoral problem of unprecedented dimensions'?[113] Even those who have extolled the virtues of the medieval English episcopate in general have had reservations about the bishops of the second half of the fourteenth century (the supposed golden age of the caesarian prelate), who made their careers by service at court or in government and who after their elevation paid as little attention to spiritual things as before.[114] Yet when individual cases are examined in greater detail, this judgement must be questioned. The diocese of Hereford provides a good illustration. An average bishopric, it was neither a prize for the most ambitious nor particularly impoverished. It is possible to examine its administration in detail over a long period because all the medieval episcopal registers have been printed in good modern editions.[115] What is most striking is the consistently high standard of episcopal governance over almost two centuries from the Black Death to the Reformation. None of the fifteen occupants of the see can be considered in any way scandalous, except perhaps the non-resident Italian diplomat Adrian Castellesi (1502-4). The bishops brought to their diocese a wide range of experience as king's clerks, papal officials, ecclesiastical administrators or heads of religious houses, and upon some of them very considerable demands were made beyond the bounds of their own jurisdiction. John Gilbert, for example, a Dominican (1375-89), had a thoroughly useful and cosmopolitan

---

[111] *Ibid.*, p. 419.
[112] A work on such collegiate foundations in late medieval Norfolk is promised by Benjamin Thompson.
[113] Walsh, *Fitzralph*, p. 278.
[114] E.g. D. Knowles, 'The English Bishops, 1072-1532', in *Medieval Studies Presented to Aubrey Gwynn*, ed. J. A. Watt, J. B. Morall and F. X. Martin (Dublin, 1961), pp. 283-96; on p. 290 he damns with faint praise.
[115] All the Hereford registers, from Thomas Cantilupe (1275-82) to Charles Booth (1516-35) have been printed by the Canterbury and York Society, vols 2, 5-6, 8-9, 14-15, 18, 20-23, 25-29 (1907-21). Extensive use is made of them by A. D. Frankforter, 'The Reformation and the Register: Episcopal Administration of Parishes in Late Medieval England', *Catholic Historical Review*, 63 (1977), 204-24.

career as papal chaplain, confessor to the Black Prince and treasurer of England between 1386 and 1389. He contrived to give honourable service to both king and pope at a period of tension between the two powers, and to conduct himself with integrity in a period when the internal politics of England were characterised by factionalism. Although frequently absent from his diocese, he appointed deputies who efficiently fulfilled his episcopal functions, and both clerical discipline and Christian observance were maintained by visitation. Gilbert's immediate predecessor at Hereford, William Courtenay (1369-75), by his distinguished career negates any generalised allegation that the sons of the nobility were inadequate religious leaders, for he proved subsequently to be a brave and conscientious bishop of London and archbishop of Canterbury at a time of crisis for the universal and the English Church. Of the rule of John Trilleck, bishop of Hereford from 1344 to 1360, the editor of his register states that 'the effects of orderly government can clearly be traced in improved conditions': and this in the period of initial shock caused by the first outbreak of plague.[116] Such comments are echoed in the introduction to every volume in the series of Hereford registers. As a group, the bishops of Hereford, in an age of endemic pestilence, may not have been remarkable for charismatic spirituality, but their constant application to the affairs of the universal Church, the realm and their own diocese is surely noteworthy – although not at all exceptional by the standards of the *ecclesia Anglicana*.

If anywhere it might be expected to find bishops with little inclination for the treadmill of ecclesiastical administration, it would be at Winchester, a see magnificently endowed with estates and revenues. Here, however, in the second half of the fourteenth century, the two royal servants who occupied the bishopric certainly cannot be adjudged failures as diocesans. William Edington (1346-66) attained the 'anonymity of the model civil servant', in which capacity he excelled, serving in turn as treasurer and chancellor of England.[117] His successor, William Wykeham (1366-1404), has often been regarded as the archetype of the politicised curialist bishop. During both episcopates, however, the diocese was well administered. Edington celebrated numerous ordinations in person and from his manor at Southwark issued instructions to his officials, who maintained sound administration throughout the very difficult years after 1348.[118] The greatest memorial to Wykeham must be his twin colleges of Winchester and New College, Oxford. These probably exercised greater influence on the intellectual development of the future leaders of the English church than any institution since the Norman abbey of Bec in the eleventh

[116] *Reg. Trillek*, p. iv.
[117] McKisack, *Fourteenth Century*, p. 213.
[118] *Reg. Edington*, I, vii-xiv, and *passim*.

century. It is significant that an allegedly 'political' bishop oriented his Oxford college towards the study of theology (and practical, pastoral, theology at that) rather than towards law, by which churchmen made their way in the world.[119] Wykeham's endowments provide a reminder, too, that it was the English episcopate which led the way in the 'educational revolution' of the late middle ages, the great expansion of opportunity for clerical learning and, indirectly, the increase of what has been termed 'devotional literacy' among English laypeople.[120]

Lay Piety

The most difficult question to be addressed concerns the effect (if any) of the Black Death upon the religious lives and spiritual aspirations of the English people. It is, of course, impossible to quantify spirituality, and any survey must be subjective and impressionistic. There can be little doubt, however, that the pessimism and resignation which characterised the academic theology of the fourteenth century was reflected in the religion of the people. Famine, followed by the mass mortality of the Black Death, was not conducive to triumphalist Christianity. Yet in England there is no evidence of religious hysteria. The Jews could not be blamed for the plague here, as they were in many areas of the continent, since they had been expelled by Edward I from his island kingdom in 1290. Neither did England witness those extraordinary processions of flagellants who traversed France, Germany and Italy, mortifying their own flesh in order to avert the wrath of God. English processions were rather lower key, authorised by the church authorities; they were controlled exercises of liturgical intercession, just like those ordered by the archbishops almost every year to plead for God's favour on English arms in the war with France.[121]

---

[119] R. L. Storey, 'The Foundation of the Medieval College', in *New College Oxford, 1379-1979*, ed. J. Buxton and P. Williams (Oxford, 1979), pp. 4, 20, 22.

[120] For the extent of the educational revolution, see N. Orme, *English Schools in the Middle Ages* (London, 1973), esp. pp. 194-223; and even more emphatic, J.-A. H. Moran, *The Growth of English Schooling, 1340-1548: Learning, Literacy and Laicisation in Pre-Reformation York Diocese* (Princeton, NJ, 1985). For the contribution of the bishops, see H. Jewell, 'English Bishops as Educational Benefactors in the Late Fifteenth Century', in *The Church, Politics and Patronage in the Fifteenth Century*, ed. B. Dobson (Gloucester, 1984), pp. 146-67; J. T. Rosenthal, 'Lancastrian Bishops and Educational Benefaction', in *The Church in Pre-Reformation Society*, ed. Barron and Harper-Bill, pp. 199-211. For devotional literacy, see M. Aston, *Lollards and Reformers: Images and Literacy in Late Medieval Religion* (London, 1984), pp. 101-34.

[121] W. R. Jones, 'The English Church and Royal Propaganda during the Hundred Years War', *Journal of British Studies*, 19 (1979-80), 18-30; A. K. McHardy, 'Liturgy and Propaganda in the Diocese of Lincoln during the Hundred Years War', *Studies in Church History*, 18 (1982), 215-27.

It was, in fact, the French campaigns of Edward III and Henry V which, far more than the Black Death, formulated the public image of the English Church in the late middle ages. Knighthood had been Christianised long before, in the wake of the First Crusade, but never had chivalric and military values been so vaingloriously displayed and proclaimed within an ecclesiastical setting. The English were portrayed in sermons as the mirror image of the people of Israel at war. Indulgences were granted to those praying for the success of English arms, and the pulpit was utilised to publicise official denunciations of the war crimes of the French and the Scots.[122] In 1348 Edward III, in the wake of his great victory at Crécy, founded the Order of the Garter as a parody, albeit profoundly serious, of a religious community.[123] Heraldic devices were emblazoned in the windows and on the facades of churches, and tombs of war heroes, sited in parish churches as well as in great private colleges, became increasingly grandiose.[124] In terms of political rhetoric it was in this age, as it has nicely been put, that 'God became an Englishman'.[125] The captains of the Hundred Years War, however, rather like the commanders of the New Model Army in the English Civil War, were leaders in the new fashion of introspective piety. There is no better illustration than Henry, duke of Lancaster, one of the first knights of the Garter, who before his death during the plague of 1361 wrote his *Livre de Seyntz Medicines* in which, using the analogy of battlefield surgery, he applied remedies to sins which he had discovered after an intensive examination of his conscience.[126]

The increasing emphasis on conscience and contemplation which is apparent in confessors' manuals and in devotional literature aimed at the laity owed much to the mystical theology of the northern recluse Richard Rolle, who himself died in 1349, and whose spirituality was channelled to a wider audience by Walter Hilton, suitably modified so as to complement rather than to undermine public religion.[127] Hilton tailored this affective

[122] H. J. Hewitt, *The Organisation of War under Edward III* (Manchester, 1966), pp. 160-63.

[123] For the best recent account, see D'A. J. D. Boulton, *The Knights of the Crown* (Woodbridge, 1987), pp. 96-166.

[124] For example, in Suffolk, the armorial windows of the Augustinian friary of Clare, 'A Description of the Windows in the Friars' Church', *Proceedings of the Suffolk Institute of Archaeology*, 20 (1930), 36-42; and the heraldry displayed in stonework on the gatehouse of Butley Priory, N. Pevsner, *The Buildings of England: Suffolk*, rev. edn (Harmondsworth, 1974), p. 155.

[125] J. W. McKenna, 'How God became an Englishman', in *Tudor Rule and Revolution: Essays for G. R. Elton*, ed. D. J. Guth and J. W. McKenna (Cambridge, 1982), pp. 25-43.

[126] Pantin, *English Church in the Fourteenth Century*, pp. 231-35.

[127] D. Knowles, *The English Mystical Tradition* (London, 1961), pp. 48-66, 100-18; for Hilton's most influential work, see *The Ladder of Perfection*, trans. L. Sherley-Price (Harmondsworth, 1957).

piety to suit the needs, and the obligations, of those whose lives were spent in the administration of estates or of businesses, rather than enclosed in the hermitage. In this, Hilton was following the example of Archbishop John Thoresby of York (1353-73), who had conducted a vigorous and coherent programme of reform in the north in the wake of the Black Death and whose greatest memorial is the *Layfolks' Catechism*, which provided a simple guide for the conduct of the Christian life and emphasised the virtues of social responsibility.[128] The impact of Rolle and Hilton was undoubtedly great, but the spirituality which they propagated was not the direct result of the misfortunes suffered by English people in the fourteenth century. The piety of Rolle and of the fifteenth-century Carthusian writers who disseminated the same message originated in the monastic cloisters of the twelfth century, and the determination, expressed in different ways by both Thoresby and Hilton, that such religious devotion should be expressed in a social rather than in a solitary context, reflected the views of the pastoral theologians of late twelfth-century Paris whose teachings had been transformed into a programme of religious education inaugurated by Pope Innocent III at the Fourth Lateran Council of 1215.[129]

Late medieval religion was increasingly Christocentric: much greater popular attention was focused upon the life, death, teachings and example of Jesus. This development, too, represents the gradual laicisation of the theological advances and monastic spirituality of the twelfth century. There was far greater preoccupation, too, with the Holy Family, which, as the religion of the upper levels of the laity became increasingly familial, provided a role model for the conduct of life.[130] Yet this concentration on the founder of the faith and on feasts specifically associated with Him – most notably Corpus Christi – was not, as is sometimes implied, at the expense of the cults of the saints.[131] St Thomas Becket's shrine at Canterbury flourished financially in the wake of the first outbreak of the Black Death, and the translation of St Thomas Cantilupe on 25 October 1349 was believed to have caused the abatement of the pestilence in

---

[128] For the wider significance of the work of Thoresby and Hilton, see J. Hughes, *Pastors and Visionaries: Religion and Secular Life in Late Medieval Yorkshire* (Woodbridge, 1988).

[129] For the monastic context, see C. A. J. Armstrong, *England, France and Burgundy in the Fifteenth Century* (London, 1983), p. 149. For the absorption into popular religion of twelfth-century intellectual advances, see J. van Engel, 'The Christian Middle Ages as an Historiographical Problem', *American Historical Review* 91 (1986), 519-52.

[130] J. Bossy, *Christianity in the West, 1400-1700* (Oxford, 1985), pp. 10-11.

[131] For feasts associated with Christ, see R. W. Pfaff, *New Liturgical Feasts in Late Medieval England* (Oxford, 1970); for Corpus Christi, see M. Rubin, *Corpus Christi: the Eucharist in Late Medieval Culture* (Cambridge, 1991).

England.[132] In the longer term, in the north of England new cults flourished: those of Rolle, St John of Bridlington and Archbishop Scrope. Older shrines, such as those of St Wilfred at Ripon and St William at York, were revitalised in the early fifteenth century.[133] Yet devotion to saints, as to Christ Himself, appears to have been more personal than in the earlier middle ages; the saints were regarded now as exemplars of a good life as much as miraculous healers.

The most obvious psychological consequence of greatly increased and sudden mortality was an almost desperate fear of oblivion after death. The immediate impact of the first outbreak of plague is captured by the Rochester chronicler, William of Dene:

> The mortality swept away so vast a multitude of both sexes that none could be found to carry the corpses to the grave. Men and women bore their own offspring on their shoulders to the church and cast them into a common pit. From these came such a stench that hardly anyone dared to cross the cemeteries.[134]

At Sandwich in June 1349 the old graveyard was full to overflowing, and the earl of Huntingdon gave a new plot, which was hastily consecrated by the suffragan bishop.[135] Such a situation must have been extremely traumatic, yet even here some caution is necessary. It was in 1301, almost half a century before the plague, that the abbot of Bury St Edmunds had been so distressed by the bones lying around in the churchyard that he had endowed a charnel chapel for their interment, staffed by two chaplains to provide liturgical commemoration.[136] Medieval people were constantly confronted by the reality of death in a way in which the inhabitants of England today seldom are. Nevertheless, the shock of mass mortality in 1348-49 was unprecedented.

The desire for commemoration brings us to the doctrine of Purgatory: the belief, which certainly did not originate with the Black Death but appears to have entered far more strongly into popular consciousness in its wake, that there existed between Heaven and Hell an intermediate place; by passing through this, the souls of the dead might purge themselves of guilt for sins committed in this world by suffering a range of divine punishments of varying severity.[137] Purgatory has often been considered an

[132] R. C. Finucane, *Miracles and Pilgrims: Popular Beliefs in Medieval England* (London, 1977), pp. 179, 193.

[133] Hughes, *Pastors and Visionaries*, pp. 298-346.

[134] *Anglia Sacra*, ed. Wharton, I, pp. 375-76.

[135] Historical Manuscripts Commission, *Eighth Report*, p. 336, cited by Gasquet, *Great Pestilence*, p. 103.

[136] Cambridge University Library, MS Ff ii 33, fols. 85v-86v.

[137] For Purgatory, see J. Le Goff, *The Birth of Purgatory*, trans. A. Goldhammer (London, 1984). For an excellent positive account of the practical consequences of the doctrine, see C. Burgess, ''A Fond Thing Vainly

oppressive doctrine, symptomatic of the neuroses and uncertainties of the late medieval period, although in fact the belief was precisely formulated by theologians in the late twelfth century, conventionally seen as an age of buoyant confidence; and as presented by Dante in his *Divine Comedy* it has been described as 'a place of hope, an initiation into joy, a gradual emergence into light'.[138] However much they might suffer, the souls in Purgatory were destined for salvation, and their torment might be foreshortened by the prayers of the living, especially by masses. The general commemoration of the faithful departed was hardly sufficient, for it was the popular belief that the benefit accruing to an individual soul decreased in proportion to the number of the dead for whom prayers were offered. It was considered necessary, therefore, to make generous provision for soul masses. A glance through the index of wills proved in the name of Archbishop Chichele (1414-43) demonstrates that those with sufficient resources required intercessory celebrations in their hundreds and thousands, which places in proper perspective the oft-quoted testamentary provision of King Henry VII for ten thousand masses.[139] It was the greatest act of charity to endow masses for the souls of kindred and friends. Late medieval religion has been well described as 'a cult of living friends in the service of dead ones', while it has been suggested that never, even in Counter-Reformation Spain, has God been bombarded with such a barrage of masses as rose from late medieval England.[140]

The chantry has been considered the most characteristic institution of late medieval religion. This was a foundation, established by an individual, family or group, the central purpose of which was to provide daily or weekly masses for the spiritual benefit of named persons. Although there are many earlier examples, from the first half of the twelfth century, it was certainly in the fourteenth century that such liturgical commemoration became the common aspiration of men and women of wealth and status. The fashion started at the apex of lay society. In the fourteenth and fifteenth centuries eighty-five noble families, virtually all the higher aristocracy of late medieval England, founded chantries which, since they could not foresee the predatory nature of post-Reformation Tudor

---

Imagined": an Essay on Purgatory and Pious Motive in Medieval England', in *Parish, Church and People: Local Studies in Lay Religion, 1350-1700*, ed. S. Wright (London, 1988), pp. 56-84.

[138] Le Goff, *Purgatory*, p. 346.

[139] *Registrum Henrici Chichele, Archiepiscopi Cantuariensis AD 1414-1443*, ed. E. F. Jacob and H. C. Johnson, 4 vols, Canterbury and York Society, 42, 45-47 (1938-47), II, index, *s.v.* Commemoration of the dead.

[140] J. Bossy, 'The Mass as a Social Institution, 1200-1700', *Past and Present*, 100 (1977), 29-61, p. 42; N. Saul, 'The Religious Sympathies of the Gentry of Gloucestershire, 1200-1500', *Transactions of the Bristol and Gloucestershire Archaeological Society*, 98 (1980), 99-112, p. 102.

government, they confidently expected to function until the end of the world.[141] Many of the more lavish institutions contained magnificent tombs, such as those of the Beauchamp earls in St Mary's, Warwick, or of the FitzAlans at Arundel. At the other end of the scale were numerous simple altars set up by gentry and prosperous merchants in the side aisles of their parish churches. Least costly of all, mass might be celebrated on a portable altar set on top of a tomb-chest – and this, rather than constant travel, surely explains the proliferation of papal indults for such altars in the fifteenth century.

Such aspirations for continual intercession cannot be attributed to the Black Death alone. In some English counties, certainly, the peak of chantry foundations came in the half-century after 1350, but this was not the case elsewhere, or indeed nationally. The greatest numbers of perpetual chantries established in any fifty-year period were founded in the first half of the fourteenth century.[142] In York Minster, for example, at least thirty out of sixty chantries were founded before 1350.[143] For Bristol, 'it may be emphasised that foundation was most profuse in the two decades before the Black Death', and the slight decline after the first outbreak possibly reflects a fall in property rentals in the town, or perhaps indicates that the uncertainties of the social situation were a deterrent to plans for eternity.[144] Certainly the rise of chaplains' wages after the Black Death caused the impoverishment of many chantries. It was a recurrent complaint of the trustees of many small institutions that it was impossible to find a priest to serve them, and often in the late fourteenth century the obligations of cantarists were reduced in order to make the job more attractive.[145] It became increasingly common in the wake of the plague to endow a chantry for a term of years (often long) rather than in perpetuity, a reflection of confidence in the efficacy of intercessory prayer, but also of hesitancy over the continuing stability of family fortunes.[146] While chantry foundations were rooted in the desire for individual and familial salvation, both

[141] J. T. Rosenthal, *The Purchase of Paradise: the Social Function of Aristocratic Benevolence, 1307-1485* (London, 1972), esp. pp. 31-52.
[142] A. Krieder, *English Chantries: the Road to Dissolution* (Cambridge, Mass., 1979) pp. 86-7; Wood-Leigh, *Church Life under Edward III*, pp. 89-126, at p. 125.
[143] Krieder, *English Chantries*, p. 95; cf. R. B. Dobson, 'The Foundation of Perpetual Chantries by the Citizens of Medieval York', *Studies in Church History*, 4 (1967), 21-38.
[144] C. Burgess, 'Strategies for Eternity: Perpetual Chantry Foundation in Late Medieval Bristol', in *Religious Belief and Ecclesiastical Careers*, ed. Harper-Bill, pp. 1-32.
[145] K. L. Wood-Leigh, *Perpetual Chantries in Britain* (Cambridge, 1965), p. 93.
[146] *Ibid.*, p. 96. There was a sharp decline in the number of royal licences for alienation in mortmain after the Black Death: see S. Raban, *Mortmain Legislation and the English Church, 1279-1500* (Cambridge, 1982), p. 191.

perpetual and temporary chantries did benefit the local community both spiritually, as at Doncaster, where a mass was celebrated every hour of the day from 5 a.m. to 10 p.m., and also practically, as has been demonstrated both generally by Professor Krieder's assessment of the educational and pastoral role of English cantarists and locally by Dr Burgess's detailed studies of their contribution to the parochial life of late medieval Bristol.[147]

Not everyone could afford to endow single-handed a chantry, even a temporary one. For the multitude of the population liturgical commemoration could best be achieved by membership of a religious confraternity or guild.[148] These voluntary associations existed throughout the medieval period, but across western Europe they proliferated in the two centuries before the Reformation. The size and status of the membership varied according to the nature and function of each particular confraternity. The greatest enjoyed nationwide prestige and attracted distinguished brethren from far beyond their own region – such were the major guilds of Boston, Coventry and Ludlow. The vast majority, however, were local associations, firmly based in the parish. It is totally impossible to estimate how many there were in England as a whole. Over 150 have been identified in the capital, and forty-five in Norwich. The guild certificates of 1389 list seven in the small Cambridgeshire town of Bottisham, four in Crowland (Lincolnshire), and no fewer than fifty-one in King's (then Bishop's) Lynn and its suburbs. Very few of those which survived – only five in London – were functioning before the first outbreak of the plague. Some, nevertheless, were, and it has been wisely observed that 'the plague, although undoubtedly a major stimulus in specific cases, is inadequate to account for a general movement which began before 1348 and continued into the early sixteenth century'.[149] It has been suggested that the ossification of the parochial system in the thirteenth century provides a more convincing explanation; the enormous difficulties facing those who might wish to establish a new parish church left confraternities as the only means by which friends and neighbours could create a religious association.

These confraternities had many social functions, from the support of members who, through no fault of their own, had fallen on hard times, to the jovial fellowship of the annual feast. Yet their core and essence was that they were communal chantries, designed to unite their brethren in prayer for the souls of deceased members. Dr Barron has demonstrated clearly

---

[147] Wood-Leigh, *Perpetual Chantries*, p. 307; Krieder, *English Chantries*, pp. 38-70; Burgess, '"For the Increase of Divine Service"'.

[148] For general surveys stressing the significance of confraternities, see J. J. Scarisbrick, *The Reformation and the English People* (Oxford, 1984), chapter 2; B. A. Hanawalt, 'Keepers of the Lights: Late Medieval English Parish Gilds', *Journal of Medieval and Renaissance Studies*, 14 (1984), 21-37.

[149] G. Rosser, 'Communities of Parish and Guild in the Late Middle Ages', in *Parish, Church and People*, ed. Wright, pp. 29-55, at p. 32.

that, while support of distressed living members was not neglected, all London chantry ordinances focused primarily upon obligations to the dead: the arrangement of a decent funeral, well attended by the brethren in livery standing around a hearse brightly lit by candles and tapers, and subsequent commemoration.[150] Fear of oblivion in death mingled with desperate concern for the welfare of the soul. At the heart of the confraternities lay deep devotion and the desire for mutual aid in the quest for salvation. The members of guilds in the English countryside and small provincial towns could, for the most part, have afforded only modest provision for masses for their own souls, but as brothers and sisters of the confraternity they became participants in the spiritual benefits which would accrue for all time to those whose names were entered in the register. It was this spiritual suffrage which attracted membership in such large numbers; the worldly benefits were almost peripheral.

Charity and Morality

An important sphere of human activity where religious attitudes and economic conditions interact is charitable alms giving. In the twelfth and thirteenth centuries, when economic conditions favoured rural landlords, the prosperous free peasantry and the burgesses of flourishing towns, the property-owning classes were eager to distribute alms lavishly to the disadvantaged in order to acquire honour in this world by conspicuous expenditure and salvation in the next through the charity which was believed to extinguish sin. The poor were generally viewed without distinction as the image of Christ.[151] In this earlier period such indiscriminate charity was normally dispensed through the mediating agency of a monastic or quasi-monastic institution: for example, the various hospitals administered by the great Benedictine abbey of Bury St Edmunds.[152] After the Black Death, because labour was in such high demand in town and countryside, the need for charitable relief became less widespread, although none the less real for those who were marginalised. In general, the income and resources of the propertied classes were in decline, just as the wages of labourers were rising. Now that labour was at a premium, non-productive members of society were no longer pitied, but rather were reviled as parasites who were seeking wilfully to undermine the prosperity of the respectable elements. Those who remained poor in an age when the conditions of the labouring class in general had improved so markedly were seen as a threat.

[150] C. M. Barron, 'The Parish Fraternities of Medieval London', in *The Church in Pre-Reformation Society*, ed. Barron and Harper-Bill, pp. 13-37.

[151] For what follows, see M. Rubin, *Charity and Community in Medieval Cambridge* (Cambridge, 1987), esp. pp. 289-99.

[152] *Victoria County History of Suffolk*, II, pp. 133-36. Five of the six hospitals were founded in the twelfth century, the last sometime between 1248 and 1252.

It is impossible in the medieval period to distinguish between piety and charity, since so many chantries had attached to them hospitals, almshouses and schools. It would be easy, indeed, to gain the impression that charity increased in the later middle ages, due to the survival of so many wills (not extant in large numbers before the mid-fourteenth century) and to the impossibility of calculating how great a proportion of the alms given in an earlier period to monasteries was channelled to the poor. Charity was not, however, now dispensed unconditionally, as it had been in the earlier middle ages. Monastic alms-giving was far less discriminating than the increasingly self-satisfied urban elite of late medieval England would have liked. They had little time for such distributions as occurred at Gloucester Abbey in the early fourteenth century, when the chronicler remarked that the dole charged on the manor of Standish was the occasion of much unseemly behaviour – 'brawling, swearing, blasphemy and fighting' – as sick and unthrifty persons flocked to the abbey gate.[153]

From the mid-fourteenth century there was a withdrawal of support from institutions which provided lodging and care for the poor. The complaint of the men of Cirencester in 1343 that the abbey had misappropriated the funds of two hospitals was certainly provoked by the long-running dispute over the canons' refusal to concede borough status, but also by disagreement as to how the two hospitals should be run. A good example of the shift of emphasis is provided by Reading. There the two hospitals annexed to the abbey were dissolved in the fifteenth century, but around 1500 other institutions emerged to take their place: Barnes hospital and Leches almshouse, both founded by the burgesses, neither attached to the monastery, and both more stringent in the requirements placed upon their inmates.[154] This is typical of the reduction of the church's discretion in the disposition of charity, as town corporations and guilds administered by laymen increasingly took over the direction of institutionalised alms giving.

A clear distinction began to be made in the late fourteenth century between deserving and undeserving poor, and this was eventually enshrined in the post-Reformation poor law. As Dr Rubin has observed in her study of *Charity and Community in Medieval Cambridge*, which has implications far wider than the immediate locality, after the Black Death 'charity was measured carefully, began and often remained at home'.[155] It became more discriminating – or perhaps, rather, more exclusive. There was a general move to restrict charity to specific groups or individuals who were suffering through no fault of their own, respectable and productive members of society who were very like the donors but who had suffered blameless misfortune, and to exclude those who seemed to their 'betters' to

[153] *Victoria County History of Gloucestershire*, II, p. 60.
[154] *Ibid.*, II, pp. 122-23; *Victoria County History of Berkshire*, II, pp. 97-99.
[155] Rubin, *Charity and Community*, p. 299.

be feckless idlers. There was an increasingly frequent insistence in the foundation documents of charitable institutions that the poor who benefited therefrom should be worthy; now 'weaker members of society are seen as *others* rather than brothers'.[156] It was economic resentment resulting from the consequences of plague which led to the rejection and punishment of the 'sturdy beggar'. The charitable benefactions of the later middle ages mirrored the attitude expressed in the Ordinance and Statute of Labourers. The work ethic in England long pre-dated the Protestantism with which it is conventionally associated.

The church itself cannot escape blame for this situation. One of the most distinguished modern students of canon law has observed how little lead the canonists gave in the formulation of a new approach to poor law in radically changed social and economic circumstances.[157] Problems were discussed, but only by the endless repetition of earlier, pre-plague, legal authorities. William Lyndwood, for example, the most distinguished of late medieval English canonists, wrote complacently of the capacity of English ecclesiastical benefices to sustain the canonical responsibilities of hospitality to the poor and needy in an age when parochial revenues had, in real terms, declined markedly. He made no reference to the problem of vagabondage in mid-fifteenth-century England, or the need to reconcile the law of the church on hospitality with secular legislation designed to suppress vagrancy. Lyndwood and his fellows were content to reiterate the traditional, but by now simplistic, distinction between the able-bodied and impotent poor. Among the able-bodied they did not distinguish between the idle, those eager to work but unable to find employment, and those who had abandoned their home villages and would only work elsewhere on better terms; nor did they consider the problem of the dependent or the wilfully unemployed. It was perhaps reasonable, in the changed economic circumstances, that greater emphasis was placed on the obligations of parishioners, rather than of the incumbent, to support the poor. It is regrettable, however, that no guidance was given which might restrain the prejudices in this matter of the still relatively prosperous laity. In this age, in the court of chancery, the canon law and its practitioners moderated, by the application of equity, the severity of the common law of England; but in the realm of poor law a similar opportunity was lost. 'If the secular laws against vagabonds from the fourteenth century are seen as excessively harsh in their treatment of men who were sometimes genuinely unemployed, the canonists must bear some share of the blame in that they, who by tradition and training were best fitted to analyse such a problem,

---

[156] *Ibid.*
[157] B. Tierney, *Medieval Poor Law: a Sketch of Canonical Theory and its Application in England* (Berkeley and Los Angeles, California, 1959), pp. 114-33.

failed to provide adequate guidance on the matter.'[158]

Another characteristic of the religious sociology of late medieval English religion was an increasing preoccupation with sexual morality. This was not an intellectual or theological shift. 'The period between the demographic disaster of the Black Death and the religious revolution of the sixteenth century saw surprisingly little change in the law and theology of sex and marriage.'[159] Yet countless ordinances for almshouses and hospitals from the late fourteenth century onwards insist on chastity (and sobriety) as an essential prerequisite for the receipt of alms.[160] The records of the church courts, moreover, reveal the determination not so much of bishops and priests, but rather of respectable lay society as represented by the churchwardens, to root out every case of adultery, fornication or sexual horseplay.[161] There was a great campaign to clean up the city of London in the 1390s, and a century later the mayor and aldermen so resented the leniency of the church courts in cases of sexual misdemeanour that they took matters into their own hands, sentencing prostitutes and adulterers to the pillory or ducking stool, whereas before an ecclesiastical judge they would have escaped with a fine.[162] By the early fifteenth century, too, it has been suggested that pastoral theologians were showing greater concern about sexual faults. Hitherto such misconduct had been considered wrong insofar as it caused social disruption: the hatred of the cuckold for the seducer, the problems caused by the birth of bastards. Now there was increased determination, expressed most vociferously by the great French theologian Jean Gerson (d. 1429), to root out the most private of sins; lust never fulfilled must be confessed and pardoned.[163] In one sense this

[158] *Ibid.*, p. 132.
[159] J. A. Brundage, *Law, Sex and Christian Society in Medieval Europe* (Chicago, Illinois, 1987), p. 487.
[160] For example, the 1447 statutes of Ellis Davy's almshouse in Croydon stipulate that inmates should be sober, chaste and honest: *Register of John Morton, Archbishop of Canterbury 1486-1500*, ed. C. Harper-Bill, 3 vols, Canterbury and York Society, 75, 78 and forthcoming (Leeds and Woodbridge, 1987-), I, no. 180.
[161] For a survey of church court proceedings, with references to specialist literature, see C. Harper-Bill, *The Pre-Reformation Church in England, 1400-1530* (London, 1989), pp. 54-63.
[162] Du Boulay, *Age of Ambition*, p. 106; R. M. Wunderli, *London Church Courts and Society on the Eve of the Reformation*, Medieval Academy of America *Speculum* Anniversary Monographs, 7 (Cambridge, Mass., 1981).
[163] J. Bossy, 'The Social History of Confession in the Age of the Reformation', *Transactions of the Royal Historical Society*, 5th series, 25 (1975), 21-38; for an eminent advocate of this strict, interiorised morality, see D. C. Brown, *Pastor and Laity in the Theology of Jean Gerson* (Cambridge, 1987), esp. pp. 63-67, 151-58. Bossy has serious reservations, and sees Gerson's preoccupations as exceptional rather than typical ('Social History of Confession', pp. 33-38). For

represents the filtering down to practical, pastoral, theology of Peter Abelard's view, revolutionary in the early twelfth century, that God takes account of intention rather than consequence. In another context, if the proposition is correct, it may be that it was the fear of God's wrath, as manifested in the plague, which led to this more rigorous attitude towards private sin. The desire for scrupulousness in confession and for greater severity in the punishment of moral transgression was perhaps the more measured English counterpart of the extravagant penitential processions of the continent – a desperate effort to avert divine anger.

Lollardy and Orthodoxy

While in any discussion of English religion in the late middle ages it is impossible to ignore the Lollard heresy, that popular creed which developed from the theological and ecclesiological propositions of the Oxford academic John Wyclif, the rise of the sect has in fact little to do with the Black Death, except perhaps that the teachings of the master and the beliefs of his adherents reveal an exaggerated manifestation of the pessimism which affected Christianity as a whole. Since heretical movements had proliferated on the continent from the twelfth century, it would be unwise to explain Lollardy in terms of the consequences of the plague. Between the 1380s and the first decade of the fifteenth century the movement, or at least certain of its tenets, attracted some measure of support from certain academics, from members of the court circle of Richard II and Henry IV, and from elements of the articulate and literate laity; but it never captured the hearts and minds of the English people as a whole.[164] The denial of transubstantiation, the real presence of Christ upon the altar, struck at the heart of common religious belief at a time when the efficacy of the mass for the redemption of souls was most accentuated. The Lollard emphasis on predestination denied to ordinary Christians any means by which they might contribute to their own salvation or that of their departed kindred. Lollard attacks on images and pilgrimages sought to undermine those tangible manifestations of religion which were crucial to

the moralistic tone of guild regulations, see B. R. McRee, 'Religious Gilds and the Regulation of Behaviour in Late Medieval Towns', in *People, Politics and Community in the Late Middle Ages*, ed. J. Rosenthal and C. Richmond (Gloucester, 1987), pp. 108-22.

[164] For very positive assessments of early Lollardy, see Aston, *Lollards and Reformers*; A. Hudson, *Lollards and their Books* (London, 1985); Hudson, *The Premature Reformation*. For the blurring of the distinction between Lollard and orthodox beliefs, see J. A. F. Thomson, 'Orthodox Religion and the Origins of Lollardy', *History*, 74 (1989), 39-55. See also R. G. Davies, 'Lollardy and Locality', *Transactions of the Royal Historical Society*, 6th series, 1 (1991), 191-212, who emphasises the integrity of Wycliffite beliefs in those areas where Lollardy did continue to flourish over a long period.

those – the vast majority – who lacked the intellectual or spiritual capacity to make an interior pilgrimage within their own hearts. Lollard suspicion of sumptuous tombs and elaborate requiems threatened to deny to knights, gentry and urban oligarchs their ambition of remembrance in this world and eternal beatitude in the next. These things were the essentials of medieval popular religion, and the needs had been accentuated, rather than diminished, by the Black Death. The religion which the Lollards attacked was that which is revealed in Chaucer's *Canterbury Tales*, of which conviviality and communal endeavour were the essential strengths. The Lollards simply attempted to overthrow too much of the mentality and apparatus of late medieval religion, at a time of disaster when these supports were most needed.

Lollardy was already in decline by 1414, in which year Henry V defeated the pathetic band of heretical rebels gathered by Sir John Oldcastle on St Giles' Field outside London. After 1414 the Lollard knight, who had provided the only hope for the worldly success of the movement, was extinct, as a public figure at least. It has, however, been suggested by Professor Colin Richmond, in two learned and extremely persuasive articles, that in the period between the Black Death and the Reformation the religion of the English gentry began to diverge to a dangerous degree from that of the majority of the population.[165] The upper echelons of English society, according to his argument, withdrew into religious privacy, worshipping normally in domestic chapels and, when they did come to the parish church, sitting in pews, often enclosed, now for the first time reserved for them, and reading therein their devotional books. Their participation in communal religion became merely a backdrop to their own spiritual experience; their presence was now a matter merely of social obligation, no longer of active commitment. For a few of the gentry and the urban oligarchy this was because they had absorbed the new emphasis on conscience and contemplation, which made the liturgical round seem merely peripheral; for the majority it was merely that literacy had now been

---

[165]   C. Richmond, 'Religion and the Fifteenth-Century English Gentleman', in *Church, Politics and Patronage*, ed. Dobson, pp. 193-208, and 'The English Gentry and Religion', *c.*1500' in *Religious Belief and Ecclesiastical Careers*, ed. Harper-Bill, pp. 121-50. Although my own interpretation of what we agree to be the disaster of the 1530s is rather different from that of Professor Richmond, in that I believe the changes to have been more sudden and to have arisen from the policies of a faction rather than the shift of religious sensibilities of a social class, I would like to express my admiration for his extraordinarily sensitive work on late medieval English religion. For an alternative view, based on Warwickshire evidence, see C. Carpenter, 'The Religion of the Gentry of Fifteenth-Century England', in *England in the Fifteenth Century: Proceedings of the 1986 Harlaxton Symposium*, ed. D. Williams (Woodbridge, 1987), pp. 53-74.

added to superiority of birth and to wealth as a factor dividing the elite from the multitude. Whatever the motivation of individuals, however, Professor Richmond argues that there developed in the late middle ages a two-tiered religion, which was the essential precondition of the Reformation.

Despite the strength of these arguments, it is possible to see the contemplative, private, elements in the religion of the late medieval English gentry as a response to the invitation issued by the Church, since the Fourth Lateran Council of 1215, to participate more personally and intimately in the observance of the Christian religion.[166] The texts read by the literate told the same story as the wall paintings which were the medium of instruction for the great majority. If they often prayed in private, the leaders of society emerged to take the lead in parochial religion at the great festivals of the Christian year. It might be argued that there was no *greater* gap in religious belief and practice between those who exercised power and the rest in 1500 than there had been in 1100. The gulf was not increasing, because even the illiterate were far better informed about the fundamentals of the faith in the period from 1350 to 1530 than they had been in the twelfth and thirteenth centuries, supposedly the golden age of Latin Christianity. This was due to the pastoral revolution of the late middle ages, inaugurated by great speculative theologians such as Peter Abelard and Thomas Aquinas, but carried to completion by prelates such as Archbishop Thoresby of York and the numerous writers of pastoral and confessional manuals. Everything we know of the religious observance of the vast majority of the gentry and urban oligarchy in the 180 years after the Black Death suggests that they were content, to say the least, with a Catholic faith which permitted a certain pomposity among the mighty of this world, most particularly in their funeral arrangements.

In the wake of the Black Death, for sure, English parish churches became the mausolea of the great, and of those not so influential. The site of interment was moved from the graveyard, or from the side-aisle of the church, to a much more prominent position. In Suffolk, for example, illustrations are provided by Burgate, where the tomb of Sir William Burgate (d. 1409) and his wife stands before the high altar, cutting it off from the village congregation; and Dennington, where the most impressive feature of the church is the chantry chapel of Lord Bardolf, a hero of Agincourt.[167] In the urban context, Holy Trinity church in Hull is replete with the tombs of wealthy late medieval merchants.[168] The aristocracy and

[166]   L. G. Duggan, 'The Unresponsiveness of the Late Medieval Church: a Reconsideration', *Sixteenth-Century Journal*, 9 (1978), 3-26. For an amplification of the points made below, see C. Harper-Bill, 'Who Wanted the English Reformation?', *Medieval History*, 2, i (1992), 66-77.

[167]   H. Munro Cautley, *Suffolk Churches*, 5th edn (Woodbridge, 1982), pp. 248-49, 277.

gentry continued to pour their money into parish churches, taking the lead in a massive re-endowment to which the widow also contributed her mite. The documentary evidence for the generosity of the English people to the Church in the post-plague period is contained in wills which survive in ever-increasing numbers from the 1350s onwards, and in the rare parochial records, such as those from Bodmin, Eye and Swaffham, which indicate that munificence was not merely a death-bed safeguard but was also the norm for those in good health.[169] The most obvious and the most important evidence is the architectural legacy of the late middle ages in England. Of some eight thousand surviving medieval parish churches, three-quarters are built wholly, or were substantially rebuilt, in the Perpendicular style which flourished from the mid-fourteenth to the early sixteenth centuries.[170] The legacy is plain to see in all parts of the country, but most particularly in wealthy areas such as East Anglia, the Cotswolds and Somerset. There was nothing to compare with this activity since the half-century after the Norman Conquest, or until the nineteenth-century programme of urban evangelisation, and the impetus for this architectural revolution came almost entirely from the laity. Of course these buildings were manifestations of dynastic pride (in the case of all those Yorkshire churches where the local gentry sought consistently to build the tower higher than that of their neighbours) or of civic consciousness (in urban churches such as St Peter Mancroft at Norwich or St Mary Redcliffe at Bristol). Yet it cannot be denied that the channel for the expression of these grandiose mundane sentiments was the lavish endowment of the Catholic Church and of orthodox religion and the creation of ever more impressive shrines for the celebration of its central mystery. The evidence of parochial architecture demonstrates clearly that if there was a tendency towards disinvestment in charity, there was no such reluctance to divert resources towards the local church.

[168] P. Heath, 'Urban Piety in the Late Middle Ages: the Evidence of Hull Wills', in *Church, Politics and Patronage*, ed. Dobson, pp. 209-34.
[169] For accessible collections of pre-Reformation wills, see *Somerset Medieval Wills*, ed. F. W. Weaver (repr. Gloucester, 1983); *Bedfordshire Wills Proved in the Prerogative Court of Canterbury, 1363-1548*, ed. M. McGregor, Bedfordshire Historical Society, 58 (Hitchin, 1979). For Eye, Historical Manuscripts Commission, *Tenth Report* (1885), Appendix 4, pp. 527-31; 'Receipts and Expenses in the Building of Bodmin Church, A.D. 1469 to 1472', ed. J. J. Wilkinson, *Camden Miscellany VII*, Camden Society, new series, xiv (Westminster, 1874); J. F. Williams, 'The Black Book of Swaffham', *Norfolk Archaeology*, 33 (1965), 243-53.
[170] Scarisbrick, *Reformation and the English People*, pp. 12-15; C. Platt, *The Parish Churches of Medieval England* (London, 1981), pp. 88-146.

Conclusion

Very much work has been accomplished in the past decade to demonstrate that English religion in the fifty years before the Reformation was in no way moribund. Under the sound leadership of the episcopate, the literate laity engaged themselves actively in the organisation of the church and responded eagerly to the invitation, extended to them since the early thirteenth century, to participate fully in the spiritual life of an increasingly Christocentric religion. In their endeavours they were actively encouraged by the religious texts which emanated from the vigorous enclosed monastic communities newly established in late medieval England. There had certainly been a crisis of confidence in the late fourteenth century. This had been resolved by the spiritual initiative of Walter Hilton and his fellows and, in the next generation, by the firm action, in so many spheres of ecclesiastical life, of King Henry V, aided by an extremely able bench of bishops.[171] Of course abuses were not entirely eliminated. Visitation records, far more prolific than for the thirteenth century, reveal occasional instances of immorality and mismanagement in monastic communities, and of neglect of their pastoral duties by parish priests. Such had always been the case, as Coulton, ever critical of the record of the medieval Catholic Church, realistically recognised.[172] There is, however, in the period after the Black Death, far more evidence of a concerted effort to eliminate such abuses, whether financial or moral.[173]

By the late fifteenth century the recovery of the English church was complete, and the most recent study of religion in the immediate pre-Reformation period has demonstrated conclusively that late medieval Catholicism was a vibrant faith which satisfied all levels of society.[174] This was essentially a 'broad church', catering admirably for all but the tiny minority who rejected its basic tenets. In this sense the assessment of Cardinal Gasquet, a much maligned historian,[175] was correct, and it may be

---

[171] For the crucial role of Henry V, see J. Catto, 'Religious Change under Henry V', in *Henry V: the Practice of Kingship*, ed. G. L. Harriss (Oxford, 1985), pp. 97-115.

[172] See above, p. 79.

[173] See, e.g., the visitation returns for the diocese of Lincoln: *Visitations of Religious Houses in the Diocese of Lincoln, 1420-49*, ed. A. Hamilton Thompson, Lincoln Record Society, 7, 14, 21 (Horncastle and Lincoln, 1914-29), and Canterbury and York Society, 17, 24, 33 (London and Oxford, 1915-27); *Visitations in the Diocese of Lincoln, 1517-31*, ed. A. Hamilton Thompson, Lincoln Record Society, 33, 35, 37 (Hereford, 1940-47).

[174] E. Duffy, *The Stripping of the Altars: Traditional Religion in England, 1400-1580* (London and New Haven, 1992). This remarkable book puts flesh upon the bones of the so-called 'revisionist' interpretation of the English Reformation.

[175] For a critique of Gasquet, see D. Knowles, 'Cardinal Gasquet as an Historian', in his *The Historian and Character* (Cambridge, 1963), pp. 240-63. While Gasquet can be faulted on points of detail, particularly as an editor of

that the impact of the plague accentuated the anxiety of literate elements of the laity to participate in the widening of personal religious experience and to embrace a view of Christian conduct first propounded in the lecture halls of Paris and in the Cistercian cloisters of the twelfth century.[176]

---

medieval texts, it is remarkable the extent to which he anticipated interpretations of late medieval religion and the English Reformation which have gained popularity in the last decade.

[176] For the radical changes of the twelfth century, in scholarship and spirituality, see C. Morris, *The Discovery of the Individual, 1050-1200* (London, 1972).

Figure 1: Incised Slab at Middleton, Essex, to Sire James Samson, Rector of the Parish, who died in the plague of 1349. From the *Transactions of the Essex Archæological Society*, new series, 8 (1903), plate opposite p. 1.

124

The Black Death and English Art:
A Debate and Some Assumptions

PHILLIP LINDLEY

Death came driving after him and dashed all to dust
Companies of kings and knights, kaisars and popes.
Learned or unlearned, he let no man stand
That he hit squarely who ever stirred afterward.
Many a lovely lady and their love-knights
Sank down swooning for sorrow of Death's blows.[1]

Introduction

It is a surprising feature of the vigorous debates about the plague's effects now taking place between social, economic, ecclesiastical and political historians that there has been no accompanying dialogue amongst art and architectural historians about the immediate, short-term impact of the Black Death in England or about the centrality of the role played by endemic plague – and the massive depopulation it caused – in the radical changes in art and architecture from 1350. This short essay can make no pretence at providing the detailed regional studies or the wider-ranging national analyses which are essential if art historians are to make a serious contribution to our understanding of the consequences of the plague. Rather, it attempts to stimulate new research by gathering together the scattered remarks and often unjustified assumptions about the plague's effects found in the literature of English art history. There is also an important and illuminating contrast to be drawn between the piecemeal research in England and the sequence of thesis and counter-thesis which has occurred in the study of the Black Death's effects on art in Trecento Italy – the area where, traditionally, large numbers of art and architectural historians have concentrated their research efforts.

Meiss's Paradigm

Millard Meiss's classic study *Painting in Florence and Siena after the Black Death* has, in the four decades since it was first published, generated intense discussion amongst students of Trecento Italian art.[2] The ramifications of

[1] William Langland, *Will's Vision of Piers Plowman*, trans. E. Talbot Donaldson (London and New York, 1990), p. 233. A version of this paper was first delivered at the 'Age of Chivalry' exhibition symposium in 1987, work on it being undertaken while I was a research fellow at St Catharine's College, Cambridge. Thanks are due to Paul Williamson, Sophie Oosterwijk, Dr S. F. E. Baylis and Prof. B. Cassidy for commenting on earlier drafts.

[2] M. Meiss, *Painting in Florence and Siena after the Black Death: The Arts, Religion and Society in the Mid-Fourteenth Century* (Princeton, NJ, 1951, revised edn

this debate provide an instructive model for any attempt to examine the effects of the plague on English art and architecture. Meiss's work, which will be familiar to every student of fourteenth-century art, claimed that there was a profound change in both the style and taste of Florentine and Sienese painting after the visitation of the plague to those cities in 1348. He argued that much of the painting of the third quarter of the century showed a reaction against the innovations of Giotto and his followers: plastic design and perspectival illusionism were supplanted by a paradoxical definition of space both in architecture and figure organisation, and for the equilibrium of the earlier paintings was substituted an uneasy tension between the planar and spatial aspects of compositions. Saturated and hard colours, together with the widespread employment of tooled gilding, revived Duecento emphases on abstract patterning and austere frontality. In iconography, realistic narratives were abrogated in favour of hieratic ritualism and instead of the humanity and intimacy characteristic of the treatment of religious themes in the work of Giotto, figures were distanced from each other and isolated. An increased exaltation of God and the church was accompanied by the recovery of earlier medieval symbolism: figures, rather than the symbols substituted for them by Giotto in the Arena Chapel, were again trampled underfoot.

The stylistic outline advanced by Meiss was not new: indeed, as Henk van Os has perceptively revealed,[3] it echoes that in G. Gombosi's 1926 study of Spinello Aretino. But Meiss's distinctive contribution – and the one which surely accounts for his work's enduring importance – was his rooting of these stylistic changes in a series of disasters which struck Florence and Siena in the 1340s, following a period of great expansion in the first decades of the century. In 1341 the Pisans captured Lucca and the aggressive expansion of Milan posed an increasingly serious threat to Florence, against a background of economic crisis precipitated by King Edward III's defaulting on his debts: in 1343 the Peruzzi declared bankruptcy, to be followed two years later by the Bardi.[4] By 1346, according to the chronicler Giovanni Villani, the Florentine companies had lost about 1,700,000 florins[5] and a difficult economic position was worsened by crop failures throughout Tuscany in 1346 and 1347.[6] These crises were followed by a far greater calamity, the Black Death, which struck Florence and Siena in 1348. Bowsky has estimated that the population of Siena prior to the plague may have been over 50,000 with perhaps another 100,000 in the rest

1964).

[3] H. van Os, 'The Black Death and Sienese Painting: A Problem of Interpretation', *Art History*, 4 (1981), 237-47, p. 237.

[4] Meiss, *Painting*, pp. 61-62. Both families had, of course, been patrons of Giotto.

[5] Quoted by Meiss, *Painting*, p. 62.

[6] Meiss, *Painting*, p. 64.

of the contado.[7] Nearly half the population died in the Black Death.[8] Some of the economic effects of the catastrophe are undisputed: the plague was followed by a great wave of immigration from the smaller towns and farms into the cities and the rise of a nouveau riche class.[9] It is of this class that a chronicler complained, 'In those days, the administration and government of the city of Florence had passed in part – and not a small part – to people newly arrived from the territory of Florence, who had little experience in civic affairs, and to people from more distant lands who had settled in the city'.[10] The structural changes in the ruling elites were even more far-reaching in Siena, where in 1355 the oligarchy of the Nove was thrown from power and the Dodicini, a wider group, took its place, only to be displaced in its turn thirteen years later.[11]

Meiss argued that painting reflected the social and economic changes after the Black Death, or rather the taste and the quality of piety which they brought into prominence. Viewing the religious and pictorial ideals of the *homines novi* as still rooted in the late thirteenth century, Meiss argued that they neither understood nor appreciated the art of Giotto.[12] Petrarch, he thought, seemed to testify to exactly this attitude when, writing in his will of 1370 about a Madonna by Giotto, he said that 'though its beauty is a source of wonder to the masters of the art, the ignorant do not understand it'.[13] The wide diffusion of conservative tastes among people who had acquired wealth and influence broadened acceptance of the new retrogressive styles, whilst in the wake of the disasters the established families also welcomed a less worldly and less humanistic art than that of the earlier years of the century. Meiss contended that the attitude of profound pessimism and renunciation of life evinced by flagellant processions and manifested in Jacopo Passavanti's penitential sermons also underlies and explains the marked change in painting before and after the plague.[14] He cited contemporary chroniclers such as the Sienese Agnolo di

7   W. M. Bowsky, 'The Impact of the Black Death upon Sienese Government and Society', *Speculum*, 39 (1964), 1-34. *Idem, A Medieval Italian Commune: Siena under the Nine, 1287-1355* (Berkeley, California, 1981).

8   Meiss, *Painting*, p. 65; Bowsky, 'Impact', p. 18.

9   Bowsky, 'Impact', pp. 26-27. See also the sumptuary legislation of 1349 in Siena, cited in Bowsky, *Siena*, p. 71.

10   Filippo Villani, quoted by Meiss, *Painting*, pp. 69-70.

11   Meiss, *Painting*, p. 64; Bowsky, *Siena*, chapter 8.

12   Meiss, *Painting*, pp. 70ff.

13   E. H. Wilkins, *Petrarch's Later Years* (Cambridge, Massachusetts, 1959), pp. 182-83. *Cf.* Meiss, *Painting*, pp. 70-71. The point seems in Petrarch to be more a contrast between the cognoscenti and the vulgar herd than a comparison between the new men and their predecessors.

14   Meiss, *Painting*, pp. 83-84. Flagellant processions also came to England (from the Low Countries): *Robertus de Avesbury, De Gestis Mirabilibus Regis Edwardi Tertii*, ed. E. M. Thompson, Rolls Series, 93 (London, 1889), pp. 407-08 but

Tura and the Florentine Matteo Villani; the latter, taking up the writing of his brother's chronicle after Giovanni had succumbed to the plague, 'decided, after many grave misfortunes and with a greater awareness of the dire state of mankind than the period of its prosperity had revealed to me, to make a beginning with our varied and calamitous material at this juncture ... Having to commence our treatise by recounting the extermination of mankind ... my mind is stupefied as it approaches the task of recording the sentence that divine justice mercifully delivered upon men...'[15] Boccaccio, in the *Decameron*, writes of Florence, that 'they dug for each graveyard a huge trench, in which they laid the corpses as they arrived by hundreds at a time, piling them up tier upon tier as merchandise is stowed in a ship, each covered with a little earth, until the trench would hold no more'.[16]

For Meiss, then, the stylistic and iconographic mutations in the art of Florence and Siena in the second half of the century were both explained and caused by the socio-economic, demographic and spiritual crises which resulted from the cataclysm of the Black Death.

Applying the Model: The English Perspective

No survey of the effects of the Black Death on English art and architecture comparable to Meiss's brilliant overview has ever been attempted. Nevertheless, it has for long been axiomatic for many architectural and art historians that the plague did exert a considerable impact on the arts in England. E. S. Prior, for example, writing early this century, thought that 'the decrepitude of [English] art following the Black Death is one of the most dramatic incidents in the whole history of art'. Prior claimed that it had four main results for English architecture: first, it put a decisive stop to monastic dominance of church-building; secondly, it let 'down the curtain on the splendid and characteristic art of the Yorkshire builders'; thirdly, it helped to curtail local building traditions, facilitating the spread of the Perpendicular style; and, finally, 'the gradual secularizing of church building was largely the outcome of the Black Death'.[17] Francis Bond, in a contemporary monograph on English Gothic, put it even more brutally:

were not an indigenous development.

15 Meiss, *Painting*, pp. 65-66.

16 Giovanni Boccaccio, *Decameron*, ed. C. S. Singleton (Baltimore, 1974), pp. 6-7. The translation is largely from Meiss, *Painting*, p. 65. See also the appalling simile of lasagna used by Marchionne di Coppo Stefani to describe how bodies were laid in layers with earth shovelled on top of them (J. Henderson, 'The Black Death in Florence: Medical and Communal Responses', in *Death in Towns: Urban Responses to the Dying and the Dead, 100-1600*, ed. S. Bassett (Leicester, 1992), p. 145).

17 E. S. Prior, *The Cathedral Builders in England* (London, 1905), pp. 78, 82; *idem*, *A History of Gothic Art in England* (London, 1900), pp. 426-7; R. Crawfurd, *Plague and Pestilence in Literature and Art* (Oxford, 1914), chapter vii.

'unfinished work was everywhere stopped; and for a whole generation little new work was begun'.[18] A popular view of the 1930s is expressed by Cox and Ford, who blamed the Black Death for the end of the Decorated style, and believed that Perpendicular design was 'immeasurably simpler in its setting out and rendering' than the Decorated. 'With the scarcity of skilled labour that followed the Pestilence...', they continued, 'it must have been hailed as a godsend by the many scratch teams of raw or half-trained workmen who were now called upon to wrestle with the quite considerable problems of church building and extension. Such causes were undoubtedly instrumental in the almost universal adoption of Perpendicular towards the close of the century'.[19] Paradoxically, Professor Jean Bony, writing in 1979, although agreeing that the Black Death had a devastating effect on architecture, claimed that 'the final triumph of the Perpendicular was delayed by [the plague]'.[20] A decade later, Christopher Wilson tentatively suggested that the Perpendicular style may have been welcomed as 'soberer and more spiritual' than the Decorated style.[21]

In manuscript painting, the plague's impact seemed absolutely unequivocal to Eric Millar. He blamed it for 'the almost complete disappearance of materials when English illumination was at the highest point of its perfection'. He thought that there were no significant manuscript illuminations painted in England from the Luttrell Psalter, which he dated to c.1340, until the Bohun manuscripts of about 1360. English manuscript illumination, he concluded, never really recovered from this catastrophic collapse.[22] A strong case could also be made that changes in the design of seals and monumental brasses occurred after the plague. The series A monumental brasses classified by J. P. C. Kent begin with two at Cobham, dating from several years after the plague, and these tough and regularised monuments are rightly regarded as far removed stylistically from the calligraphic complexities of the best pre-plague brasses.[23]

[18] F. Bond, *Gothic Architecture in England* (London, 1905), p. 136. See also p. 499, where he argues that 'the simplicity of Gloucester stone-craft, the superiority of Gloucester glass, made their appeal at the right moment to a sobered England ... for the future the architecture of England was to be conditioned by glass and not by stone. Cathedral church and abbey church were content to sit at the feet of Gloucester.'

[19] J. C. Cox and C. B. Ford, *Parish Churches* (London, 1934, rev. ed. 1961), p. 95.

[20] J. Bony, *The English Decorated Style* (Oxford, 1979), p. 61.

[21] C. Wilson, *The Gothic Cathedral* (London, 1990), p. 212.

[22] E. G. Millar, *English Illuminated Manuscripts of the XIVth and XVth Centuries* (Paris, 1928), p. 24.

[23] J. P. C. Kent, 'Monumental Brasses – a New Classification of Military Effigies c.1360-c.1485', *Journal of the British Archaeological Association*, 12 (1949), 70-97; see also R. Emmerson, 'Monumental Brasses: London Design c.1420-85', *Journal of the British Archaeological Association*, 131 (1978), 50-77.

Similarly, episcopal seals of the 1350s show an interest in spatial illusionism rare before that date. According to Francis Bond, even the style of choir stalls was radically changed by the plague: there was, he writes, 'a great change... [in] design', namely, 'the great multiplication and predominance of the vertical line'.[24] Figure sculpture, for Prior and Gardner, was sadly affected by the plague: it 'became monotonously regular for something like a hundred and fifty years'; it was increasingly seen as mere architectural furniture, and the qualitative gap between the best and the worst work started to widen. They conclude, 'some work of the later fourteenth century can claim to have preserved the sculptural expression that fifty years earlier had been a matter of course: but after 1400 the trivial and mannered reproduction becomes increasingly characteristic, and though the art of fifteenth-century sculpture in England was often respectable it can never, we think, be called fresh or inventive'.[25] Lawrence Stone, although sensitive to the need for a more sophisticated analysis of the plague's effects, situating it within the context of other social and economic changes, also inclines to the view that the middle of the fourteenth century was a period of transition, which witnessed a 'noticeable shift of emphasis both in style and in choice of field'.[26] Monumental effigies, instead of lying in dynamic and contorted poses, are laid flat on their backs in rigid repose, precisely paralleling the change in brass design, and perfectly suiting the representation of plate armour. 'The virtual disappearance after 1348 of the gifted and prolific school of sculptors at Beverley' may, Stone thinks, be ascribed to the plague.[27] In the sphere of stained glass, John Knowles saw a notable break in the flourishing York school of glass painting at the Black Death, and linked it with the death of designers, deploying an analysis of the York Freemen's Rolls to demonstrate the high mortality rate. Subsequently, he claimed, York lagged behind centres such as Oxford and Winchester, and when the east window of York's choir was commissioned in 1405, the contract went to John Thornton of Coventry.[28] It has also been argued that the use of impressment by Edward III to obtain glaziers for royal projects such as St Stephen's Chapel, Westminster, was a consequence not so much of the king's desire to hasten the completion of the project – and the glazing of St Stephen's *was* accomplished

---

[24] F. Bond, *Wood Carvings in English Churches, I, Stalls and Tabernacle Work* (London, 1910), pp. 40, 45-47.

[25] E. S. Prior and A. Gardner, *An Account of Medieval Figure-Sculpture in England* (Cambridge, 1912), pp. 390-91.

[26] L. Stone, *Sculpture in Britain: The Middle Ages* (Harmondsworth, 1972), p. 177.

[27] *Ibid.*

[28] J. Knowles, *Essays in the History of the York School of Glass-Painting* (London, 1936), chapter xv; see also J. Knowles, 'The Periodic Plagues of the Second Half of the Fourteenth Century and their Effects on the Art of Glass-Painting', *Archaeological Journal*, 79 (1922), 343-52.

extraordinarily rapidly in 1350-52 – but of the dearth of skilled glaziers to make up a workshop which included at one time six or seven designers, eleven painter-glaziers and fifteen glaziers cutting and fitting the glass, working simultaneously.[29]

Finally, the plague has been connected with the rise of the vernacular. John Trevisa, Higden's first translator, traced its growth to the effects of the 'furste moreyn', after which translation from Latin was increasingly made into English instead of French at grammar school. The result was that children learned grammar much more quickly than before, but with the disadvantage, as Trevisa picturesquely puts it, that 'they conneth na more Frensch than can here lift heele'.[30] Between 1362 and 1364, three successive parliaments were opened by speeches in English and in 1362 a statute ordered that pleadings in the law courts were to be conducted in English, on the grounds that French was no longer sufficiently understood.[31] It has frequently been concluded, then, that the Black Death exerted as decisive an influence on English art as it did on that of Siena or Florence.

Meiss Rebutted: Style and Artistic Change

In recent years, however, it has increasingly been doubted whether the plague really did have the impact on Sienese and Florentine painting that Meiss claimed for it. The commonest line of attack on his thesis is that many of the phenomena which Meiss dated after 1348, and which he regarded as characteristic of the third quarter of the Trecento, should in fact be dated before 1348. The frescoes of Barna da Siena in S. Gimignano, employed by Meiss to demonstrate a violent eruption of 'the inner conflict and repressed excitement' of art after the plague, are viewed by Van Os and others as antedating it, whilst Polzer, on the basis of iconographic

[29]   For this suggestion, see R. Marks, *Stained Glass in England during the Middle Ages* (London, 1993), p. 166. The figures in Knowles, 'Periodic Plagues', p. 345 are far from reliable. See L. F. Salzman, 'The Glazing of St Stephen's Chapel, Westminster 1351-2', *Journal of the British Society of Master Glass Painters*, 1 (1926-27), 14-16 (where it is pointed out that work on the windows actually began in 1349 and the position of John de Chestre – head of a team of 5 or 6 master glaziers at first until he loses his superior wage rate from 25 July 1350 and disappears from 13 Feb 1352 – is discussed) and 31-35.

[30]   B. Cottle, *The Triumph of English 1350-1400* (London, 1969), pp. 17-21. Trevisa also ascribes the decay of fluency in French to the fact that gentlemen had stopped teaching their children the language. See also P. Ziegler, *The Black Death* (London, 1969), p. 253.

[31]   *The Brut or The Chronicles of England*, ed. F. W. D. Brie, 2 vols, Early English Texts Society, 131, 136 (London, 1906-08), II, p. 315. The oldest private legal instrument in English dates from 1376; the Mercers' petition to parliament of 1386 is the first piece of parliamentary English and the oldest English wills in the London court of probate are of 1387.

arguments, has proposed a dating of 1330-35 for the Triumph of Death frescoes in the Camposanto at Pisa.[32] Luciano Bellosi, who ascribes them to the shadowy figure of Buonamico Buffalmacco, places them in the mid-1330s, whilst claims in favour of a dating round 1342 have been advanced, in the course of an excellent résumé of the previous literature, by Antonino Caleca.[33] Far more serious for Meiss's argument was Miklos Boskovits's rejection of the whole outline of stylistic change on which it was based. For Boskovits, the significant changes in Florentine art took place not after 1350 but in the 1320s: indeed, he sees the work of Orcagna and Nardo di Cione as a 'revival' of Giotto's art.[34] Cristina de Benedictis could see no direct reflections of the plague in Sienese art of the sixth decade of the century, which she characterises instead as marked by the persistence of Lorenzettian motifs and a renewed interest in the art of Simone Martini.[35] Indeed, there now seems to be a widespread belief amongst art historians working in this period that the changes in art, whenever they actually occurred, should be attributed not to historical factors but to autonomous stylistic ones.[36]

Exactly the same points can be made about the hypothetical connections of the Black Death and English art. It would, indeed, be a simple matter to draw together sceptical assessments of the plague's impact and to weld a revisionist view from them. It is important to recall, though, that the sequence of hypothesis and counter-thesis which is so marked a feature of the literature on the Italian Trecento is not found in England. Diametrically opposed views co-exist simultaneously in uneasy tension.

[32] H. B. J. Maginnis, 'The Literature of Sienese Trecento Painting, 1945-75', *Zeitschrift für Kunstgeschichte*, 40 (1977), 276-309 (301-04). See also M. Meiss, 'Notable Disturbances in the Classification of Tuscan Trecento Paintings', *Burlington Magazine*, 113 (1971), 178-86. For J. Polzer's latest work, see his 'Aspects of the Fourteenth-Century Iconography of Death and the Plague', in *The Black Death: the Impact of the Fourteenth-Century Plague*, ed. D. Williman (New York, 1982), pp. 107-30.

[33] See the important review of L. Bellosi, *Buffalmacco e il Trionfo della Morte* (Turin, 1974), by H. B. J. Maginnis in *Art Bulletin*, 58 (1976), 126-28. A. Caleca, G. Nencini and G. Piancastelli, *Pisa – Museo delle Sinopie del Camposanto Monumentale* (Pisa, 1979), p. 55. The traditional dating for Orcagna's tabernacle in Orsanmichele, 'a star witness' in Meiss's argument for a post-plague style, has recently been questioned by B. Cassidy, 'The Financing of the Tabernacle of Orsanmichele', *Source*, 8/i (1988), 1-6.

[34] M. Boskovits, *Pittura Fiorentina alla vigilia del rinascimento* (Florence, 1975).

[35] C. de Benedictis, *La Pittura Senese 1330-1370* (Florence, 1979), p. 35, argues that social instability and the climate of violence which led to either irresponsible vitality or intense devotional practices 'non sembrano trovare a mio avviso un diretto e dimostrabile riflesso nella cultura cittadina posteriore alla metà del secolo'.

[36] This point is explicitly made by Van Os, 'Black Death', p. 241.

A major obstacle to a banal theory of linkage between plague and architectural style in England has long existed in the form of Robert Willis's 1860 analysis of the south transept at Gloucester Cathedral, now widely regarded as the first work in the new Perpendicular style (Plates 1 and 2).[37] The Gloucester chronicle which, in the absence of fabric rolls, provides the only documentary evidence for the rebuilding, states unequivocally that the work of remodelling the transept was begun and finished in six years during the abbacy of John Wigmore, who died in 1337.[38] At the latest estimate, work must have begun in 1331, a full seventeen years before the plague. The south window of the Gloucester transept – which contains the basic Perpendicular motifs of the mullion cutting the arch, a transom and the rigid systematisation and hierarchy of elements – may reflect a revision of the lateral transept window designs, intended to assimilate it to the windows of the chapter house and cloister of Old St Paul's (begun in 1332). The influence could instead, perhaps, be in the other direction. Whether the former or latter argument is correct – or, indeed, whether both buildings are related primarily through their common sources – is for my purposes unimportant.[39] What is significant is that both of the first examples of the Perpendicular style – at Old St Paul's and Gloucester – considerably antedate the Black Death. It seems clear that the Perpendicular style may, in origin at least, be viewed purely as an autonomous stylistic development. Already, in 1949, Joan Evans severely criticised the theory that the plague had any real effect on architecture: she pointed to the continuance of the Decorated style in the east and north, citing the Carlisle east window of 1363-82 as an example, and denied that there was any important break in church construction. She highlighted Gloucester as a monastic church where the building programme continued straight after the plague. 'It is easy to say that [the Decorated style's] knell was sounded beside the plague-pits of 1349, but it is not true...'; and she concluded, 'the Black Death ... did little or nothing to change the standards of artistic luxury'.[40]

[37] The most recent analysis is that by Wilson, *Gothic Cathedral*, pp. 204-07.

[38] See *Historia et Cartularium Monasterii Sancti Petri Gloucestriae*, ed. W. H. Hart, 3 vols, Rolls Series, 33 (London, 1863-67), I, p. 46. The best extended study is that of C. Wilson, 'The Origins of the Perpendicular Style and its Development to *ca*.1360', University of London Ph.D. thesis (1979), chapter 3.

[39] The former is a suggestion of J. H. Harvey, *The Perpendicular Style* (London, 1978), p. 79, based on the fact that the south window revises features of the east and west windows of the south transept (notably, they do not include the device of the mullions cutting the arch).

[40] J. Evans, *English Art 1307-1461* (Oxford, 1949), pp. 36, 46. See also p. 75, 'There was ... no appreciable slowing down in the work of church building in the years following the Black Death.' See also, for instance, Etchingham

In seal design, Sandy Heslop has recently shown that a revolution, every bit as decisive as the beginning of the Perpendicular style in architecture, occurred in the second seal of Richard of Bury, in 1335.[41] Its spatial illusionism was taken up by Bishop Stratford's seal of 1340.[42] In other words, here too the important changes occurred well before the plague. For manuscript illumination, Francis Wormald showed that two groups of manuscripts, one centring round the Egerton Genesis, and the other round the Fitzwarin Psalter, could be attributed to the post-plague years. 'Even during the dark days of the third quarter of the century', he claimed, 'England was producing a vigorous and individual style of her own in the traditional manner and was not entirely struck down by the disaster of the middle of the century.'[43] The break in manuscript production between 1348-49 and the 1360s was by no means as complete as Millar had believed. William Courtenay has argued that – for Oxford at least – the plague did not have the effect on higher education often ascribed to it: 'the mortality rate was not particularly high, either of the brilliant or of marginal scholars and masters'.[44] Charles Tracy's redating of the beginning of work on the Hereford choir stalls to before the plague would, if correct, remove the evidence for any significant effect of the Black Death in this sphere too, and a strong case could be made for believing that the critical phase in monumental brass design occurred not in 1348-49 but in 1331, on the death of Adam of Corfe, in whose shop, John Blair has convincingly claimed, the Camoys-style brasses were produced.[45]

---

church in East Sussex, cited by Pevsner as an example of the survival of pure Decorated into the late 1380s (I. Nairn and N. Pevsner, *Sussex* (Harmondsworth, 1965), pp. 48-49, 496-97).

[41] T. A. Heslop, 'Seals of the Mid-Fourteenth Century', in *Age of Chivalry: Art in Plantagenet England 1200-1400*, ed. J. J. G. Alexander and P. Binski, exhibition catalogue (London, 1987), p. 493 and cat. no. 675. Heslop convincingly argues for a foreign origin for the matrix. See further *idem*, 'The Episcopal Seals of Richard of Bury', *Medieval Art and Architecture at Durham Cathedral* (Leeds, 1980), pp. 154-62, where he suggests that the matrix comes from 'Avignon or the French Court' (p. 159).

[42] *Age of Chivalry*, cat. nos. 675, 676.

[43] F. Wormald, 'The Fitzwarin Psalter and its Allies', *Journal of the Warburg and Courtauld Institutes*, 6 (1943), 71-79.

[44] W. J. Courtenay, 'The Effect of the Black Death on English Higher Education', *Speculum*, 55 (1980), 696-714.

[45] C. Tracy, *English Gothic Choir-Stalls 1200-1400* (Woodbridge, 1987), p. 32, suggests 'a protracted period of manufacture, starting in the early 1340s and culminating with the completion of the canopy of the bishop's throne some ten years later'. Tracy argues that the north range of stalls 'may be a little later in date than the south, perhaps interrupted by a visitation of the plague', but sees no significant time-lag between them. For the brasses, see J. Blair, 'English Monumental Brasses before 1350: Types, Patterns and Workshops',

In figure sculpture the picture has been complicated by the near total loss of work in the capital from the 1350s, particularly unfortunate in view of the documentary evidence that William Patrington and Richard Lakenham were busily carving imagery for the chapel of St Stephen, Westminster.[46] Their work was accompanied by the joinery and carpentry work of the chapel's stalls, at first in the hands of William Hurley and William Herland, with misericords by Robert Burwell, and subsequently in the charge of Master Edmund of St Andrew, an Augustinian canon from Newstead Abbey in Nottinghamshire, and one of the few English sculptor-joiners of the Gothic period who is known to have been a cleric.[47] It is at least possible that in the work of Patrington and Lakenham one would have seen a transition from the still movemented but smooth and mannered coldness of the alabaster effigy of John of Eltham (d. 1336) to the austerity of works from the 1370s. If the row of kings on the west front of Lincoln Cathedral (Plates 3 and 4), carved whilst John de Welbourne was treasurer there, are London works of the 1360s, as Lawrence Stone has suggested, we may see further evidence that the stylistic transition in sculpture was not so dramatic as it seems.[48] The head types seem to him to be a natural development of works such as the head of Edward II carved a generation earlier, though he differentiates the Lincoln kings' graceful naturalism of poise from the theatricality of the Eltham weepers of c.1340, which he ascribes to the same sculptor as was responsible for Edward II's effigy.[49] Certainly, it is time to jettison Prior and Gardner's wrong-headed evaluation of the quality of all late fourteenth-century sculpture in England. Works such as the tombs of Edward III (Plate 5), Richard II and Anne of Bohemia or the Westminster Hall kings commissioned by Richard II in 1385 (distorted though their rhythms have been by whitewash and sometimes ineptly restored attributes) do not bear witness to any decline

---

in *The Earliest English Brasses: Patronage, Style and Workshops 1270-1350*, ed. J. Coales (London, 1987), pp. 167, 169: 'most if not all brasses made in London between c.1305 and c.1335 came from one big workshop, in which standard patterns were mass-produced with a strong continuity of design over the thirty-year period'. This conclusion is strongly supported by the stylistic analysis presented by Paul Binski in the same volume.

[46] H. M. Colvin, 'St Stephen's Chapel', in R. A. Brown, H. M. Colvin and A. J. Taylor, *The History of the King's Works* I, *The Middle Ages* (London, 1963), pp. 521-23. See also J. H. Harvey, *English Medieval Architects: a Biographical Dictionary Down to 1550* (Gloucester, 1984), *s.v.*

[47] Colvin, 'St Stephen's', pp. 520-21. Robert Burwell was doubtless a relative of the John Burwell who carved the central boss of the lantern of Ely Cathedral, where William Hurley had been the designer of the timber structure.

[48] Stone, *Sculpture*, p. 181.

[49] *Ibid.*, p. 161. See also L. Southwick, 'The Armoured Effigy of Prince John of Eltham in Westminster Abbey and Some Closely Related Military Monuments', *Church Monuments*, 2 (1987), 9-21.

from the 1340s. Their current conservation has, indeed, tended to emphasise the exceptional quality of the best of the kings.[50]

Post-revisionism

In the Italian Trecento sphere, the argument seems to have moved away from a position which deployed the Black Death to account for nearly every significant change in art to one which denies it almost any importance: Meiss's thesis has been, in effect, replaced by a position which takes almost exactly the opposite view. J. M. W. Bean has justly remarked that 'the removal of cataclysms is almost an occupational disease of modern historians because a critical approach to contemporary evidence leads quite naturally to suspicion of contemporary stress on the consequences of great events or of the work of professional colleagues whose reputations are based on the discovery of crises'.[51] No doubt the debate will continue. But there are numerous reasons for caution in taking the revisionist argument too far when applying it to English art and architecture of the second half of the fourteenth century. Even if this tendentious thesis is correct for Florence and Siena and the plague had no discernible impact on artistic production in these cities, the economic, artistic, social, political and demographic situation in England in this period presents major contrasts with that obtaining in the Italian city states. We must be wary, in criticizing the crude causal links between plague and change postulated in the past, of missing signs of a subtler and more complex relationship. Any consideration of the plague's impact on art in England has to start from an analysis of what actually happened when it swept the country in 1348-49. On the most conservative estimates something like one third of the total population died and the true total might be much higher. For parish priests and monks it almost certainly was.[52] Now, whatever the economic, political and social effects the plague had (and these are likely to be the subject of continuing dispute), a country cannot lose at least a third of its population in under two years without some fairly drastic dislocation. It may well be, as Professor Ormrod has shown, that Edward III's government responded remarkably efficiently to the crisis under the direction of men such as William Edington and William Shareshull, and here Edward's government provides a strong contrast to the collapse of the Valois financial machinery.[53] But, in

---

[50]   See P. G. Lindley, 'Absolutism and Regal Image in Ricardian Sculpture', in *The Wilton Diptych*, ed. D. Gordon, C. Barron and C. Elam (forthcoming, London, 1995).

[51]   J. M. W. Bean, 'The Black Death: the Crisis and its Social and Economic Consequences', in *Black Death*, ed. Williman, p. 23.

[52]   See Harper-Bill, above, pp. 85-86, 97-98. For a cautionary view of medieval demography, see N. Siraisi, 'Introduction' in *Black Death*, ed. Williman, p. 11.

[53]   W. M. Ormrod, 'The English Government and the Black Death of 1348-49', in *England in the Fourteenth Century: Proceedings of the 1985 Harlaxton*

some areas of the arts at least, it can be proved that the plague did have an immediate and quantifiable impact.

In the first place, it killed a significant number of the top designers (just as it did in Siena in 1348 when, for instance, both Ambrogio and Pietro Lorenzetti seem to have died). Three of the Ramsey family of masons died in 1349, the most important of whom was William, the designer of Old St Paul's chapter house and cloisters, and king's master mason from 1336. William Ramsey's successor, John atte Grene, did not even last until May the next year, never having a chance to influence architectural design.[54] He must stand for countless other artists of unknown potential whose careers were abruptly terminated. John Harvey hypothesises that the great designer William Joy, to whom he ascribes the Wells Cathedral presbytery, also died in the plague, together with the master mason of Westminster Abbey, Walter le Bole, and lesser talents such as the Yarmouth carpenter John de Gunton; other masons – Thomas de Pacenham (master mason of York Minster) and Henry de Snelleston (master mason to the Black Prince), for instance – do not re-emerge in the records after 1349.[55] In London all eight wardens of the Cutlers' Company died, all six of the hatters and four of the goldsmiths, and it is therefore highly probable that deaths amongst other London artists were just as high.[56] When the leadership of artistic innovation is concentrated in relatively few hands, high mortality amongst this group will clearly have a disproportionate effect on the arts.

John Maddison, in an exceptionally valuable study of one region, has argued that in the diocese of Lichfield the transition from the Decorated style to the Perpendicular is directly attributable to the plague: change 'was brought about not through the gradual permeation of local design by advanced features from the south but rather by a much more sudden and dramatic shift which can only be explained by the disruption and eventual extinction of the lodge of masons working in the Yorkshire manner and by the completion of their unfinished buildings as much as thirty years later by one clearly identifiable master mason whose experience was gained in a

---

Symposium, ed. W. M. Ormrod (Woodbridge, 1986), pp. 175-88.

[54] For both architects, see Harvey, *English Medieval Architects*, s.v. The appointment of 30 June 1349 to John atte Grene to hire workmen for Westminster is in *Calendar of Patent Rolls, 1348-50*, p. 387.

[55] See Harvey, *English Medieval Architects*, s.v. For Joy, see also *idem, Perpendicular Style*, p. 82. *Ibid.*, p. 267, n. 44, states that of 87 master masons and carpenters whose careers began between 1325 and 1349, 12 died in the plague years 1348-49. *Idem, Medieval Craftsmen* (London, 1975), pp. 133-34, mentions John de Mymmes as a London imager who died in the plague. See *Calendar of Wills Proved in the Court of Hustings, London, AD 1258-AD 1688*, ed. R. R. Sharpe (London, 1889), p. 558 (and for his widow, a painter: p. 576).

[56] Ziegler, *Black Death*, p. 159.

very different background'.[57] Even the masonry base for St Werburgh's shrine in Chester Cathedral seems to have been left incomplete when the plague struck. Maddison's study needs to be buttressed by further detailed work in other regions, but his conclusion that the deaths of individuals, coupled with short-term regional collapse, dramatically affected not just the prosecution of ecclesiastical architecture in the diocese, but also its style, seems entirely convincing.

The fine engraver responsible for the remarkable brass of Sir Hugh Hastings at Elsing and for that at Wimbish in Essex may also have died in the plague: it is otherwise difficult to account for the sudden extinction of his sophisticated style after a very brief florescence.[58] It may be that the disappearance of such a gifted individual in the crucial interregnum following Adam of Corfe's death explains why Flemish brasses started to penetrate the English market.[59] In this, they were apparently following the importation of incised slabs, such as the two in Essex commemorating priests who died in 1349 (Figure 1), presumably from the plague.[60] Apparently none of the sculptors who worked on the vast programme of imagery in the Lady Chapel of Ely Cathedral – where only twenty-eight monks survived the plague (one of the victims being the obedientiary, John of Wisbech, who had been responsible for the chapel's direction for over twenty-eight years) – or those responsible for sculptural decoration in a group of 'Fenland' churches, is found again after the plague.[61] Lynda Dennison's re-evaluation of the Fitzwarin Psalter group of manuscripts accounts for the abrupt cessation of work in the Vienna Bohun Psalter by the artist responsible for other works of the 1340s such as Bodleian MS Douce 131 (Plate 6) by his death in the plague; the same cause, she argues, explains the termination of the Fitzwarin artist's contribution to the Vienna

[57] J. M. Maddison, 'Master Masons of the Diocese of Lichfield: a Study in 14th-Century Architecture at the Time of the Black Death', *Transactions of the Lancashire and Cheshire Antiquarian Society*, 85 (1988), 107-72.

[58] P. Binski, 'The Stylistic Sequence of London Figure Brasses', in *Earliest English Brasses*, ed. Coales, p. 122: 'The disappearance of this style was probably a result of the Black Death.'

[59] *Ibid.*, p. 125. A detailed study of the Flemish brasses of *c.*1330-80 is provided by L. Dennison, 'The Artistic Context of Fourteenth Century Flemish Brasses', *Transactions of the Monumental Brass Society*, 14/i (1986), 1-38.

[60] M. Christy and E. B. Smith, 'Two Essex Incised Slabs', *Essex Archaeological Society Transactions*, 8 (1903), 1-7; F. A. Greenhill, *Incised Effigial Slabs*, 2 vols (London, 1976), II, p. 3.

[61] D. J. Stewart, *On the Architectural History of Ely Cathedral* (London, 1868), pp. 136, 207; P. G. Lindley, *Gothic to Renaissance. Essays on Sculpture in England* (Stamford, 1995), p. 21. William Patrington (*fl.*1351-72) may be a survivor of the Beverley group of sculptors, one or more of whom also worked at Ely. A good deal more detailed work needs to take place on these sculptors before this suggestion can be substantiated.

manuscript.[62] The implication of her redating of the Fitzwarin artist's working life is that there really was a serious hiatus in English manuscript illumination.[63] In this medium, at least, the Black Death may be a watershed. Professor E. W. Tristram puts forward a balanced view of its effects on wall painting, claiming that 'in the poorer churches and more remote areas a decline is evident in quality. However ... there was no diminution in the richness and brilliance of the best work, but rather the reverse. The magnificent decoration of St Stephen's Chapel in ... Westminster was in fact begun with the pestilence at its height, and though the work had been substantially completed by 1351 it was elaborated at intervals over a period of some years' (Plate 7). On the other hand, in 'ordinary country churches, after 1350, comparatively few extensive schemes were put in hand, as they had been earlier'.[64] Richard Marks has argued that the stained glass of the thirty years after 1350 is an anticlimax after the achievements of York, Wells, and Ely and connected this with the plague. For him, the wide-ranging quest for glaziers at St Stephen's may testify to a shortage of competent craftsmen.[65] In other words, standards could be maintained, but only by drawing from an exceptionally wide geographical area.

One effect of population losses was undoubtedly the rapid escalation of wage rates. In 1349 the crown tried to check this, issuing the first Ordinance of Labourers, to order that wages and prices should remain at their former levels. It seems to have had little effect, for it was reinforced and issued as a statute in 1351, with a clause specifically concerned with the building trade.[66] In 1350, the city of London issued an ordinance to regulate wages and prices, opening with an assertion of the 'damages and grievances which the good folks of the City, rich and poor, have suffered and received within the past year, by reason of masons, carpenters, tilers and all manner of labourers, who take immeasurably more than they have been wont to take'.[67] It seems probable, as Salzman suggests, that it was

[62] L. Dennison, 'The Fitzwarin Psalter and its Allies: a Reappraisal', in *England in the Fourteenth Century*, ed. Ormrod, pp. 42-66.

[63] Dennison, 'Fourteenth Century Flemish Brasses', states (pp. 29-33), 'The Black Death clearly had a devastating effect on manuscript production in England ... with the result that when it was again revived, under the patronage of the Bohun family around 1355, it was necessary to import a Flemish artist.'

[64] E. W. Tristram, *English Wall Painting of the Fourteenth Century* (London, 1955), p. 3. He adds that the increased popularity of St Christopher may have been associated with the plague (p. 115).

[65] Marks, *Stained Glass*, pp. 166-67. Tristram, *Wall Painting*, makes the same point about the wall painters (p. 30).

[66] M. McKisack, *The Fourteenth Century 1307-1399* (Oxford, 1959), p. 335; L. F. Salzman, *Building in England down to 1540* (Oxford, 1967), p. 72.

[67] For discussion, *ibid.*, pp. 72-75. *Memorials of London and London Life*, ed. H. T.

because the city wage rates were so much higher than statutory that many craftsmen employed at Westminster Palace went off to work for other employers. In 1353 proclamation was made that they should be brought back and that no one should employ such men on pain of imprisonment and forfeiture.[68] In 1360 the Statute of Labourers was strengthened by increasing its penalties, specifically including carpenters and masons, and forbidding them to form unlawful confederations in order to boost wages.[69] William of Dene, the Rochester chronicler whose harrowing account of plague mortality has already been cited, complained that 'the labourers and skilled workmen became so rebellious that neither the king, nor the law, nor the justices...were able to punish them'.[70] Of course, breaches of the statutes were frequent and in 1391 John Sampson, perhaps the master sculptor of William of Wykeham's New College, had the case against him dismissed 'for that he is a master freestone mason and extremely knowledgeable and skilful in that art and in carving'.[71] One consequence of the shortage of labour was that the crown had increasingly to resort to impressment to obtain its workforce: peacetime impressment was used before the plague, but it was most widely employed between 1350 and 1380.[72] The continuator of Higden's chronicle complained that 'almost all the masons and carpenters throughout the whole of England were brought to [Windsor], so that hardly anyone could have any good mason or carpenter except in secret'.[73] In such circumstances, discipline became a serious problem and many workmen left the king's employment for the higher rates of pay offered by other patrons. The king's furious complaints were of little use and in August 1360 he was himself forced to authorise the clerk of the works at Westminster and the Tower to offer wages well above the statutory rate: 'within a few years the rise in wages had become general and

Riley (London, 1868), pp. 253-58.

[68] *Memorials*, pp. 271-72.

[69] Salzman, *Building*, p. 73. *Statutes of the Realm*, 11 vols (London, 1810-28), I, pp. 366-67, cited in R. A. Brown and H. M. Colvin, 'Towards a Central Organisation 1272-1377', in *History of the King's Works*, I, p. 184, n. 6. Salzman, *Building*, p. 73.

[70] F. A. Gasquet, *The Black Death of 1348 and 1349* (London, 1908), p. 231. See also Harper-Bill, above, p. 110.

[71] Harvey, *English Medieval Architects*, s.v.

[72] Brown and Colvin, 'Central Organisation', p. 182: 'Though Edward III was already impressing men for his works before the Black Death, the shortage of labour resulting from the great pestilence undoubtedly forced him and his ministers to make greater use of his compulsory powers.' See also D. Knoop and G. P. Jones, 'The Impressment of Masons in the Middle Ages', *Economic History Review*, 1st series, 8 (1937-38), 57-67, p. 64.

[73] *Polychronicon Ranulphi Higden Monachi Cestrensis*, ed. C. Babington and J. R. Lumby, 9 vols, Rolls Series, 41 (London, 1865-86), VIII, p. 359. The translation is that of Brown and Colvin.

was afterwards maintained'.[74]

According to John Harvey, regional differences in the effects of the Black Death may account for the fact that so many royal masons of the second half of the century, such as Henry Yeveley, John Palterton and Simon Roucestere, were of north midlands origin, filling the vacuum left by the deaths of East Anglian masons such as the Ramseys.[75] East Anglia, indeed, seems to have been particularly hard hit by the plague. Norwich, with a population of well over 13,000 before the plague, lost over half its citizens and not only did it never recover its position in relation to the rest of England but, in absolute terms, had barely regained its vanished population by the end of the sixteenth century.[76] This must surely be part of the reason for the end of the rich tradition of manuscript painting in Norwich. At the cathedral priory of Ely, where nearly half the monks died in 1348-49, the death of workmen and a hiatus in the work may perhaps account for the inept handling of the relationship between the vault and wall-surfaces of the Lady Chapel.[77] The Lady Chapel's stained glass after 1349 is dramatically simpler than that executed before the plague.[78] Undoubtedly, the Black Death affected the prosecution of other building projects, such as Nantwich in Cheshire, or Great Yarmouth, the latter of which was never completed, whilst the maintenance of some parish churches was affected by the decline of population: in 1365-66, two Cambridge parishes – All Saints and St Giles – had to be united owing to the losses, and there are frequent accounts, in East Anglia and elsewhere, of parish churches standing desolate and ruinous after demographic losses in the region.[79]

The traditional view that the grand-scale rebuilding of the great monastic churches was severely checked by the plague now seems more convincing than Evans's counter-argument: of the four examples she cites to highlight continuing building programmes,[80] at Westminster Abbey, there *was* no major building programme at the time of the plague so to claim that there is no special break in the fabric rolls is irrelevant. Gloucester – where the choir was rebuilt after the plague – is exceptional, for the presence of Edward II's tomb seems to have led to munificent

---

[74]   Brown and Colvin, 'Central Organisation', pp. 184-85.

[75]   Harvey, *Perpendicular Style*, p. 97; *idem*, *English Medieval Architects*, p. 359.

[76]   I am here paraphrasing Ziegler, *Black Death*, p. 170.

[77]   P. G. Lindley, 'The Monastic Cathedral at Ely, *c.*1320 to *c.*1350: Art and Patronage in Medieval East Anglia', University of Cambridge, Ph.D. thesis (1985), p. 123.

[78]   *Ibid.*, p. 223.

[79]   Ziegler, *Black Death*, p. 172. *Sixth Report of the Royal Commission on Historical Manuscripts* (London, 1877), p. 299.

[80]   Evans, *English Art*, p. 46.

donations.[81] At Ely Cathedral, new building was henceforth confined to the monastic buildings, with some minor additions and alterations to the church (the western tower's octagon, and new fenestration); at Winchester, Bishop Edington's work on a new west front was clearly interrupted, not to be resumed for some years – perhaps not until 1371 in the episcopate of his successor, William Wykeham, according to the most recent analysis – and one very likely cause of such an interruption is the plague (Plate 8).[82]

For the secular cathedrals, the situation was not much better. York Minster, which Evans claimed was given its nave vault in 1354, is viewed by John Harvey in rather a different light. Pointing out that the vaulting was not completed for many years 'probably because of the great pestilence', he shows that timber was still being sought in January 1356 and does not think work was completed until 1360; moreover, although the rebuilding of the choir had already been envisaged in 1348, it was not actually begun until 1361 and was finally completed only after 1405.[83] Exeter, contrary to what Evans and even Lawrence Stone believed, presents an even more revealing instance of the plague's disruption.[84] All the recent work on the west facade sculpture of the cathedral (and the related material on Christchurch's great reredos) has helped to emphasise the significance of the plague. It has been proposed that the Exeter facade screen was originally 'started as a single-tier construction' (Plate 9).[85] The sculptures of this first tier of niches seem to belong to three different campaigns: a first group completed by c.1350, a second group of 1374-75 and a final group of c.1380.[86] Paul Williamson has concluded: 'it is highly likely that the output of [the] early workshop at Exeter was cut short by the

[81] *Historia et Cartularium Monasterii Sancti Petri Gloucestriae*, I, p. 46. Gloucester is exceptional also in its revival of monastic numbers: see Harper-Bill, above, p. 98.

[82] J. Crook and Y. Kusaba, 'The Perpendicular Remodelling of the Nave: Problems and Interpretation', in *Winchester Cathedral: Nine Hundred Years*, ed J. Crook (Chichester, 1993), p. 221 and n. 23 (where the plague's visitation is, however, incorrectly dated).

[83] J. Harvey, 'Architectural History from 1291 to 1558', in *A History of York Minster*, ed. G. E. Aylmer and R. Cant (Oxford, 1977), 149-92 (pp. 158-69).

[84] Stone, *Sculpture*, p. 175 (where the same statuary is at once dated 'unlikely [to be] ... carved any later than 1360' and 'hardly carved much earlier than 1360').

[85] J. P. Allan and S. R. Blaylock, 'The West Front I: The Structural History of the West Front', in *Medieval Art and Architecture at Exeter Cathedral* (Leeds, 1991), pp. 94-115. Although this proposal seems unlikely, it seems evident that there *was* a significant constructional break between the completion of the lower tier of niches and the construction of the upper tier.

[86] P. Williamson, 'Sculptures of the West Front', in *Exeter Cathedral: a Celebration*, ed. M. Swanton (Exeter, 1991), p. 78 (the upper tier of images was not populated for another century). Compare Allan and Blaylock, 'West Front', pp. 102-03.

Black Death in 1348-49, leaving some of the niches at the north end of the screen empty, not to be filled for another twenty-five years'.[87] At Exeter, the plague seems to have had a devastating effect, severely retarding one of the most ambitious and lavish sculptural programmes of fourteenth-century England. Just as in Siena, where the days of the great commissions were now over,[88] at Ely, nothing comparable with the great programme of works from c.1320 to 1350 would ever be attempted again. At Exeter, the large-scale sculptural programme was halted for a quarter century and work on Winchester Cathedral would probably not resume until 1371 or even later.[89] At Ely and Exeter, then, the Black Death may really have been the unique cause of a decisive break in building and marked a watershed in these commissions; elsewhere, as at Winchester and York, the plague may have been an important contributory factor in delaying the architectural and sculptural enterprises of other churches.

It is always a difficult matter to differentiate a specific cause from other contributory factors. This is particularly the case when the evidence is so fragmentary and susceptible to widely differing interpretations. In many instances the roots of change may be seen before the plague's first outbreak. However, the temptation to discount the effects of the plague in the 1370s and '80s, when its effects cannot be so clearly distinguished from other longer-term developments, should be resisted. Economic historians increasingly emphasise that the most significant effects of the Black Death should be looked for not in the 1350s, but in the 1360s and later: the commutation of services for money rents and the renting out of demesne lands instead of keeping them in hand really accelerated in the generation after the plague. In considering this we do well to remember that the first outbreak was not the only one: there were severe visitations in 1361-62, 1368-69, 1375 and 1390.[90] We clearly are, therefore, entitled to wonder if

[87]   *Ibid*: 'it seems likely that the plague brought construction to a halt in 1347... In our view ... the image screen and its earliest sculptures, including that in Grandisson's chapel, should be dated c.1342-47.' The implication that the sculptors died or that patronage was curtailed needs further work. It should also be noted that the Italian influence on the early sculptures is not seen thereafter either, and the plague seems to have had the longer-term effect of reducing the relationship between English and Italian art which is so notable a feature of the first half of the century. There is an important study by X. Muratova, 'Exeter and Italy: Assimilation and Adaptation of a Style; The Question of Italian Trecento Sources in the Sculptured Front of Exeter Cathedral (Fourteenth Century)', in *World Art: Themes of Unity in Diversity*, ed. I. Lavin (University Park, Pennsylvania, 1989), pp. 117-24.

[88]   Van Os, 'Black Death', p. 243; Wilson, *Gothic Cathedral*, p. 264.

[89]   Crook and Kusaba, 'Perpendicular Remodelling', pp. 215-30. Harvey had already noted the significance of the 1371 document (*Perpendicular Style*, p. 84). Still, it is clear that the bulk of the nave's rebuilding postdates 1394.

[90]   See the useful discussion by Bean, 'The Black Death: the Crisis and its Social

there were not also longer-term effects in the arts. Of course, analysing these effects is a complex matter, particularly as the evidence is exceptionally scanty and there have been very few of the detailed regional studies which are a pre-requisite of a more satisfactory overall picture. It is true that the development of the Perpendicular style can be understood purely in aesthetic terms, as one strand of the reaction to Rayonnant design in England. But the fact that it was also so adaptable a style, one which did not require the hugely expensive and labour-intensive sculptural enrichment which is requisite in works of the Decorated style, must have made it attractive to patrons. Similarly, the relative eclipse of monastic architectural patronage in comparison with Edward III's new enterprises at Windsor and elsewhere, to which labourers were compulsorily drawn from a wide geographical area by impressment, must be a factor in the spread of the Perpendicular style employed in the royal works.

A number of indirect effects of the plague can be traced. In the first place, the shortage in numbers of the clergy led to the foundation of at least two Cambridge colleges, Corpus Christi (Plate 10) and Trinity Hall, to repair these losses; and the plague was a contributory factor in the endowment of Canterbury and New Colleges, Oxford.[91] The quality of the clergy immediately after the plague undoubtedly declined; the usual rules governing the ordination of priests were sometimes virtually abandoned. The decline in educational standards and alleged increase in clerical cupidity were not only the subject of frequent adverse comment but were widely recognised by the ecclesiastical hierarchy, whose patronage of the universities was intended to reverse it. The plague may have increased the desire for chantry masses and chantry chapels in the second half of the century and accelerated the trend towards more pietistic devotions; though images of 'The Three Living and the Three Dead' (Plate 12) do not gain increased currency, St Christopher as an individual image becomes very popular, for he was seen not only as a guardian against sudden death, but was attributed the power to overcome sickness and sores (Plate 11).[92]

It is, of course, sensible to be profoundly sceptical of attempts to trace the direct effects of endemic plague into the mid- or later fifteenth century:

---

and Economic Consequences', pp. 23-38: his conclusion that the 'Black Death ... was a powerful but blunt instrument which left uneven injuries' is analogous to the consequences to be drawn from a consideration of its cultural impact. Compare also Siena, where the large-scale rebuilding of the cathedral was terminated and never resumed, though other factors were also involved there: Bowsky, *Siena*, p. 285. See also Bolton, above, pp. 23-29, for demographic effects.

[91]   Ziegler, *Black Death*, pp. 254-55; see also Harper-Bill, above, pp. 106-07.

[92]   H. C. Whaite, *St. Christopher in English Mediæval Wallpainting* (London, 1929), pp. 8-10. See also n. 64, above. For the effect of chantries on jobs, see Courtenay, 'Black Death and English Higher Education', p. 713.

it is for this reason that I have largely confined my comments to an analysis of the second half of the fourteenth century. Nevertheless, no student of the arts in late medieval England can fail to note that there is, in the fifteenth century, a dramatically increasing penetration of foreign art and craftsmen into English markets. Often, though, this takes place mainly in the second half of the fifteenth century. Whereas major sculptural programmes of the early and mid-fifteenth century – the Canterbury and York pulpita kings, or the chantry chapels of Richard Beauchamp, earl of Warwick, or King Henry V at Westminster – seem to be executed by indigenous craftsmen, even if influenced by the art of the Burgundian Netherlands, in the second half of the century sculptures from the Great Screen in Winchester Cathedral reveal that foreign sculptors were at work in England.[93] The major wall paintings of the same period, those in Eton College Chapel, also appear to feature a Low Countries artist.[94] It is a paradox that although in the late fifteenth and early sixteenth centuries English sculptors seem, for the first time, to attain high status and incomes, this may have been the result of mass production rather than of superlative quality or a new respect for the sculptor's craft. By the time that Henry VII's Chapel received its sculptural programme, the contrast between the Low Countries sculptors and the native artists is very marked indeed.[95] In stained glass, too, by the early sixteenth century, the most progressive artists were foreigners and in spite of a bitter and protracted struggle fought by London glaziers, royal patronage increasingly turned to alien glaziers based at Southwark.[96] In manuscript illumination, also, the pace was set not by English painters – as it had been before 1350 – but by artists in and from the Low Countries.[97] Only architecture seems to have remained a native stronghold, with English master masons capable of producing works to equal anything abroad.[98] However, whether the loss of artistic leadership resulted directly or indirectly from the catastrophic population losses

---

[93]   Stone, *Sculpture*, pp. 195-210; P. G. Lindley, 'The Great Screen of Winchester Cathedral', *Burlington Magazine*, 131 (1989), 604-17; 135 (1993), 796-807.

[94]   *Ibid.*, 805-06.

[95]   H. J. Dow, *The Sculptural Decoration of the Henry VII Chapel, Westminster Abbey* (Edinburgh, 1992), publishes a text written in 1961, and takes no account of more recent research.

[96]   Marks, *Stained Glass*, pp. 206ff. In 1474 the London glaziers were already complaining about 28 alien craftsmen at work.

[97]   A. Arnould and J. M. Massing, *Splendours of Flanders* (Cambridge, 1993); see also *Renaissance Painting in Manuscripts*, ed. T. Kren (London, 1983), and J. Backhouse, 'Founders of the Royal Library: Edward IV and Henry VII as Collectors of Illuminated Manuscripts', in *England in the Fifteenth Century: Proceedings of the 1986 Harlaxton Symposium*, ed. D. Williams (Woodbridge, 1987), pp. 23-42.

[98]   Harvey, *Perpendicular Style*, chapters 7 and 8.

caused by the plague, or whether it was determined essentially by fashion or other factors altogether is not very clear as yet.

Major issues still demand attention. Was there perhaps a shift in the pattern of patronage towards parish churches, chantry chapels and domestic architecture, rather than an overall decline in the period 1350-1400? Or did the recovery come later? How significant are regional variations? Did production methods and training change? Did female employment proportionately increase?[99] Much more work is needed into the production and development of the arts in fifteenth-century England. It is certainly also rather misleading to treat the years 1350-1550 as a unitary entity.

As scholars of Italian art have already realised, even the most cataclysmic of disasters seldom stands in a simple relationship to artistic change. The central problem with Millard Meiss's work is its assumption of a direct connection between art and society, of the 'organic unity' of a period.[100] In the English context it is apparent that different arts were affected differently. In some, the effects of the plague were immediate and catastrophic, in others the results were more complex and diffused over time. But what is unequivocal is that the Black Death did have a dramatic effect on cultural production in England.

[99]   D. Knoop and G. P. Jones, *The Mediaeval Mason* (Manchester, 1967), pp. 71 and 73, for such issues.

[100] This is a central problem, too, in the work of Erwin Panofsky and others who draw on a Hegelian historical tradition. This intellectual indebtedness is as important, perhaps, as the experience of the Second World War in providing a parallel and model for Meiss's analysis of the effects of disaster on the survivors.

The Politics of Pestilence:
Government in England after the Black Death[1]

W. M. ORMROD

Introduction

Historians of the Black Death, traditionally preoccupied with the demographic, economic and social effects of plague, have rarely given more than passing consideration to the impact that pestilence may have had on the political and governmental framework of later medieval England. The neglect, though misguided, is not perhaps surprising. Much of the structure of late medieval administration was already in place by 1348 and many of the principal political issues that dominated parliament over the following hundred years – the technicalities of the common law, the state of overseas trade and, above all, the management of the French wars – had little or nothing, at least in a direct sense, to do with the Black Death. Furthermore, recent research has emphasised that medieval attitudes both to government and to natural disaster were not sufficiently developed to allow even the Italian cities, let alone the large monarchical states, to develop what might be called 'plague policies' before the end of the fifteenth century.[2] To draw such sharp distinctions between 'government' and 'society' is, however, to ignore the fact that the notions of authority that underpinned both central and local administration grew out of precisely the same theories of order, hierarchy and responsibility that conditioned the whole socio-economic fabric of medieval England.[3] Far from being peripheral to the subject, then, governance in many ways stands at the very heart of any discussion about the re-ordering of English society in the period after the Black Death. This contribution aims not so much to provide a comprehensive and definitive

---

[1] All unpublished documents cited here are in the Public Record Office. I am indebted to Dr A. J. Verduyn for comments on an earlier draft of this essay. R. C. Palmer, *English Law in the Age of the Black Death, 1348-1381. A Transformation of Governance and Law* (Chapel Hill, NC, 1993), appeared only after this was completed, and I have thought it better to reserve my response to this important study for another occasion.

[2] P. Slack, 'Introduction', in *Epidemics and Ideas. Essays on the Historical Perception of Pestilence*, ed. T. Ranger and P. Slack (Cambridge, 1992), 1-20, pp. 15-17 and the sources cited there.

[3] The characteristically narrow definition given to the word 'politics' in English historiography has recently, for example, led F. R. H. Du Boulay to argue that since William Langland had so little to say about the court he cannot legitimately be labelled a 'political poet': *The England of Piers Plowman: William Langland and his Vision of the Fourteenth Century* (Woodbridge, 1991), pp. 7-8.

vindication of that assertion as to explore some of the areas in which further research on this subject might be most beneficial.

One of the principal reasons why historians have chosen not to pursue the interplay between plague and government lies in the comparative rarity of specific and detailed references to the Black Death in the English state archive. Although Cardinal Gasquet long ago demonstrated the importance of various series of records compiled by the royal chancery and exchequer in supplying additional data on the economic impact of the first plague, the apparent decline in such information after the 1350s, coupled with a marked reluctance on the part of administrative historians to undertake the sheer labour of searching through the mass of mostly unpublished primary evidence, has produced an assumption either that the impact of plague itself has been exaggerated or that government was not sufficiently deeply rooted in society to have to concern itself with the profound economic and social changes brought about by the plague.[4] It must be admitted, of course, that the state, represented in the more limited sense by the crown and a centralised bureaucracy, played a much smaller part in the life of the country than was to be the case in the sixteenth, let alone the twentieth, century: despite the notable experiment in the aftermath of the plague with what would now be called a wages policy, there were whole spheres of economic management over which the crown had no authority and which were decided and administered at the level of the individual estate or business. On the other hand, the shortage of colourful accounts of plague devastation in the public records should certainly not be taken to indicate the immunity of central and local government to the effects of the Black Death. The royal clerks who drew up the records of the chancery and exchequer, the common law courts and parliament, were trained not to chronicle catastrophes but to preserve that information most crucial to the procedures of government. The constant repetition of the laconic phrase 'on account of the pestilence' may therefore represent not so much the indifference of the government as a succinct rendering of the much greater dramatic detail often reaching the central administration in the form of petitions.[5] In assessing the wider impact of the Black Death on English government it is therefore necessary to look beyond these standardised references and consider some of the broader issues that helped determine the course of later medieval politics and which might be said to have their

[4]   F. A. Gasquet, *The Great Pestilence (A.D. 1348-9)* (London, 1893); W. M. Ormrod, 'The English Government and the Black Death of 1348-49', in *England in the Fourteenth Century: Proceedings of the 1985 Harlaxton Symposium*, ed. W. M. Ormrod (Woodbridge, 1986), p. 175.

[5]   See, among much else, the commissions set up to examine such pleas: *Calendar of Inquisitions Miscellaneous*, III, nos 258, 605; IV, no. 125; *Ancient Petitions Relating to Northumberland*, ed. C. M. Fraser, Surtees Society, 176 (Durham and London, 1961), pp. 34-35.

origins in, or found added impetus from, the great socio-economic changes precipitated by the plague.

Plague and the Governing Elite
It is natural to begin with the question of how the successive outbreaks of plague affected the mechanics and personnel of royal government at the central and local level. The Black Death was no more a respecter of public office than it was of ecclesiastical rank or artistic expertise, and the mortality rate among certain sections of the administrative hierarchy during periods of epidemic disease could, on occasions, reach significant proportions. Appendix 1 provides details of some members of the central administration who are known to have died, or at least disappeared from the records, during the first four national outbreaks of plague in 1348-49, 1361-62, 1368-69 and 1375.[6] The list is restricted to the upper levels of the administration: unfortunately, it is largely impossible to establish the turnover among the mass of lesser functionaries employed in all these departments. This is regrettable, since the civil service tended to recruit from within, and a quantitative analysis of its lower ranks might well have provided some clue to any possible changes in the quality and experience of men promoted into the upper echelons of the bureaucracy during the second half of the fourteenth century. What little evidence does exist therefore allows only for rather subjective comment. I have suggested elsewhere that the decline in the standards and efficiency of central government between the 1350s and the 1380s owed most to a decline in the real or perceived quality of those holding the offices at the top of the hierarchy as chancellor, treasurer, keeper of the privy seal and chief justices of king's bench and common pleas.[7] On the other hand, it is at least worth exploring in a little more detail the possibility that the general disruption

---

[6]   The plague of 1371 leaves no mark in administrative records of the crown and is omitted here. It must be stressed that the lists provided in Appendices 1 and 2 are imperfect. Not the least of the problems in studying the later plagues is the lack of a proper chronology of epidemics. The dates provided by J. M. W. Bean, 'Plague, Population and Economic Decline in England in the Later Middle Ages', *Economic History Review*, 2nd series, 15 (1962-63), 423-37, pp. 427-31, are hardly adequate for such purposes. In tracing the deaths of officials, it should also be remembered that contemporary administrators were not always accurately informed. In 1351, for example, proceedings to collect the debts of Guy St Clair, 'deceased' sheriff of Cambridgeshire and Huntingdonshire, were already in hand when it was discovered that St Clair was in fact alive: E368/123, m. 14d.

[7]   W. M. Ormrod, *The Reign of Edward III: Crown and Political Society in England, 1327-1377* (London, 1990), pp. 70-94; W. M. Ormrod, 'The Peasants' Revolt and the Government of England', *Journal of British Studies*, 29 (1991), 1-30, pp. 28-29.

created by plague did indeed have an impact on the lower levels of the bureaucracy and affected the way in which the central offices functioned.

What, then, of the record of the central administration in maintaining the processes of government during the actual outbreaks of plague that struck England periodically after 1348? In 1349 both the central courts of king's bench and common pleas closed down for the Trinity term, and while the chancery and the exchequer persevered, their business was much curtailed.[8] In 1361 king's bench, common pleas, and the upper exchequer were all shut down from mid-May until they reconvened at Michaelmas, and in 1368 all three of these departments were again closed for the Trinity term.[9] These adjournments represented not only the natural concern of state servants for their own safety within the capital but also the very substantial drop in the amount of business they had to do during such emergencies. Indeed, even the exchequer of receipt, which was kept open during these periods, sometimes found its dealings drastically reduced: in 1368 it did only three days' work between the start of the Trinity term and the opening of the new financial year in late September.[10] That these formal and informal closures created disruption for those of the king's subjects who had business with the central administration seems obvious enough. That they created any real challenge to the efficiency of the offices of state is, however, much more questionable. In 1348-50 there were some uncharacteristic muddles in the composition and custody of the records of king's bench and common pleas, while in 1364-65 it was claimed that certain illicit payments had been made out of the royal treasury during the closure of the exchequer of account in 1361.[11] In general, however, there is remarkably little to suggest that adjournments as a result of plague created a serious challenge to regular administrative procedures. While it is

---

[8] Ormrod, 'English Government and Black Death', pp. 176-77. The profits of the hanaper of chancery fell from £761 in 1347-48 to £422 in 1351-52: E101/212/4, 7. The farmer of the deputed great seals of the courts of king's bench and common pleas also had to be excused his payment to the exchequer in 1350 because of loss of business during the plague: E159/126, m. 87.

[9] 1361: *Calendar of Close Rolls, 1360-64*, pp. 181-2, 197-8; E159/137, Recorda, Pasch, m. 14; E368/133, Recorda, Pasch, mm. 14d-15; *Select Cases in the Court of King's Bench*, ed. G. O. Sayles, 7 vols, Selden Society, 55, 57, 58, 74, 76, 82, 88 (London, 1936-71), VI, p. xlviii. 1368: *Calendar of Close Rolls, 1364-8*, p. 426; *Select Cases in King's Bench*, VI, p. xlix. See also *List of Plea Rolls of Various Courts*, Public Record Office Lists and Indexes, 4 (repr. New York, 1963), pp. 7, 36.

[10] E401/493; E403/434.

[11] B. H. Putnam, *The Place in Legal History of Sir William Shareshull* (Cambridge, 1950), p. 83; SC8/179/8936 (certain records of common pleas not in the custody of the chirographer 'since the pestilence'); *Calendar of Close Rolls, 1364-68*, p. 116.

possible that the closure of the exchequer as well as the courts during the epidemics of the 1360s may have been symptomatic of a general shift away from the particularly aggressive and determined fiscal policies pursued by Edward III's administration in the 1350s, it needs to be stressed that there were in fact no further formal adjournments of the exchequer, or of king's bench and common pleas, on account of plague until the time of Edward IV.[12] Consequently, any crisis of control resulting from the closure of central government has to be measured very much in the short term and in the context of individual cases.

This is not to say, however, that the Black Death did not influence more general changes that came about in the actual composition of the royal bureaucracy. In particular, it is possible that plague speeded up the process whereby an administrative hierarchy previously dominated by churchmen became, by the fifteenth century, largely the preserve of the laity. The laicisation of the English civil service had its origins long before the Black Death and was, if anything, temporarily reversed during the regime of Archbishop Thoresby and Treasurer Edington in the 1350s.[13] By the end of the fourteenth century, however, the breakdown of the clerical monopoly was becoming evident even in the royal chancery. That high mortality during the pestilences of the previous decades had contributed to this broadening of the recruitment pool is at least suggested by the fact that the chancery, which had previously had a strictly clerical and celibate personnel, lost three of its twelve senior clerks not only in 1348-49 but again in 1361-62 and 1375. It may even be hypothesised that the particularly hostile complaints about the cupidity of chancery officials in the later fourteenth century owed something to a change in the social profile and a breakdown of the earlier collegiate ethos within this group.[14] To move this argument further, and suggest that the Black Death had a direct bearing on the quality of the central administration in the late middle ages, is, however, to push things rather too far: even the supposed decline of a common identity and joint responsibility consequent upon the intrusion of larger numbers of laymen into royal government in the

[12]   For fiscal policy in the middle decades of the century see W. M. Ormrod, 'The Protecolla Rolls and English Government Finance, 1353-1364', *English Historical Review*, 102 (1989), 622-32. Later adjournments: *Calendar of Close Rolls, 1461-68*, pp. 224-25, 424; *List of Plea Rolls*, p. 39; M. Blatcher, *The Court of King's Bench 1450-1550: a Study in Self-help* (London, 1978), pp. 23-24, 169 n. 2.

[13]   J. R. Strayer, *Medieval Statecraft and the Perspectives of History* (Princeton, NJ, 1971), pp. 251-65; W. M. Ormrod, 'Edward III's Government of England, c.1346-1356', University of Oxford D.Phil. thesis (1984), pp. 232-33.

[14]   B. Wilkinson, *The Chancery under Edward III* (Manchester, 1929), pp. 59-64; T. F. Tout, *Collected Papers*, 3 vols (Manchester, 1932-4), II, pp. 143-71, esp. pp. 168-69.

fifteenth century has yet to be shown to have had any really adverse effect on the actual procedures and efficiency of the state.[15]

Similar caution must be expressed about the long-term impact of the plague on office-holding at the local level. The English state depended not on professional clerks but on local landowners to provide the part-time and mainly unpaid staff required for the administration of the counties. The evidence relating to the mortality of royal agents in the shires is again imperfect, but provides some particularly interesting perspectives on the perils of public office in the later fourteenth century. Appendix 2 supplies details of those sheriffs and escheators who died in office during the national epidemics of plague between 1348 and 1375. Given the very small sample from which these data are drawn, no specifically demographic significance can of course be read into the material represented here. It is worth pointing out, however, that the particularly high level of mortality among sheriffs in the plague of 1361-62 was reflected in other local government posts as well: no fewer than 21 of the men appointed as commissioners of the peace early in 1361 were reported dead and replaced during the second pestilence, whereas just one commissioner had to be replaced as a result of infirmity in 1369 and only a single justice died in office in 1375.[16] If this discovery is set alongside the conspicuously high death rates noted by K. B. McFarlane for the peerage and by J. C. Russell for the lay tenants in chief of the crown in the plague of 1361-62, it at least calls into question some of the assumptions (derived largely from the possibly atypical mortality of beneficed clergy in the diocese of York), that the second pestilence was far less devastating than that of 1348-49.[17]

[15] For laicisation see R. L. Storey, 'Gentleman-bureaucrats', in *Profession, Vocation, and Culture in Later Medieval England*, ed. C. H. Clough (Liverpool, 1982), pp. 90-129. For the efficiency of government in the 15th century see G. L. Harriss, 'Political Society and the Growth of Government in Late Medieval England', *Past and Present*, 138 (1993), 28-57; pp. 34-39.

[16] 1361-62: *Calendar of Patent Rolls, 1361-64*, pp. 63-66, 66-67, 150, 205, 208, 209, 210, 213 (and see also the report that a Norfolk commissioner was too ill to act: *ibid.*, p. 66). 1369: *Calendar of Patent Rolls, 1367-70*, p. 264. 1375: *Calendar of Patent Rolls, 1374-77*, p. 228. A. J. Verduyn, 'The Attitude of the Parliamentary Commons to Law and Order under Edward III', University of Oxford D.Phil. thesis (1991), pp. 109-10, has demonstrated that approximately a third of the keepers of the peace may have died in the plague of 1348-49.

[17] K. B. McFarlane, *The Nobility of Later Medieval England* (Oxford, 1973), pp. 168-71; J. C. Russell, *British Medieval Population* (Albuquerque, 1948), pp. 215-18; A. Hamilton Thompson, 'The Pestilences of the Fourteenth Century in the Diocese of York', *Archaeological Journal*, 71 (1914), 97-154, p. 115. If the use of replacement rates for beneficed clergy still has any validity as a demographic indicator, then it is worth noting that high replacement rates have been identified (though not as yet properly calculated) for other dioceses in 1361-62: J. F. D. Shrewsbury, *A History of Bubonic Plague in the British Isles*

More importantly for present purposes, however, this material demands some comment on the number of men left to take up county offices at a time when, principally as a result of the emergence of the justices of the peace as a permanent element within the judicial structure, the range of responsibilities in the shire administration was expanding considerably. There are some indications of a temporary crisis resulting from the deaths of serving sheriffs during the plagues of the 1360s, as the sons or deputies of deceased officials were appointed as lieutenants of the counties until more suitable candidates could be found.[18] The summoning of three members of the local political community to Westminster in 1369 to determine which of them should be appointed sheriff of Essex and Hertfordshire may also signify a temporary breakdown in the channels of communication that normally provided the council with its choice of candidates for local office.[19] It is much more probable, however, that any shortage of recruits thus implied was more an indirect result of the plague, as the financial liabilities imposed on the sheriff made his an increasingly onerous and less attractive post than that, for example, of commissioner of the peace, and as the range and status of families from which the crown selected its principal county officials became significantly smaller.

This latter point is of particular importance in providing a key to longer-term changes in English governance after 1350. What little work has been attempted on the subject suggests that the development of a more refined hierarchy of offices, coupled with the growing insistence of the county communities on the appointment of local men, meant the emergence of a more restricted and static political elite within each shire between 1300 and 1400.[20] This did not necessarily mean an absolute

---

(Cambridge, 1970), p. 129; C. Dyer, *Lords and Peasants in a Changing Society: The Estates of the Bishopric of Worcester, 680-1540* (Cambridge, 1980), p. 225; *The Register of William Edington, Bishop of Winchester, 1346-1366*, ed. S. F. Hockey, 2 vols, Hampshire Record Series, 7, 8 (Winchester, 1986-87), *passim*; Harper-Bill, above, p. 86.

[18] In 1361 Edmund Fourneux was appointed to replace his father as sheriff of Cambridgeshire and Huntingdonshire, though when the account fell due the sheriffdom had to be handed over to Thomas Cheyne, who had apparently been acting for the Fourneux family throughout the year: *List of Sheriffs for England and Wales*, Public Record Office Lists and Indexes, 9 (repr. New York, 1963), p. 12; E368/134, Recorda, Mich., m. 1d; Recepta, Mich., m. 5. In 1369 Henry Puys was promoted from under-sheriff in Staffordshire explicitly until another sheriff was found: *Calendar of Fine Rolls*, VIII, p. 19. Note also the very high turnover of sheriffs of Essex and Hertfordshire in 1368-70: *List of Sheriffs*, p. 44.

[19] Ormrod, *Reign of Edward III*, p. 155.

[20] N. Saul, *Knights and Esquires: The Gloucestershire Gentry in the Fourteenth Century* (Oxford, 1981), pp. 160-64; see also the comments of K. S. Naughton, *The Gentry of Bedfordshire in the Thirteenth and Fourteenth Centuries*, University of

decline in numbers; even if it did, it must be remembered that the extinction rate among gentry families was always high and may have owed as much in this period to the perils of war as to the ravages of plague.[21] On the other hand, the Black Death almost certainly had an indirect impact on the number of men considered to be qualified for public office by speeding up the process of social stratification and drawing a sharper distinction between what historians now call the 'county gentry' (men of the rank of knight and esquire) and the larger, more amorphous group of 'parish gentry'.[22] The property qualifications that were fixed for most of the senior posts in the county administration during the later fourteenth and fifteenth centuries were themselves a demonstration of this deliberate attempt to create a pyramidal structure within the elite.[23] Although much was said in defence of this oligarchy – principally, that men of substance were less likely to be tempted by the illicit profits to be made from extortion and bribery – it is also noticeable that the period after 1350 witnessed no respite in the stream of complaints against the oppressions committed by the crown's local agents, oppressions which were themselves increasingly perceived as a product of the sinister links between royal office-holders and magnate affinities.[24] It is not surprising, then, that contemporaries sometimes expressed their doubts about the quality of men selected for office in terms of the apparently diminishing pool from which they were drawn. In 1421 the commons in parliament bemoaned the loss of so many men of substance and integrity through the twin perils of pestilence and war and requested that the rule concerning the annual replacement of sheriffs, observed since the 1370s, might now be relaxed in order to

---

Leicester Department of English Local History Occasional Papers, 2 (1976), esp. pp. 50, 53. I have benefited from G. Dodd, 'A Comparative Study: The Political Community of Buckinghamshire 1307-1327 and 1509-1529', University of York B.A. dissertation (1993).

[21] S. J. Payling, 'Social Mobility, Demographic Change, and Landed Society in Late Medieval England', *Economic History Review*, 2nd series, 45 (1992), 51-73, argues that the redistribution of land after the Black Death meant the recruitment of considerable numbers of 'new' gentry.

[22] C. Given-Wilson, *The English Nobility in the Late Middle Ages: The Fourteenth-Century Political Community* (London, 1987), pp. 69-73 and the works cited there.

[23] Saul, *Knights and Esquires*, pp. 106-67; S. M. Wright, *The Derbyshire Gentry in the Fifteenth Century*, Derbyshire Record Society, 8 (Chesterfield, 1983), pp. 1-6, 93-118; S. J. Payling, *Political Society in Lancastrian England: The Greater Gentry of Nottinghamshire* (Oxford, 1991), pp. 109-10; E. Acheson, *A Gentry Community: Leicestershire in the Fifteenth Century* (Cambridge, 1992), pp. 107-34; C. Carpenter, *Locality and Polity: A Study of Warwickshire Landed Society, 1401-1499* (Cambridge, 1992), pp. 263-77.

[24] E. Powell, *Kingship, Law, and Society: Criminal Justice in the Reign of Henry V* (Oxford, 1989), pp. 107-14 and the works cited there.

preserve this office for the most senior and trustworthy families in each county community.[25] Ironically, of course, the willingness of Henry V's government to concur with this request simply made it easier for small groups of leading landholders to establish effective monopolies over the premier offices in their counties. Consequently, the Black Death may be seen to have been an important turning-point in the transformation of the political communities at the shire level from relatively 'open' to increasingly 'closed' elites; and although the quality of local administration and justice did not necessarily deteriorate in absolute terms, the higher standards demanded and increasingly articulate criticism offered by the wider political community were at least occasionally expressed in terms of the adverse demographic, economic and social consequences of plague.

Issues in Government: Justice

If those who remained politically empowered were so often dissatisfied with the state of government in the years after the Black Death, how much greater was the sense of alienation among the great mass of the population that had no direct control over or access to the machinery of the state. Although the insurrections that took place all across Europe in the later fourteenth century have always tended to be interpreted primarily within a socio-economic context, there is much to be said for the idea that the English Peasants' Revolt of 1381 emerged from the growing political disillusionment of those classes that found their status and interests increasingly threatened by changes within the structure of government. In many ways, indeed, the direct challenge to public as well as to seigneurial authority offered by the rebels of 1381 was a greater threat to political stability, in both the short and the long term, than any of the violent natural disasters that preceded it. This is not the place in which to recount the events of and the great variety of issues that contributed to the English Rising. Instead, the following two sections of this essay will attempt to examine what were the two principal issues of public debate in England after 1348 and, arguably, the two principal driving forces behind the revolt of 1381: namely, the structure of royal justice and the burden of royal taxation.

The advent of the Black Death coincided with a period of intense debate over and profound change in the English legal system and helped to precipitate a major transformation both in the scope and in the administration of royal justice.[26] The most important, though not the only,

[25] *Rotuli Parliamentorum*, 6 vols (London, 1783), IV, p. 148. It is possible that this request was precipitated by the recent deaths in office of Robert Corbet and Humphrey Halghton, sheriffs of Shropshire and Staffordshire respectively: *List of Sheriffs*, pp. 118, 127.

[26] The following section depends heavily on B. H. Putnam, 'The Transformation of the Keepers of the Peace into the Justices of the Peace,

contribution to this transformation came in those celebrated pieces of fourteenth-century legislation, the Ordinance and Statute of Labourers (1349 and 1351 respectively). So much has been written about these laws that it is sometimes forgotten what a radical change they represented in the range of human activities that were, or were not, subject to state control. Although the English government had made various attempts to control prices before 1348, this was the first time that the contracts, wages and other terms of employment offered to agricultural, building and manufacturing labourers became subject to detailed and systematic legislation by the crown.[27] The administration of Edward III was not alone in its reaction to the plight of employers during the emergency of the first plague: ordinances of a similar nature and intent were issued in a number of European states during and immediately after the great European pandemic of 1347-50.[28] What really distinguished the Ordinance and Statute of Labourers from so much continental – and indeed from so much other English – legislation of the later middle ages was the particular attention given to its enforcement. For the first decade after the Black Death, the labour laws were administered by special standing commissions in the shires served by members of the local gentry. Not only were these men naturally motivated to uphold the interests of employers, but they were also given a share of the profits of their sessions and, for a time, allowed to use the remaining proceeds for the relief of the tax burden in their shires. These special commissions were withdrawn in 1359, partly perhaps because they had always been intended as an extraordinary response to a temporary crisis but principally because of another shift in royal priorities away from law keeping and towards the prosecution of a major military campaign in France. After the conclusion of the treaty of Brétigny in 1360, however, political pressure applied in parliament necessitated the reinstatement of the legislation and ensured that its enforcement was placed in the hands of the justices of the peace, permanent commissioners again drawn, in the main, from the local gentry and indeed including some of those who had earlier acted as justices of labourers. From this point onwards, the need for the permanent implementation of the labour legislation became the very watchword of the local political community and therefore, by extension, of the state.

1327-1380', *Transactions of the Royal Historical Society*, 4th series, 12 (1929), 19-48; A. Harding, 'The Revolt Against the Justices', in *The English Rising of 1381*, ed. R. H. Hilton and T. H. Aston (Cambridge, 1987), 165-93; Verduyn, 'Attitude of the Commons'.

[27] For royal edicts on prices and other economic legislation before the Black Death see R. H. Britnell, *The Commercialisation of English Society 1000-1500* (Cambridge, 1993), pp. 90-97.

[28] R. S. Gottfried, *The Black Death* (London, 1983), p. 95; J. N. Hillgarth, *The Spanish Kingdoms 1250-1516*, 2 vols (Oxford, 1976-78), II, pp. 4-5.

The evolution of what were originally perceived as emergency measures into a permanent element within the judicial system was itself to some degree a product of the economic challenges brought on by the return of the plague. If it is true that the statute of 1361 reciting the powers of the justices of the peace was issued before the second pestilence had properly established itself, it is also true that the full range of the labour laws was not formally included in the peace commissions until the full effects of that epidemic had been felt, in November 1362.[29] It is also significant that after withdrawing from the peace commissions the right to judge felonies and cases against the labour laws in 1364, the crown chose to hand back such powers in May 1368 at exactly the time that the latest outbreak of plague reached the capital.[30] Furthermore, the 1360s also witnessed a notable extension in the other economic concerns over which the justices of the peace had competence. Forestalling and regrating (interfering with supply to, and therefore prices in, the open market) as well as the use of irregular weights and measures, both of which had long been matters of deep concern to the king's subjects and frequent causes of complaint in fourteenth-century parliaments, now at last became subject to inquiry and prosecution by the local commissions of the peace.[31] Consequently, the labour laws became only one of a whole range of measures by which the landed classes, who dominated the bench, were able to shore up their economic interests and enhance their political authority in the regions where they held sway.

It has often been remarked that the labour laws were doomed to fail because they did not take account of the realities of the post-plague

[29] The statute of 1361 may have been provoked as much by concern over the control of disbanded soldiers as over the continuing effects of plague: *Statutes of the Realm*, 11 vols (London, 1810-28), I, pp. 364-65; Verduyn, 'Attitude of the Commons', pp. 138-41. The king's concern to secure adequate labour for the royal works may also be a factor: *Calendar of Close Rolls, 1360-64*, pp. 262-63. Although Putnam saw the absence of the labour legislation from the commissions of March 1361 as a slip on the part of the government which the justices themselves chose to ignore (*Proceedings before the Justices of the Peace in the Fourteenth and Fifteenth Centuries*, ed. B. H. Putnam, Ames Foundation (London, 1938), p. cxxii), Verduyn believes that in 1361 the crown was not yet willing to countenance this extension of authority and comments that 'it is certainly productive to examine the many changes that took place [in 1362] in the light of the second pestilence' (personal communication).

[30] The plague was said to be 'anew increasing' in London in May 1368: *Calendar of Close Rolls, 1364-68*, p. 426.

[31] For earlier enforcement of royal legislation on these matters see R. H. Britnell, 'Forstall, Forestalling and the Statute of Forestallers', *English Historical Review*, 102 (1987), 90-102; W. M. Ormrod, 'Agenda for Legislation, 1322-c.1340', *English Historical Review*, 105 (1990), 1-30, pp. 23-24; Ormrod, 'Edward III's Government', pp. 204-11.

economy. This, however, is to measure the legislation solely in statistical terms, setting the numbers of prosecutions brought for excess wages in the surviving peace rolls against the apparently inexorable escalation of wage rates recorded in so many series of manorial records from the late fourteenth and fifteenth centuries.[32] In fact, the real significance of the labour laws lies not so much in their actual application as in the threat they posed to the interests and rights of all those – about a third of the total population – that made their livelihood by selling their services on the open market. Remarkable as the policy on wages outlined in the original Ordinance of 1349 undoubtedly was, the principal force of the legislation lay in the restrictions it placed on the freedom both of that market and of the labourers who operated within it. The requirement to enter formal, binding contracts of service and not to leave the place of residence if work was available there, together with the increasingly severe punishments threatened against offenders (after 1361, outlawed fugitive labourers who had been apprehended by the sheriffs were liable to be branded on the forehead with the letter F, for falsity), all signified a major challenge to the rights of free peasants. Since those villeins who received their freedom in the period after the plague were not infrequently required to enter into labour contracts as a condition of their manumission, it is easy to see why the series of controls instituted in 1349 may have been perceived as a 'second serfdom': indeed, one of the most obvious but neglected ways of resolving the apparent anomaly between the free status of the rebels who marched on London in 1381 and the particular persistence of their demand for the abolition of villeinage lies in the increasing concern felt by many peasants about the real or potential tyranny of contracts.[33]

To that specific tyranny was added a more general distrust and dislike of the way in which the whole structure of the law seemed to be moving in favour of the social and political elite. Although the justices of the peace were supervised in a general sense by judges from the central courts, who had to be in attendance when felonies (serious crimes punishable by death) were being considered, the great bulk of the work undertaken in the new quarter sessions was dealt with by members of the local gentry who rapidly became the most numerous element in and most vociferous supporters of the peace commissions. From the perspective of the peasantry, the retreat of the royal judges who had previously controlled much of the law keeping in the shires was probably of no great significance: the high level of corruption that operated at all levels within the legal system meant that

[32] For a systematic study see S. A. C. Penn and C. Dyer, 'Wages and Earnings in Late Medieval England: Evidence from the Enforcement of the Labour Laws', *Economic History Review*, 2nd series, 43 (1990), 356-76.

[33] C. Dyer, 'The Social and Economic Background to the Rural Revolt of 1381', in *The English Rising of 1381*, ed. Hilton and Aston, pp. 25-26.

justice had always been weighted against the interests of the poor.[34] Much more important, and ominous, was the gradual encroachment of the commissions of the peace into the system of communal self-policing operated by rural society under the terms of the Statute of Winchester of 1285. It seems no accident that a high proportion of those who took part in the uprising of 1381 in south-east England had direct experience in local administration at the level of the manor, village or hundred; these men, in other words, represented precisely that upper echelon of peasant society that had traditionally provided the leaders of rural communities and participated actively in the public life of the locality. It is very interesting to notice that in Essex, one of the centres of revolt in 1381, the constables responsible for administering the Ordinance and Statute of Labourers within village communities had for some years been ambivalent about and sometimes actively hostile to the particularly ruthless enforcement of the labour legislation being pursued by the justices of the peace in that county.[35] A small number of the rebels in 1381 were of sufficient financial standing to be counted as members of the parish gentry, a class which, as has already been suggested, was also becoming somewhat politically marginalised in the more self-conscious and stratified political society of the later fourteenth century.[36] The fact that the leaders of the Peasants' Revolt were at once the economic and social inferiors of the county gentry and also the conscious inheritors of a tradition of active involvement in the administration of the locality (if not of the shire and the realm) therefore serves to emphasise both the broad scope of governance in the fourteenth century and the high degree of tension that may have arisen over the exercise of public authority in the period of turmoil following the Black Death.

Issues in Government: Taxation

Alongside these important issues of justice were those of finance. There can be few people in late twentieth-century Britain who are unaware that it was a poll tax that sparked off the Peasants' Revolt of 1381; indeed, without dwelling on what is actually an unhelpful analogy, it is at least worth remarking that the enormous problems encountered by anti-poll tax activists in mobilising opposition to the government in the 1980s may well have sharpened the historian's appreciation of the organisational achievements of the rebels of 1381.[37] To understand the exceptional

---

[34]   J. R. Maddicott, *Law and Lordship: Royal Justices as Retainers in Thirteenth- and Fourteenth-Century England*, Past and Present Supplement, 1 (Oxford, 1978).

[35]   Dyer, 'Social and Economic Background', p. 17; L. R. Poos, *A Rural Society after the Black Death: Essex 1350-1525* (Cambridge, 1991), pp. 241-42.

[36]   R. Hilton, *Bond Men Made Free: Medieval Peasant Movements and the English Rising of 1381* (London, 1973), pp. 180-81.

[37]   See in particular N. Brooks, 'The Organization and Achievements of the

animosity provoked by the collection of the 1380 poll tax, however, it is necessary to forget modern parallels and to concentrate instead on the system of royal taxation that operated in England during the half century before the Great Revolt.

Direct taxation was an extraordinary phenomenon in medieval England, linked to the making of war and to other very special financial needs of the crown.[38] The almost permanent state of hostility with France between 1337 and 1360, and again from 1369 to 1389, meant that taxation became more frequent than ever before. This is not to say, however, that either the political community that granted taxes or the urban and rural communities that paid them became automatically conditioned to such financial exactions. In 1376, in the midst of a major political crisis, parliament took up an old principle last used in the 1320s and declined a royal request for direct taxation on the grounds of impoverishment, citing the hardships that had resulted not only from human plagues but also from epidemic diseases among animals and the repeated failures of the harvest — a three-fold litany that would be much employed in the language of parliamentary politics over the following years.[39] Given that the harvest of 1376 proved to be one of the best of the century and brought about a significant reduction in grain prices, the continued inclusion of the agricultural depression among the hardships cited by parliament in the 1380s may seem somewhat disingenuous, or else be taken to reflect the selfish concerns of landholders threatened by rapidly diminishing profits.[40]

Peasants of Kent and Essex in 1381', in *Studies in Medieval History Presented to R. H. C. Davis*, ed. H. Mayr-Harting and R. I. Moore (London, 1985), pp. 247-70. On the other hand, recent research does not all point in this direction: see in particular A. J. Prescott, 'Judicial Records of the Rising of 1381', University of London Ph.D. thesis (1984); A. J. Prescott, 'London in the Peasants' Revolt: A Portrait Gallery', *London Journal*, 7 (1981), 125-43.

[38] The standard works on direct taxation of the laity are: S. K. Mitchell, *Taxation in Medieval England* (New Haven, 1951); J. F. Willard, *Parliamentary Taxes on Personal Property, 1290 to 1334* (Cambridge, Massachusetts, 1934); M. W. Beresford, *The Lay Subsidies and Poll Taxes* (Canterbury, 1963). I have benefited much from C. C. Fenwick, 'The English Poll Taxes of 1377, 1379, and 1381: A Critical Examination of the Returns', University of London Ph.D. thesis (1983).

[39] *Rotuli Parliamentorum*, II, pp. 322, 365; III, pp. 139, 147. The precedents of the 1320s were discovered by M. C. Buck, 'The Reform of the Exchequer, 1316-1326', *English Historical Review*, 98 (1983), 241-60, pp. 252-54 (though the justification for refusal in 1325 is not clear). Ormrod, *Reign of Edward III*, p. 165, argues that the refusal of 1376 was made easier by the fact that the request for taxation was put forward during a period of truce.

[40] D. L. Farmer, 'Prices and Wages, 1350-1500', in *The Agrarian History of England and Wales*, III: *1348-1500*, ed. E. Miller (Cambridge, 1991), pp. 439, 503. It is significant that when the commons pleaded poverty in 1378, they

Underpinning and validating the commons' refusal of taxation in 1376, and again on a number of occasions in the 1380s, however, was a more widespread concern about the nature and distribution of the standard system of direct taxation that had operated over the previous half-century.

Direct taxes in later medieval England were normally assessed on the basis of movable property – chiefly livestock and grain in the countryside and merchandise and household goods in the towns (it was only the beneficed clergy who regularly paid income taxes). It is important to realise that under this system the household, rather than the individual, provided the basic taxable unit. Until the early 1330s, each grant of taxation was followed by a new valuation of the tax base. In 1334, however, the crown abandoned this time-consuming practice and negotiated a series of block quotas with town and village communities, leaving the allocations for separate households to local initiative. In theory, and often in practice, contributions were still made on the basis of movable property, the 'fifteenths and tenths' representing the proportions of the value of such property payable in rural communities on the one hand and in urban areas and the ancient demesne of the crown on the other.[41] It is indeed one of the most remarkable achievements of the English state that the 1334 quotas were used and collected, with very few remissions and alterations, for every lay subsidy between 1334 and 1360. The established nature of the tax probably did much to guarantee its viability and ensure its collection even during the unprecedented emergency of 1348-49: there is a very striking contrast in this respect with the kingdom of France, where a new and otherwise promising system of tax assessment and collection foundered and collapsed in the wake of the Black Death.[42]

On the other hand, it needs to be stressed that this achievement was made possible only because direct taxation in England was very far from being a universal obligation. Prior to 1334 there had been a minimum valuation below which all householders were technically exempt; in some parts of the country over half the population had thereby escaped the obligation to pay royal subsidies.[43] After 1334 this exemption had been

---

added to their complaints of dwindling yields the fact that what produce remained was worth little: *Rotuli Parliamentorum*, III, p. 38.

[41] The idea that liability to 15ths and 10ths became attached to the holding of certain plots of land has been challenged by R. S. Schofield, 'Parliamentary Lay Taxation 1485-1547', University of Cambridge Ph.D. thesis (1963), pp. 85-95.

[42] Ormrod, 'English Government and Black Death', pp. 182-5; J. B. Henneman, 'The Black Death and Royal Taxation in France, 1347-1351', *Speculum*, 43 (1968), 309-49.

[43] W. M. Ormrod, 'The Crown and the English Economy, 1290-1348', in *Before the Black Death: Studies in the 'Crisis' of the Early Fourteenth Century*, ed. B. M. S. Campbell (Manchester, 1991), p. 156.

dropped and there was a marked increase in the number of those caught up in the system.[44] It has usually been assumed that this extension of liability made direct taxation more regressive, since the wealthy – particularly those who enjoyed influence with the county tax commissioners – were able to ignore or shake off their obligations and have the resulting shortfall charged to the poorer elements in local society.[45] In the light of what has already been suggested about the increasing social and political stratification that set in after the plague, it is indeed tempting to suggest that taxation, like justice, became an instrument of social policy after the Black Death and that the landed classes sought to offset their economic problems by throwing a still larger proportion of the tax burden of royal subsidies onto the shoulders of smallholders and newly prosperous labourers.

In reality, the picture was probably not so neat. While those communities that relied on major contributions from nobles and gentry undoubtedly suffered considerable hardships if an absentee landlord refused to co-operate or, perhaps even worse, immunised himself from liability by leasing out his demesne, there were many other villages where the distribution of the quotas applied much more evenly and progressively.[46] In Kent – the only county for which accurate evidence exists – the sub-assessors continued to observe a minimum level of liability, even if local conditions now dictated that this often fell below the 10s. worth of movables often observed in earlier subsidies.[47] It is worth stressing in this context that the people who actually undertook the job of allocating and collecting such taxes at the local level were drawn not from the county gentry but from the petty landholders and village elders, men who lacked the political and social authority to overthrow communal traditions and who were just as likely to identify with the interests of their village neighbours as with the more authoritarian regime operated by their social betters. It is

[44] Willard, *Parliamentary Taxes*, p. 177; H. A. Hanley and C. W. Chalkin, 'The Kent Lay Subsidy of 1334/5', in *Documents Illustrative of Medieval Kentish Society*, ed. F. R. H. Du Boulay, Kent Archaeological Society Records Branch, 18 (London, 1964), p. 62.

[45] E. B. Fryde, *Studies in Medieval Trade and Finance* (London, 1983), chapter I, p. 8-42; chapter V, p. 256; J. R. Maddicott, 'The English Peasantry and the Demands of the Crown, 1294-1341', in *Landlords, Peasants and Politics in Medieval England*, ed. T. H. Aston (Cambridge, 1987), p. 335. Fenwick, 'Poll Taxes', pp. 19-20, argues that it was the gentry who were under most pressure from the tax system in the 1370s.

[46] Ormrod, 'Crown and English Economy', pp. 156-57.

[47] Hanley and Chalkin, 'Kent Lay Subsidy', pp. 63-64. Fenwick, 'Poll Taxes', p. 29, is not correct in her statement that the taxable minimum in Kent remained at the 1332 level, though she provides valuable data (pp. 21-22) to demonstrate the continued immunity of large numbers of households from 15ths and 10ths in the 1370s. The Kent lay subsidy rolls deserve much closer attention.

therefore suggested here that the inequalities that came increasingly to be perceived within the system of fifteenths and tenths after the re-opening of the French war in 1369 derived not so much from variations in personal liability as from the increasingly obvious fact that certain communities, heavily depopulated and impoverished by successive outbreaks of plague, were having to bear quite unreasonable and unrealistic levels of taxation in comparison with those towns and villages that had emerged relatively unscathed, or even revitalised, in the post-plague economy.

This concern with the geographical, rather than the specifically personal, inequalities of taxation certainly explains why, when parliament turned its attention to a reform of the tax system in the 1370s, it chose first to alleviate the problem of communal quotas. In 1371, when they were asked to grant the first direct subsidy for over a decade, the lords and commons suggested that a standard figure should be charged on each parish (as distinct from town or village), and that the commissioners appointed to administer the tax should be empowered to offset the burden on poor communities by taking extra payments from rich ones. In fact, although this tax yielded almost all the £50,000 assessed, it tended to exacerbate rather than alleviate discrepancies in the tax burden as applied at the local level; this, together with the fact that the subsidy was regarded very much as a special response to a specific financial emergency, meant that the experiment was never again repeated.[48] Indeed, in 1372-73, parliament returned to the standard fifteenth and tenth as the favoured form of direct taxation; for whatever reason, the momentum for reform had apparently abated.

It comes as something of a surprise, then, to find that the last parliament of Edward III's reign, which assembled in January 1377, instigated what was probably the most radical change in direct taxation ever witnessed in later medieval England by proposing a standard poll tax of 4d. on every adult over the age of fourteen. The reasons behind this decision have never been fully understood. Many historians have seen this as the natural culmination of a deliberate policy pursued since 1334 and gathering momentum in the 1370s whereby the political classes sought to extend the basis of liability and pass on the burden of taxation to those previously exempt from direct subsidies.[49] In the light of the bitter complaints made about both free labourers and villeins in the parliaments of 1376-77, it is

[48] W. M. Ormrod, 'An Experiment in Taxation: The English Parish Subsidy of 1371', *Speculum*, 63 (1988), 59-82. Fenwick, 'Poll Taxes', p. 23, notes that this levy was to be assessed on lands as well as goods and collected, at least in theory, from all households.

[49] See, most recently, Britnell, *Commercialisation*, p. 185. A more cautious assessment is provided in a number of studies by E. B. Fryde, for example *The Great Revolt of 1381*, Historical Association general series, 100 (London, 1981), p. 10.

indeed tempting to suppose that the 1377 poll tax symbolised the deliberate extension of class conflict into the area of public finance. On the other hand, the motives behind the earlier reform of 1371, coupled with the progressive nature of the graduated poll tax of 1379 and the comments made in the parliament of 1380 about the iniquities of the fifteenth and tenth, suggest that the assembly of 1377 may have been moved as much by compassion and equity as by a desire to punish a greedy and unworthy peasantry.[50]

Two points are particularly worthy of consideration in this respect. Firstly, the 1377 poll tax was granted for a very special purpose, not merely to help subsidise the general costs of war, but to defend the realm from imminent attack by a combined French and Castilian armada: under these circumstances no delay could be countenanced and the political community was obliged to find the quickest possible means of raising the money needed to subsidise an English fleet.[51] Secondly, the decision to fix the tax at 4d. per head was probably not taken at random. The minimum valuation set for liability to a fifteenth and tenth before 1334 had meant that the lowest assessment commonly charged on individual households in rural communities outside the royal demesne was 8d., payable under normal circumstances in two equal instalments. It is particularly interesting to notice that the parliament roll records the decision of the lords and commons in 1377 to authorise a tax of 'four pence to be taken from the goods of each person of the kingdom'.[52] In practice, this was a nonsense, since the tax on heads obviously took no account of movable property; but the fact that it was expressed in this way strongly suggests that the new capitation tax was perceived by the political classes as an emergency levy representing the former standard minimum payment towards one instalment of a fifteenth and tenth. This is not to say, of course, that parliament did not appreciate the enormous changes that would be brought about in the distribution of this tax by its decision to charge the levy not on selected households but on every adult head of population. Nevertheless, the evidence surveyed here strongly suggests that the poll tax of 1377 was perceived very much as a supplement to, rather than a replacement for, the standard fifteenth and tenth, and that the startlingly regressive nature of the tax was a consequence less of some class conspiracy than of what was in

[50] *Rotuli Parliamentorum*, III, 57-58, 90. It is not clear whether the much-quoted comment of 1380 that 'the tenths and fifteenths are in many ways very oppressive to the poor community' came from the lords, the commons, or the chancery clerk who drew up the record.

[51] A comparison with the special tax arrangements worked out during an earlier invasion scare in 1360 is instructive: G. L. Harriss, *King, Parliament and Public Finance in Medieval England to 1369* (Oxford, 1975), pp. 395-400.

[52] *Rotuli Parliamentorum*, II, 364, as translated in R. B. Dobson, *The Peasants' Revolt of 1381*, 2nd edn (London, 1983), p. 105.

many ways a rather rushed and muddled response to a particular financial emergency.

This interpretation also does much to explain both the decision of 1379 to adopt an elaborately graduated poll tax based on social (rather than strictly economic) rank and the circumstances surrounding the grant of the fateful third poll tax in parliament in December 1380. The proposal of the commons in the latter assembly to raise 100,000 marks (£66,667) by means of a levy of 12d. on each adult over the age of fifteen has often been seen as a blatant attack on the economic standing of the lower classes that caused widespread resentment, resistance and eventual revolt. Again, however, a distinction needs to be drawn between the intention behind the tax and the harsher realities that emerged during its administration. The new levy was in fact intended as a kind of hybrid between the experimental subsidies of 1371 and 1377: in each town and village the total assessment, calculated by multiplying the number of persons liable by the standard rate of 12d. per head, was to be apportioned to individuals according to their ability to pay.[53] The very ambiguity both of the parliament roll and of the commissions issued to the collectors of this tax about the way in which such ability was to be judged suggests that previous tax bandings both for fifteenths and tenths and (though officially forbidden) for the poll tax of 1379 were to be important, if not actually determining, criteria.[54] In practice, as is well known, this scheme simply exacerbated the inequalities that already existed in both the geographical and the individual distribution of the tax burden. It is not surprising that these gross inequalities, coupled with the general unpopularity of the causes for which the tax was collected (chiefly to cover the crown's military debts and, in particular, to pay for the extravagant and unproductive expedition of the earl of Buckingham earlier in 1380), resulted in a good deal of opposition and evasion.[55]

On the other hand, mere local resistance to taxation – a not infrequent phenomenon in medieval England – was very different from active

---

[53] *Rotuli Parliamentorum*, III, p. 90, translated in Dobson, *Peasants' Revolt*, pp. 117-18.

[54] Fenwick, 'Poll Taxes', pp. 30, 155-56.

[55] Justification for taxation: *Rotuli Parliamentorum*, III, p. 88, translated in Dobson, *Peasants' Revolt*, pp. 113-14. The rate of concealment as calculated by C. Oman, *The Great Revolt of 1381*, 2nd edn (Oxford, 1969), pp. 27-29, 162-66, and cited most recently by E. B. Fryde and N. M. Fryde, 'Peasant Rebellion and Peasant Discontents', in *Agrarian History of England and Wales*, III, p. 771, fails to take account of the substantial differences between the poll taxes of 1377 and 1381: above all, the immunity of married women from the latter. As Fenwick, 'Poll Taxes', pp. 196, 218, 225-35 notes, the 1381 returns, though still suspicious, represent a much lower rate of concealment than has usually been thought.

rebellion.[56] It is well known that the Peasants' Revolt was precipitated not by the grant or the collection of the third poll tax but by the appointment in the spring of 1381 of commissioners to sit in selected shires and inquire into the administration of the tax.[57] What has not generally been considered is the fact that those who took up arms in opposition to these controversial commissions were not simply the passive victims of an iniquitous tax policy but included some who had been directly involved in the administration of the tax at the local level.[58] By allowing the quotas to be redistributed within communities, the government had in effect placed the 1380 poll tax, like its predecessors, in the hands of those same minor gentry and leading peasants who had long acted as sub-assessors and sub-collectors of

[56] R. Hilton, *Class Conflict and the Crisis of Feudalism: Essays in Medieval Social History*, 2nd edn (London, 1990), pp. 49-78; R. H. Hilton, 'Resistance to Taxation and to Other State Impositions in Medieval England', in *Genèse de l'état moderne: prélèvement et redistribution*, ed. J.-Ph. Genet and M. Le Mené (Paris, 1987), pp. 169-77; Willard, *Parliamentary Taxes*, pp. 170-74, 195-97; Harriss, *King, Parliament*, p. 322; Ormrod, *Reign of Edward III*, p. 156; Ormrod, 'Experiment in Taxation', pp. 75-6.

[57] It should be noted that such commissions had also been used in 1379: Fenwick, 'Poll Taxes', pp. 141-43, 217-18. Fenwick also notes (pp. 41, 153, 229-31) that although commissions were only issued for certain shires and towns in 1381, some form of re-assessment seems to have been carried out in most areas. In the light of the discussion that follows, it may be significant that the commissions of 1379 were made up of local gentry and were required to report to and work with the local collectors (*Calendar of Fine Rolls*, IX, pp. 162-64), whereas those of 1380 included an 'official' element not only from within the shire (the sheriff and escheator) but also from the central government (a king's serjeant and an exchequer clerk) and were required to report back directly to the exchequer (*Calendar of Fine Rolls*, IX, pp. 248-50).

[58] The identity of sub-collectors of taxes on movables cannot normally be established after 1334, but for the poll tax of 1377 there are a large number of acquittances issued by chief collectors naming the sub-collectors from whom they received the proceeds of the levy. These can be compared with the extant lists of rebels in 1381 found, for example, in the sources cited by Dyer, 'Social and Economic Background', p. 11, n. 4. A systematic comparison has not been made here, but a sample of hundreds in Essex reveals that the following rebels of 1381 (named in indictments in KB145/3/6/1) had been active in the administration of the first poll tax. Hinckford Hundred (acquittances in E179/107/53): Robert Warner of Gestingthorpe, sub-collector at Bocking; John Kentysh (described as 'former sub-bailiff' of the hundred in 1381), sub-collector at Braintree; William atte Hel, sub-collector at Little Henny. Tendring Hundred (acquittances in E179/107/56): Thomas Leyham of Little Bromley, constable and sub-collector at Little Bromley. Lexden Hundred (acquittances in E179/107/58): Walter Debelan, constable and sub-collector at Stanway.

fifteenths and tenths.[59] By appointing members of the county gentry reinforced by experts from the central financial and judicial agencies to make detailed inquiries into the administration of the levy and report their findings directly back to the exchequer, however, the crown was threatening the high degree of autonomy that bailiffs, constables and other village elders had come to expect over the distribution of taxation within individual communities ever since the fixing of the communal charges for fifteenths and tenths in 1334. That only certain counties were identified for such treatment may simply have increased the distrust engendered there by this fundamental challenge to the principle of local self-government.[60] As though the intrusion of the justices of the peace into the policing of urban and rural societies over the previous two decades was not enough, the very right of the vill to organise its own response to the financial demands of the state was now apparently being undermined.

This rather long excursion through the history of fourteenth-century taxation therefore suggests that the fiscal issues that surfaced during the Peasants' Revolt of 1381 were a consequence not simply of the economic dislocation and social conflict experienced since the Black Death of 1348-49 but more directly of a growing unease over the principles and practices that conditioned the governance of the realm. By medieval standards, England was exceptional in the high (some might have said excessive) degree to which the monarchy controlled the lives of its subjects. The delegation of direct administrative responsibilities to a large number of men in the localities had not only spread the influence of the crown into the provinces; it had also created a highly politicised society with a remarkably detailed knowledge of both local and national affairs. The more self-conscious stratification of the governing classes after the Black Death and the drawing together of crown, nobility and county gentry in a community of economic and political interests had the effect of marginalising those lesser landholders and greater peasants who provided the most basic points of contact between crown and people. Although the origins of the Peasants' Revolt can be traced in innumerable spheres of human activity, it may well have been governance, in the widest sense of the term, that had the most profound influence on the origins, the course, and indeed the aftermath of that rising.

[59]   Fenwick, 'Poll Taxes', pp. 56, 64-75, stresses the important role played by sub-collectors in the administration of all three poll taxes.
[60]   For the local organisation of royal taxation see A. B. White, *Self-Government at the King's Command* (Minneapolis, 1933), pp. 77-81; *Surrey Taxation Returns*, ed. J. F. Willard and H. C. Johnson, Surrey Record Society, 11 (London, 1932), p. xx.

Issues in Government: The Royal Demesne

It therefore appears that the Black Death had a formative, if often indirect, impact on the political attitudes and governmental structures that prevailed in England during the second half of the fourteenth century. Nor were the issues raised by the plague necessarily confined to the local operation of royal justice and finance. At the centre, too, in the Westminster administration and the sessions of the king's parliament, the demographic disasters and resulting challenge facing the landed classes not only created a new subject and vocabulary of complaint but also provoked significant changes in attitude and policy. Perhaps the most interesting of the issues thus raised concerned the administration of the royal demesne, a subject that tells us much about the attitudes of both crown and parliament to the radical economic changes brought on by the plague.

By the fourteenth century, the income from royal lands provided only a small proportion even of the ordinary revenues of the state; indeed, by comparison with the enormous amounts of money raised by Edward III from extraordinary taxes, the demesne in its strictest sense, as the permanent landed estate of the crown, was of very little financial significance at all.[61] With the advent of the Black Death in 1348-49, however, the central government found two reasons for focusing renewed attention on this rather neglected aspect of its fiscal system. Firstly, it was imperative that the crown should be seen to be acting in concert with the landholding classes and working hard to protect itself from any diminution in seigneurial rights and revenues resulting from the recent demographic disaster; and secondly, the deaths of large numbers of the crown's feudal tenants created an unexpected opportunity for short-term financial gain through the exploitation of royal prerogative rights. The result was that throughout the 1350s the exchequer put considerable pressure both on the sheriffs (as administrators of the demesne) and on the lessees of royal wardships to produce levels of income comparable to those achieved before the plague.[62] While the king himself might sometimes intervene to relieve the burden on a favoured courtier or confidant, the official line was remarkably severe and compared well with the general policy of a return to the *status quo ante* being pursued on so many of the great estates in this

[61] The only estimates that are of any relevance here are those for the revenue from the sheriffs' farms. The receipt rolls suggest that these brought in about £4,000 a year in the 14th century: see Harriss, *King, Parliament*, pp. 146-47, 489, 524-26; A. Steel, 'The Distribution of Assignment in the Treasurer's Receipt Roll, Michaelmas 1364-5', *Cambridge Historical Journal*, 2 (1926-28), 175-85, p. 180; G. Holmes, *The Good Parliament* (Oxford, 1975), p. 70. It should be remembered that the farms derived from the profits of justice and administration as well as from land.

[62] Ormrod, 'Edward III's Government of England', pp. 243-9, 259-60.

period.[63] To the extent that the king still identified himself as the greatest landholder and feudal suzerain of the realm, the decade after the first outbreak of the plague therefore probably did much to convince other members of the elite of the crown's commitment to supporting the restoration of their seigneurial rights and economic advantages.

The main problem with this policy, however, was that the sheriffs and lessees of the crown were themselves drawn from the landed classes and inevitably resented the undue pressures brought to bear on them in the difficult economic climate prevailing after 1348. It is therefore significant that after the second plague, and particularly after the widespread damage caused by the freak storm of February 1362, the exchequer seems to have been rather more inclined to accept pleas from such agents for remission of their outstanding debts.[64] This is not to say that the crown was altogether neglectful of its rights. A petition in the parliament of 1363 that the king should turn a blind eye to the leasing of those lands held by tenants in chief left ruinous since 'the pestilences and great winds' inevitably received a rather sharp response from the council, while the campaign that got under way after the third plague for the formal reduction of certain shrieval fee farms long remained a point of issue between the exchequer and the county communities.[65] The crown was therefore faced with the considerable problem of balancing a necessary sensitivity to individual

[63] Ormrod, 'English Government and Black Death', p. 182, n. 64.

[64] For chronicle accounts of the storm see C. E. Britton, *A Meteorological Chronology to A.D. 1450*, Meteorological Office Geophysical Memoirs, 70 (1937), pp. 144-45. For damage to the economic infrastructure see K. C. Newton, *Thaxted in the Fourteenth Century* (Chelmsford, 1960), pp. 25-26; J. Titow, 'Le climat à travers les rôles de comptabilité de l'évêché de Winchester (1350-1450)', *Annales: économies, sociétés, civilisations*, 25 (1970), 312-50, p. 320. For relief offered by the crown as a result of storm damage see *Calendar of Close Rolls, 1360-64*, p. 336; *Calendar of Fine Rolls*, VII, p. 341; *Calendar of Inquisitions Miscellaneous*, III, nos. 605, 743; E368/135, Precepta, Pasch, mm. 5-6 (John Boys, sheriff of Lincolnshire, excused £157 on account of the storm).

[65] 1363 petition: *Rotuli Parliamentorum*, II, p. 279. Shrieval fee farms: *ibid.*, II, p. 301. The latter issue was taken up particularly by the twin shires of Essex and Hertfordshire (*ibid.*, II, pp. 349, 370; III, pp. 19, 45, 94), but despite granting *ad hoc* remissions (*Calendar of Close Rolls, 1360-64*, p. 336), the crown was only finally prepared to accept the permanent reduction of the old fee farm in return for a fine of £2,000 levied on these shires in 1398: *Calendar of Charter Rolls, 1341-1417*, p. 371; E179/242/83. For other shires, see Ormrod, *Reign of Edward III*, p. 162; and for the continuation of the debate on a general level into the 15th century see R. Virgoe, 'The Crown, Magnates, and Government in Fifteenth-century East Anglia', in *The Crown and Local Communities in England and France in the Fifteenth Century*, ed. J. R. L. Highfield and R. Jeffs (Gloucester, 1981), pp. 73-74.

needs against the possible charge that it was squandering its landed resources and thereby failing to provide a proper example to the proprietary classes. The decision of Edward III to exempt himself from the labour legislation in order to ensure adequate supplies of manpower for the royal building works at Windsor during the 1360s hardly suggested that the community of interests between crown and employers symbolised in the original Ordinance of Labourers still stood particularly firm.[66] Over the next two decades, the collapse of that alliance was to be expressed specifically in bitter criticism of the administration of the royal demesne.

In the Good Parliament of 1376 the commons requested that the king take compassion on the great poverty that had befallen his subjects through repeated pestilences and that the income from 'archbishoprics, bishoprics, abbacies, baronies, escheats, fines, ransoms, wardships, marriages, and all profits belonging and escheating into the king's hand' should be reserved and used for the defence of the realm and ease of the people.[67] This was the first statement of an idea that was to be developed considerably in a series of parliamentary petitions over the following decade.[68] The commons were not necessarily suggesting that the reservation of regalian and feudal incidents and other royal prerogative revenues would be sufficient to allow the king to 'live of his own' during peace time, and even less that such a policy would be an adequate means of covering the particularly exorbitant costs of war. Instead, their primary concern seems to have arisen from a perception that the crown's feudal resources had gradually come to be used as a form of patronage rather than of income. In the decade 1349-59, the exchequer had consistently used the farms of royal wardships (together, more occasionally, with the revenues from alien priories and vacant ecclesiastical temporalities) for the upkeep of the king's household.[69] Although the financial support thus provided for the domestic expenditure of the court had proved comparatively modest, this targeting of resources was precisely the system so often recommended by critics of the crown's finances in later reigns and may even have provided something of a model for the remedial schemes they proposed. The policy, dropped in 1359 when the royal wardrobe resumed its function as a war office, had not been revived in the period of peace during the 1360s, despite the notably large number of wardships that fell into the king's hands during the plague of 1361-62; and by the 1370s many of the crown's most valuable feudal

---

[66] R. A. Brown, H. M. Colvin and A. J. Taylor, *The History of the King's Works* I, *The Middle Ages* (London, 1963), pp. 84-85.

[67] *Rotuli Parliamentorum*, II, pp. 355-56.

[68] *Ibid.*, III, 15-16, 115, 139, 147. For the general context see B. P. Wolffe, *The Royal Demesne in English History* (London, 1971), pp. 72-75; C. Given-Wilson, *The Royal Household and the King's Affinity: Service, Politics and Finance in England 1360-1413* (London, 1986), pp. 110-30.

[69] Ormrod, 'Edward III's Government', pp. 243-49, 258-61.

perquisites were being used not to benefit the royal coffers but to reward the small and controversial group of courtiers that gathered round the aged Edward III. The belief, articulated in 1378 and 1404, that Edward had further impoverished the crown by permanent alienations from the demesne towards the end of his reign can only have given added credence to the argument that the safeguarding of the crown's fiscal prerogatives (coupled, as was suggested in 1378, with a selective resumption of alienations) was the necessary first step in restoring the viability, as well as the economy and efficiency, of royal finances.[70]

In a general sense, furthermore, this political programme also aimed to relieve the burden of taxation on the king's hard-pressed subjects. It is particularly significant in the context of this chapter that the rhetoric of the debate on the crown's resources repeatedly drew attention to the poverty and distress experienced by the king's subjects through plague and other natural disasters and their inability to contribute to the costs of the state.[71] Even in the years immediately after 1348, when parliament had been so generous in its grants of direct taxation to Edward III, the commons had asked for compassion as a result of their suffering in the recent pestilence.[72] After 1381 the plea of poverty, coupled with worries about further tax revolts, proved to be the surest and most potent of the commons' reasons for rejecting outright the crown's requests for direct subsidies.[73] That the debate over the use of the crown's landed resources and the extent of the country's financial obligations under Edward III and Richard II was stimulated and justified by the Black Death and its economic effects therefore does much to emphasise the continued relevance and importance of plague within the political life of later fourteenth-century England.

The Fifteenth Century

By the early fifteenth century, however, this was no longer the case: plague, though still a regular hazard, had largely ceased to inform either the political language or the administrative policies of the ruling elite. Inevitably, the Black Death and its injurious consequences continued to appear among the lists of hardships put forward by those individuals or corporations seeking favours from the crown: in particular, the epidemics of the 1430s seem to have set an agenda for the many petitions subsequently lodged with the crown by urban communities anxious to secure remission

---

[70] See the sources cited in Ormrod, *Reign of Edward III*, p. 59.

[71] *Rotuli Parliamentorum*, II, pp. 355-6; III, pp. 139, 147.

[72] *Ibid.*, II, pp. 227, 237.

[73] J. A. Tuck, 'Nobles, Commons and the Great Revolt of 1381', in *The English Rising of 1381*, ed. Hilton and Aston, pp. 204, 208-9. For the effect upon military strategy see A. Tuck, 'Richard II and the Hundred Years War', in *Politics and Crisis in Fourteenth Century England*, ed. J. Taylor and W. Childs (Gloucester, 1990), pp. 117-31.

from their fee farms and tax quotas.[74] But by this stage those political issues that were discussed at a national rather than a local or personal level seem no longer to have been articulated specifically within a plague context. From the 1390s, for example, the public debate over royal finance became a good deal more specific in its criticisms and more ambitious in the remedies that were offered. It was the extravagance of the king's household and the escalating costs of the royal affinity that now provoked calls for economy, while the issue of whether or not 'public' money should be used to support such 'private' expenditure concentrated not on the general poverty of the taxpaying population but on the extent of the country's constitutional responsibility to support the king in peace as well as in war.[75] Although this shift of emphasis was in many ways a natural development from the more guarded political debate of the 1370s and '80s, it is also possible that it represented the very different economic, social and political conditions prevailing in the country by 1400.

The general shift away from the direct management of the land and towards the leasing of demesnes, which took off rapidly in the last decades of the fourteenth and first decades of the fifteenth centuries, profoundly altered the legal and economic relationship between lords and peasants. As the exploitation of seigneurial rights gave way to the negotiation of rents, the total burden of lordship, formerly represented by services in money, kind and labour, now declined both in range and in quantity. This, together with a marked drop in the cost of staple foodstuffs after the 1370s, meant a significant, if not always very secure, improvement in the standard of living of a substantial proportion of the peasant population. Those landholders who continued to run their home farms and other demesnes with the use of contract workers and the increasing number of yeomen farmers who were now beginning to employ labour on their holdings all continued to have a vested interest in the preservation of the labour laws. Increasingly, however, the terms of contracts and rates of wages offered to agricultural labourers had of necessity to reflect the relative shortage of human resources. Consequently, wage labourers probably gained more in proportional terms from the new economic dispensation than any other group within the peasantry.[76] But while the growing prosperity of agrarian society in the fifteenth century has long been a source of comment, little attention has been paid to the governmental and political implications of this situation. In France, it would appear that any economic benefit derived

[74] D. M. Palliser, 'Urban Decay Revisited', in *Towns and Townspeople in the Fifteenth Century*, ed. J. A. F. Thomson (Gloucester, 1988), pp. 3-7.

[75] Given-Wilson, *Royal Household*, pp. 113-14, 126-41; G. L. Harriss, 'Theory and Practice in Royal Taxation: Some Observations', *English Historical Review*, 97 (1982), 811-19.

[76] C. Dyer, *Standards of Living in the Later Middle Ages: Social Change in England c. 1200-1520* (Cambridge, 1989), pp. 27-48, 109-50.

by the peasantry from the retreat of seigneurial authority after the Black Death was largely negated by the great increase in the financial demands of the state from the 1360s.[77] In England, however, the situation was very different. To understand the broader changes that came about in English government during the century after the Peasants' Revolt it is necessary to return to the most frequent and contentious point of contact between crown and people in the later middle ages, namely taxation.

Although they did not know it at the time, the English rebels of 1381 were at least in part responsible for a profound change in the operation of royal taxes. Not only were there no further poll taxes for the rest of the fourteenth and fifteenth centuries, but the king's subjects seem actually to have benefited from the decision to return to the apparently outdated fifteenth and tenth. Three factors may be said to have contributed to making this system more palatable to the ordinary taxpayer. Firstly, the general improvement in the economic status of the peasantry undoubtedly made it easier for many taxpayers to meet their commitments to the state. Secondly, and more significantly, the period after 1381 witnessed an appreciable decline in the number and frequency of fifteenths and tenths charged on the realm; indeed, although the burden increased again during the early years of the fifteenth century, not even the extremely generous subsidies awarded to Henry V in the aftermath of Agincourt broke through the apparent ceiling of sustainability that had been fixed during the 1370s.[78] Finally, and most importantly, it is also possible that taxation, for all its inherent anomalies, became a good deal less socially divisive than it had been in the generations immediately following the Black Death.

This last suggestion is borne out by a number of features within the late medieval tax system. The restoration of the fifteenth and tenth meant not only a return to the household as the basic tax unit but also the revival of a crude but vital correlation between the tax charge and the ability to pay. What little we know of the distribution of late medieval lay subsidies suggests that, although the communal quota charged on each community was often spread over a large number of households, individual assessments still varied widely; and there is no reason to doubt that in most cases the scale of these assessments represented, however crudely, the relative economic capacity of each contributor.[79] Furthermore, the fact that at least

---

[77] G. Bois, *The Crisis of Feudalism. Economy and Society in Eastern Normandy c.1300-1550* (Cambridge, 1984), pp. 277-345.

[78] The fiscal data collected by me on which this statement is based are stored in the European State Finance Database, deposited in the Economic and Social Research Council Data Archive at the University of Essex, and may be accessed via JANET (e-mail: archive@essex.ac.uk). See in particular for present purposes the dataset \orm\engm010.ssd.

[79] See, in particular, *The Bailiffs' Minute Book of Dunwich 1404-1450*, ed. M. Bailey, Suffolk Records Society, 34 (Woodbridge, 1992), pp. 5-6, 7-8, 50-52,

some communities in the fifteenth century came to use additional or alternative criteria to the valuation of movable property as a means of distributing the burden of the fifteenth and tenth also suggests a growing sensitivity to the basic principle of fiscal equity.[80] That the common funds to which numerous late medieval testators left land or money were used at least in some cases to provide relief from the communal tax quota provides striking evidence of the way in which even the payment of the king's subsidies could be used to demonstrate both personal piety and public spirit.[81]

This is not to say, of course, that the fifteenth century was a golden age of the English taxpayer. The absence of further tax revolts before the outbreak of opposition to the Tudor subsidies does not in itself prove that taxation was now perceived as progressive: it may simply be that medieval society had a much greater tolerance of the unfairness of taxation than is the case today.[82] Nonetheless, the extent to which both the crown and the political elite were prepared to go to endorse the general principle of equity remains remarkable. From the beginning of the fifteenth century there were a number of attempts – some of them admittedly rather misguided – to reduce the worst of the anachronisms that had emerged in the 1334 communal valuations as a result of the fall in population and redistribution of wealth since the Black Death, and from 1404 there were occasional, if again rather modest, attempts to redress what was in many ways the worst imbalance in the tax system by imposing income taxes on the upper levels of English society.[83] Most striking of all, perhaps, was the refusal of parliament before 1514 to pursue the tax policies adopted by the English church and reinstate poll taxes as a means of raising supplementary revenue from those who normally escaped the standard forms of direct taxation.[84]

55-56, 74-76, 102-04, 111-13, 138-41.

[80] Schofield, 'Parliamentary Lay Taxation', pp. 85-95.

[81] W. K. Jordan, *The Charities of Rural England 1480-1660: The Aspirations and the Achievements of the Rural Society* (London, 1961), pp. 143-5; Schofield, 'Parliamentary Lay Taxation', pp. 99-100; Dyer, *Standards of Living*, p. 256. Dr Verduyn points out that the preamble to the Charitable Uses Act of 1601, which included reference to bequests made for the relief of 15ths and 10ths (*Statutes of the Realm*, IV, 968-69), was not actually repealed until 1960.

[82] Hilton, *Class Conflict*, pp. 12-18, argues that tax revolts were more likely to be occasioned by corrupt administration than by general inequality.

[83] For the artificial way in which remissions were allocated to the quotas for the 15th and 10th see A. R. Bridbury, *Economic Growth*, 2nd edn (Brighton, 1975), pp. 96-97; M. W. Beresford, 'A Review of Historical Research (to 1968)', in *Deserted Medieval Villages*, ed. M. Beresford and J. G. Hurst (London, 1971), p. 10. For income taxes see European State Finance Database \orm\engd 011.ssd.

[84] For clerical poll taxes see European State Finance Database \orm\engd 017.ssd. For the 1514 poll tax see R. S. Schofield, 'The Geographical

Significantly enough, it was only foreigners, so much hated and criticised in the fifteenth century for their supposed domination of trade, who were made subject to a new series of parliamentary poll taxes after 1439; judging from the extreme xenophobia of most of English society in the late middle ages, these punitive levies would have incited nothing but praise if and when the king's ordinary subjects learned of their operation.[85]

The easing of the burden of direct taxation and of the social tensions that had so often revolved around the levying of the king's subsidies in an earlier period may therefore have been symptomatic of a new dispensation gradually emerging in response to the long-term economic and political effects of the Black Death. The initial decision to return to a reliance on the fifteenth and tenth may certainly have represented the inertia, not to say the fear, of the political elite in the face of continued threats of insurrection during the 1380s and '90s, while the refusal of parliament to countenance a full-scale reform of the tax system during the fifteenth century says more about its suspicion of the Lancastrian monarchy's attempts to extend the circumstances under which subsidies might be demanded than it does about its often spurious concern for social welfare.[86] Nevertheless, there remains a sense in which the period after 1400 did indeed witness the dissipation, if not the complete disappearance, of those conflicts and concerns that were earlier identified as the basis of so much political dissatisfaction in the revolt of 1381. While the upper gentry showed no particular sign of releasing the stranglehold they had established over the major public offices in the shires, the rapid increase in the size of the bench meant that, in theory at least, a larger proportion of those within the elite became actively involved in local administration than ever before.[87] Furthermore, the general participation of other classes in the government of the shire had not, in the end, been eliminated. Lesser gentry became increasingly important as chief tax collectors while yeomen established a considerable degree of autonomy in the individual

---

Distribution of Wealth in England, 1334-1649', *Economic History Review*, 2nd series, 18 (1965), 483-510, pp. 492-3 and notes.

[85] European State Finance Database \orm\engd013.ssd; S. L. Thrupp, 'A Survey of the Alien Population of England in 1440', *Speculum*, 32 (1957), 262-73. For attitudes to aliens see J. L. Bolton, *The Medieval English Economy 1150-1500* (London, 1980), pp. 305-14.

[86] Harriss, 'Political Society and the Growth of Government', pp. 42-43 and the works cited there.

[87] Carpenter, *Locality and Polity*, pp. 273-74; A. L. Brown, *The Governance of Late Medieval England 1272-1461* (London, 1989), pp. 126-28. For the problem of the numbers of JPs actually attending the quarter sessions see Payling, *Political Society*, pp. 180-82; J. R. Lander, *English Justices of the Peace 1461-1509* (Gloucester, 1989), pp. 58-74.

distribution of royal subsidies at the village level.[88] As the powers of the justices of the peace were extended, so the co-operation and participation of the constables of hundreds and vills became ever more important.[89] Above all, perhaps, the minor gentry and greater tenantry won a significant, if sometimes token, acknowledgement of their role in public affairs through the fixing of the minimum property qualification for the election of parliamentary representatives at the level of the 40s. freeholder in 1429-30.[90] Finally, the sheer sophistication of the late medieval state, represented above all by the great expansion in private litigation that it countenanced during the fifteenth century, offered innumerable possibilities for men of relatively humble status to create careers, and sometimes considerable fortunes, for themselves in the provision of all manner of legal, financial and administrative services.[91] In the end, then, the apparently ominous divisions that had opened up within an increasingly stratified governing elite in the immediate aftermath of the Black Death were to a large extent healed, and the revolutionary aims that some had identified among the rebels of 1381 were discarded in favour of the more specifically political objectives of a series of provincial uprisings culminating in Cade's Rebellion of 1450.[92]

Conclusion

In 1439 the commons in parliament made an unusual request of King Henry VI.

> ... how that a sickness called the pestilence, commonly through this your realm more commonly reigneth than hath been usual before this time,

[88]   Saul, *Knights and Esquires*, pp. 143-44, suggests that pressure from the lesser gentry may account for the increase in the size of the tax commissions towards the end of the 14th century. This increase is demonstrated conveniently in *Surrey Taxation Returns*, ed. Willard and Johnson, pp. 97-109.

[89]   *Proceedings before the Justices of the Peace*, ed. Putnam, pp. xxxvii-xxxviii, xcix.

[90]   S. J. Payling, 'The Widening Franchise: Parliamentary Elections in Lancastrian Nottinghamshire', in *England in the Fifteenth Century: Proceedings of the 1986 Harlaxton Symposium*, ed. D. Williams (Woodbridge, 1987), pp. 167-85; R. Virgoe, 'Aspects of the County Community in the Fifteenth Century', in *Profit, Piety and the Professions in Later Medieval England*, ed. M. Hicks (Gloucester, 1990), pp. 7-11.

[91]   E. W. Ives, *The Common Lawyers of Pre-Reformation England* (Cambridge, 1983), pp. 285-417; Payling, 'Social Mobility', pp. 66-7; N. Ramsay, 'Scriveners and Notaries as Legal Intermediaries in Later Medieval England', in *Enterprise and Individuals in Fifteenth-Century England*, ed. J. Kermode (Stroud, 1991), pp. 118-31; N. Ramsay, 'What was the Legal Profession?', in *Profit, Piety and the Professions*, ed. Hicks, pp. 62-71.

[92]   Dobson, *Peasants' Revolt*, pp. 336-42; Fryde and Fryde, 'Peasant Rebellion', pp. 797-807; Poos, *A Rural Society*, pp. 252-62; I. M. W. Harvey, *Jack Cade's Rebellion of 1450* (Oxford, 1991).

the which is an infirmity most infective, and the presence of such so infect[ed] most to be eschewed, as by noble physicians and wise philosophers before this time plainly it hath been determined and as experience daily showeth. Wherefore we ... beseech your most noble grace, in conserving of your most noble person, and in comfort of us all ... graciously to conceive how where that any of your said commons, holding of you by knight service, oweth in doing to you homage, by your gracious suffrance to kiss you, to ordain and grant by the authority of this present parliament, that each of your said lieges, in the doing of the said homage, may omit the said kissing of you, and be excused thereof at your will...[93]

This petition provides a nice illustration of the very different part that plague had come to play in the government of the realm by the middle years of the fifteenth century. Although epidemic disease was still very much a threat to life, it was no longer perceived as a challenge to the social and political organisation of the realm. Significantly, the rhetoric of government and politics had ceased to employ the plague and its effects as a means of justifying or conditioning the administrative policies of the crown, and the periodic outbreaks of pestilence in the fifteenth century were seen merely as a temporary hazard to those in public life, forcing a series of regrettable but necessary adjournments to sessions of parliament.[94] It was not until the sixteenth century, and then only very gradually, that the English state found it necessary to adopt a conscious strategy towards the management of epidemic disease.[95] If political society had therefore inured itself to the more devastating implications of the Black Death, it was because the economic and social upheaval predicted by so many in the aftermath of the first plague had not in fact come about and the interests of the elite had been maintained without the coercive and divisive policies that had been deemed necessary in the years between 1348 and 1381. In a broader sense, however, the very structure of royal government on which that elite increasingly relied to maintain its pre-eminence had been profoundly affected by the demographic shockwaves of the later fourteenth century and permanently influenced by the new social and economic conditions that came in their wake. If government can indeed be said to be an expression of the society in which it exists, then the suggestions offered here about the link between pestilence and politics may indeed represent but a small part of a more profound series of changes brought about by the Black Death in late medieval England.

[93] *Rotuli Parliamentorum*, V, p. 31.
[94] *Ibid.*, IV, p. 420; V, pp. 67, 143, 171, 172, 238, 618; VI, p. 99.
[95] P. Slack, *The Impact of Plague in Tudor and Stuart England* (London, 1985), pp. 199-226.

APPENDIX 1
KNOWN AND ASSUMED DEATHS OF OFFICIALS IN CENTRAL GOVERNMENT DURING PERIODS OF PLAGUE, 1348-75

The Plague of 1348-49

OFFICE	NAME	POST HELD	CIRCUMSTANCES
Chancery	John Offord	Chancellor	d. May 1349
	Henry Edwinstowe	C. of 1st grade	dis. after May 1348
	Thomas Cottingham	C. of 1st grade	d. by Apr. 1350
	John Morton	C. of 1st grade	d. by Dec. 1349
Exchequer	Thomas Cross	Royal chamberlain	d. by Jan. 1349
	Peter Delagh	King's chamberlain	dis. after Apr. 1349
King's Bench	John Lincoln	King's attorney	dis. after Oct. 1349
Common Pleas	John Clun	King's attorney	dis. after Oct. 1349
Household	Nicholas Buckland	Auditor of chamber	d. by May 1349
	Thomas Clopton	Keeper of wardrobe	d. by July 1349

The Plague of 1361-62

OFFICE	NAME	POST HELD	CIRCUMSTANCES
Chancery	Thomas Brayton	C. of 1st grade	dis. after Feb. 1361
	William Emeldon	C. of 1st grade	d. by Feb. 1361
	Elias Grimsby	C. of 1st grade	d. by May 1362
Exchequer	Hugh Appleby	King's remembrancer	d. by Oct. 1362
Courts	William Fyfield	King's serjeant	dis. after June 1361
Household	John Newbury	Keeper of great wardrobe	d. June 1361

The Plague of 1368-69

OFFICE	NAME	POST HELD	CIRCUMSTANCES
Chancery	John Coddington	C. of 1st grade	dis. 1369
Exchequer	Robert Charwelton	Treasurer's remembrancer	d. by Oct. 1368
	William Hull	Controller of great roll	dis. after Dec. 1368
	John Weye	Apposer of sheriffs' foreign summonses	d. by May 1368

The Plague of 1375

OFFICE	NAME	POST HELD	CIRCUMSTANCES
Chancery	John Branketre	C. of 1st grade	d. Sept. 1375
	William Mirfield	C. of 1st grade	dis. after July 1375
	Nicholas Spaigne	C. of 1st grade	d. early 1375
Exchequer	James Palmer	C. of great roll	d. by May 1375
	Robert Wygeley	Controller of great roll	dis. after Oct. 1375
	Sir William Tauk	Chief baron	d. by Oct. 1375

Sources
B. Wilkinson, *The Chancery under Edward III* (Manchester, 1929); D. M. Broome, 'The Exchequer in the Reign of Edward III: A Preliminary Investigation', University of Manchester Ph.D. thesis (1922); J. C. Sainty, *Officers of the Exchequer*, Public Record Office List and Index Society special series, 18 (1983); *Select Cases in the Court of King's Bench under Edward III*, ed. G. O. Sayles, Selden Society, 82 (London, 1965); T. F. Tout, *Chapters in the Administrative History of Mediaeval England*, 6 vols (Manchester, 1920-33).

Abbreviations
C.   = clerk
d.   = dead/died
dis. = disappeared

APPENDIX 2
SHERIFFS AND ESCHEATORS DYING IN OFFICE DURING
OUTBREAKS OF PLAGUE, 1348-75

The Plague of 1348-49

NAME	POST HELD	CIRCUMSTANCES	REFERENCES
William Bret	S, Essex and Herts; E, Essex, Herts and Middx	d. 23 May 1349	E199/10/12; E368/121, m. 186; *L. of Escheators*, p. 43
Thomas atte Fenn	S, Cornwall	d. by July 1349	*Reg. Black Prince* II.13
Simon Ruggeleye	S, Staffs	d. 9 Aug. 1349	*CIPM* IX. no. 437
John Vaux	S+E, Notts and Derbs	d. before Oct. 1349	*L. of Sheriffs*, p. 103; *L. of Escheators*, p. 109

The Plague of 1361-62

NAME	POST HELD	CIRCUMSTANCES	REFERENCES
John Fourneux	S, Cambs and Hunts	d. by Aug. 1361	E368/134, Precepta, Mich., m. 5
John Potenhale	S, Hants	d. by Aug. 1361	*CFR*, VII. 154
William Fililode	E, Northants and Rutland; Holderness	d. 7 Aug. 1361	*L. of Escheators*, pp. 98, 199
Walter Parles	S, Northants	d. 13 Aug. 1361	*CIPM*, XI. no. 173
William Hatton	E, Surrey, Sussex, Kent and Middx	d. by Oct. 1361	*L. of Escheators*, p. 163
Thomas Monyngton	E, Glos, Herefords and Welsh March	d. 27 Oct. 1361	*L. of Escheators*, p. 52
John Burton	S, Salop	d. by Nov. 1361	*L. of Sheriffs*, p. 118
William Overton	S, Rutland	d. by Jan. 1362	*CFR*, VII. 154
John Northwode	S, Essex and Herts	d. 1 Jan. 1362	*CIPM*, XI. no. 252
John Musard	S, Staffs	d. by Feb. 1362	*CIPM*, XI. 443; E368/134, Precepta, Mich., m. 9

The Plague of 1368-69

NAME	POST HELD	CIRCUMSTANCES	REFERENCES
Nicholas Beek	S, Staffs	d. by July 1368	*CFR*, VIII. 19
John Tye	E, Surrey, Sussex, Kent and Middx	d. 23 Oct. 1368	*L. of Escheators*, p. 163
Thomas Cheyne	E, Devon	d. 4 Apr. 1369	*L. of Escheators*, p. 33
William Beaufo	S, Rutland	d. 30 Aug. 1369	E368/142, Precepta, Mich., m. 1
Richard Chiselden	S, Devon	d. by Nov. 1369	*CFR*, VIII. 37

The Plague of 1375

NAME	POST HELD	CIRCUMSTANCES	REFERENCES
William Pymp	S, Kent	d. by Sept. 1375	*CFR*, VIII. 296; E368/148, Precepta, Mich., m. 2d
John Arden	S, Beds and Bucks	d. by Oct. 1375	*CFR*, VIII. 296; E368/148, Precepta, Mich., m. 2

Abbreviations
S = sheriff
E = escheator
d. = dead/died
L. = List
CFR = Calendar of Fine Rolls
CIPM = Calendar of Inquisitions Post Mortem

INDEX

The index attempts to be comprehensive, though many of the ideas which are covered inevitably overlap in subtle ways. References to places are followed by the traditional (not necessarily the present) English county. References to the county as a whole are also indexed but these need to be supplemented by searches for specific places. The footnotes are included where they supplement the main text, though not for bibliographical references without comment; '74 + n.133' refers to both the main text and the note; '74: n.133' refers only to the note. References to the ideas of modern historians, when labelled in the main text, are also indexed. The compiler was the publisher, Shaun Tyas.

182

Basque country, 56
'bastard feudalism', 59
Bath and Wells, bishop of, 84, 85, 86
Battle Abbey (Sussex), 101
Bean, J. M. W., historian, 4: n.11; 59, 136; 149: n.6
Beauchamp family, earls of Warwick, 112, 145
  Richard, earl of Warwick, 145
Beaufo, William, sheriff, 181
Beaulieu Abbey (Hampshire), Cistercian community at, 99, 100
Beauvale (Nottinghamshire), Charterhouse at, 104
Bec, Norman abbey of, 100, 106
Becket, St Thomas, 109
Bedfordshire, 59, 60, 181
Beek, Nicholas, sheriff, 181
beer, see ale
Belford (Northumberland), 24
Bellosi, Luciano, art historian, 132
Benedictines, monastic order, 98, 101, 104
Benedictis, Cristina de, art historian, 132 + n.35
Berkshire, 53, 56, 58: n.99; 59, 60
Bernard of Clairvaux, St, 91
Betley (Staffordshire), 68
Beverley (Yorkshire), 36, 130
  school of sculpture at, 130, 138: n.61
Binski, Paul, art historian, 135: n.45; 138: n.58
Bishop's Lynn, see King's Lynn
bishops' registers, as source material, 4, 84, 85, 86, 87, 88, 93, 96, 105 + n.115, 106
Black Death, see under plague
Black Prince, Edward the, 106
Blair, John, historian, 134
Blakenham (Suffolk), 100
Boccaccio, author of the Decameron, 128

Bocking (Essex), 69, 166: n.58
Bodmin (Cornwall), 121
Bohun Psalter, 129, 138-39 + n.63; plate 6
Bole, Walter le, master mason, 137
Bond, Francis, architectural historian, 128, 130
Boniface VIII, pope, 81-82
Bony, Jean, architectural historian, 129
Booth, Charles, bishop of Hereford, 105: n.115
Boskovits, Miklos, art historian, 132
Bossy, J., historian, 117: n.163
Boston (Lincolnshire), 7: n.20; 113
Bottisham (Cambridgeshire), 113
Boulay, F. R. H. Du, historian, 147: n.3
Bowsky, W. M., historian, 126-27
Boys, John, sheriff, 169: n.64
Braintree (Essex), 69; 166: n.58
branding, as a punishment, 158
Branketre, John, clerk, 178
Brantingham, Thomas, bishop of Exeter, 88
brasses, monumental, 129, 130, 134 + n.45; 138 + n.58
Brayton, Thomas, clerk, 178
bread, 10, 55, 99. See also diet, farming
Brenner, R., historian, 52, 61: n.106; 77
Brentford (Middlesex), 69
Brentwood (Essex), 12
Bret, William, sheriff, 180
Brétigny, treaty of (1360), 156
Bridbury, A. R., historian, 15, 18-19, 64, 65: n.111
Bridgettines, order of nuns, 104
Bristol, 7: n.20; 22, 92, 112, 113
  St Mary Redcliffe, 121
Britnell, R. H., historian, 31, 42, 45
Brut, the, 28
Brut, Walter, Welsh Lollard, 90

INDEX

Chipping Campden
(Gloucestershire), 68
Chipping Norton (Oxfordshire), 68
Chiselden, Richard, sheriff, 181
chivalry, 107-08 + n.124
Christ Church, Canterbury, *see*
Canterbury
Christopher, St, 139: n.64; 144;
plate 11
Church, the (in England), effects
of Black Death upon, 79-123
cathedrals, 133, 142-43
clergy, 84-96, 96-102
appropriations of income,
94-96
deaths of clergy, 22, 79, 84-87,
110, 144, 152, fig. 1 (p.124)
exchanges of livings, 93-94
recruitment difficulties, 84-96,
98-99 + n.84; 144, 152: n.17
regular (monastic) clergy,
30-31, 96-102
training of new clergy, 87-89,
90, 96-98, 98-99, 106-107, 144
churches, parish, 15, 60, 94,
113, 120-21, 128-29, 133-34:
n.40, 141, 146
churching records, as evidence,
39
collegiate institutions, 102-05,
144
episcopate, 105-07 + nn.114,
115 & 120; 122, 130
increase in anti-clericalism,
89-92 + n.43, 97, 103-04 +
n.106; 118-21, 144
increase in lay piety, 79,
103-04, 107-14, 114-18, 119-20,
144
increase in penance, 80, 102,
107, 109-10
monasteries, 94-95, 96-102,
103-04, 128, 141-42
Dissolution of, 61, 99: n.84
mendicants, 103-04

monastic debts, 99-102
monks, deaths of, 30-31, 32,
34, 46, 96-99
pilgrimage, 118
renewed emphasis on Jesus in
religion after the Black Death,
82, 109, 122
See also architecture, bishops'
registers, chantry chapels,
heresy, liturgy, Lollards,
morality, monastic orders
(headings listed), Ockham,
pessimism, philosophies
(headings listed), rental
incomes, Wyclif *and specific
locations and institutions*
Church Eaton (Staffordshire), 68
Cione, Nardo di, Florentine artist,
132
Cirencester (Gloucestershire), 115
Cistercians, monastic order, 96-97,
98, 99, 100, 101, 104, 123
civil war (1450s and '60s), *see* Wars
of the Roses
civil war (17th century), 108
Clare (Suffolk), Augustinian friary
at, 108: n.124
Clement V, pope, 82
Clement VII, anti-pope, 82
clergy, *see under* Church
climatic change, 6: n.18; 40, 44,
169
Clopton, Thomas, keeper of
wardrobe, 178
cloth industry, 7, 8, 10, 18, 25, 56,
61, 64, 65, 67
Clun, John, king's attorney, 178
Cobham (Kent), 129
Coddington, John, clerk, 178
coins/age, *see* monetary affairs
Colchester (Essex), 7: n.20; 31, 32,
37, 65, 69
Coleshill (Berkshire), 56
Colet, Dean John, 91
Colorado, USA, plague in, 25

185

Mare, Thomas de la, abbot of St Albans, 98

Marks, Richard, art historian, 139

marriage, effects of Black Death upon, 2, 5, 13, 19, 26, 29, 33, 34-40, 44, 49, 70-71, 74-75, 76-77, 117

Martini, Simone, artist, 132

Mate, M., historian, 42, 46, 49, 77

McFarlane, K. B., historian, 152

meat, 6, 8, 10, 55, 57, 61, 67. *See also* diet, fish, livestock

Meaux, Cistercian monastery of, 96

Meaux chronicle, 27

Meiss, Millard, art historian, 14, 125-28, 131, 136, 146

Melcombe Regis (Dorset), 22

merchants, *see* trade

metals/ware, trade in and manufacture of, 7, 8, 56, 67 + n.116; 73

Mid Lavant (Sussex), 95

Middlesex, 180, 181

Middleton, Baillys of, yeoman family, 54: n.88

Middleton (Essex), fig. 1 (p.124)

midlands, *see under* regional diversity

migration, *see* population / movements of *and* towns / migration into

Milan (Italy), 126

Millar, Eric G., art historian, 129, 134

Miller, E., historian, 38

Mirfield, William, clerk, 178

misericords, 135

Mollat, M., historian, 14

monasteries, *see under* Church, the

monastic orders, *see* Augustinians, Benedictines, Bridgettines, Carmelites, Carthusians, Cistercians, Dominicans,

Franciscans, Premonstratensians *See also specific institutions*

monetary affairs

barter, as means of exchange, 41, 42, 67

bullion famine, 21, 40-41

credit, 41, 42-43

debasement of coinage, 42-43

gold, 40, 41

mints, 40

monetarism (philosophy of), 42

recoinage of 1464-71, 40

money supply, 20-21, 40-43

silver base of coinage, 42-43

tokens, as alternative money, 42-43

See also government / royal demesne; rental incomes, taxation, wages

Monkton (Durham), 23

Monyngton, Thomas, escheator, 180

morality, effect of Black Death upon, 114-18 + n.163; 177. *See also* marriage, pessimism, prostitution

moral chaos/panic, 1, 10, 12, 14, 18, 118, 122

mortality, *see under* population

Morton, John, clerk, 178

Musard, John, sheriff, 180

Mymmes, John de, London artist, 137: n.55

Nantwich (Cheshire), 141

nautical matters

coastal raids, 43, 95, 101

navy, 164

See also trade / overseas

Netherlands, *see* Low Countries

New Mexico (USA), plague in, 25

Newborough (Staffordshire), 68

Newbury, John, keeper of great wardrobe, 178

Newcastle (Northumberland), 32, 65

rebellion, *see* Cade's Rebellion; Glyndwr's rebellion; labour / impressment; Oldcastle, Sir John; parliament / rejection of tax proposals; Peasants' Revolt, Sussex Rising

Reformation (16th century), 2, 79, 80, 89, 98, 105, 111, 113, 115, 119-20 + n.165; 122-23 + nn.174 & 175. *See also* Protestantism

regional diversity, 13, 20, 22-23, 31, 32, 33, 36, 44, 49, 52, 56, 57, 60, 61, 63, 65, 70, 77, 85, 86, 88, 125, 137, 141, 144, 146
  East Anglia, 23, 32, 121, 141
  eastern England, 23, 36, 53-54, 64, 100, 133
  midland England, 9, 22, 23, 26, 32, 34, 36, 54, 56, 57, 58, 65, 69, 88, 141
  northern England, 20, 23, 27, 29, 31, 32, 33, 36, 40, 43, 44, 46, 56, 57, 64, 70, 77, 89, 95, 101, 109, 110, 133
  south-western England, 22, 56, 70
  south-eastern England, 56
  southern England, 20, 32, 35, 43, 46, 54, 56, 57, 64, 88, 100.
  See also specific towns and counties

rental income, problem of declining, 8-9, 18, 20-21, 41, 45-46, 92-93, 99-102, 143, 168-71

Rhineland, 56

Richard II, king of England, 118, 135, 171

Richmond, Colin, historian, 119-20 + n.165

Rigby, S., historian, 65: n.111; 66

Ripon (Yorkshire), 110

Rocester (Staffordshire), 68

Rochester (Kent), 110
  diocese of, 92

Rochester chronicler (William of Dene), 90, 110, 140

Rogers, J. E. Thorold, historian, 17

Rolle, Richard, theologian, 108, 109, 110

Rome, 82, 90

Romford (Essex), 69

Romsey (Hampshire), nunnery of, 94

Roucestere, Simon, mason, 141

Rubin, M., historian, 14, 115

Ruggeleye, Simon, sheriff, 180

Russell, J. C., historian, 34, 152

Russell, John, bishop of Lincoln, 50

Rutland, 72, 180, 181

S. Gimignano (Italy), 131

saints, cults of, 109

Salisbury (Wiltshire), 64 + n.110

salt, industry and trade in, 55

Salzman, L. F., architectural historian, 139

Sampson, John, sculptor, 140

Samson, Sire James, fig. 1 (p.124)

Sandwich (Kent), 110

Scarborough (Yorkshire), 33, 65

Schofield, R. S., population historian, 39

Scilly Isles, 99

Scotland, 108
  Scottish raids, 43, 95

Scrope, Richard le, archbishop of York, 110

sculpture (includes masonry), 129: n.18; 130, 135-36, 137-38 + nn.55 & 61; 142-44 + nn.82, 84-87 & 89; 145; plates 3, 4 & 9

seals, designs of, 130, 134 + n.41

Second World War, disaster comparison with, 18-19, 146: n.100

servants, *see under* labour

Seven Corporal Acts of Mercy, 14-15

Shareshull, William, chief justice of king's bench, 136

1. Gloucester Cathedral, south transept (interior, looking east), showing panelling effect, characteristic of the 'Perpendicular Style' and derived from the exterior treatment of St Stephen's Chapel, Westminster (photo: P. Lindley).

2. Gloucester Cathedral, south transept, south window. The south transept dates from *c*.1331 to 1337. This window contains the basic 'Perpendicular' motifs of mullions cutting into the arch, a transom and a rigid hierarchy of decorative elements (photo: P. Lindley).

3. (above) Lincoln Cathedral, detail of the gallery of kings, inserted into the west front. These figures are ascribed by Professor Lawrence Stone to the 1360s and attributed to a London workshop (photo: P. Lindley).

4. (left) Lincoln Cathedral, detail of one of the gallery of kings. The high quality and astonishingly good preservation of the figure is evident (photo: P. Lindley).

5. Head of gilt-bronze effigy of King Edward III (d. 1377), Westminster Abbey (photo: P. Lindley).

6. (far left) Judgement of Solomon. Full page illumination in Bodleian MS Douce 131, fol. 96v. It has been argued that the artist of this psalter died in the plague, whilst working on the Vienna Psalter (photo: The Bodleian Library, Oxford).

7. (left) Nineteenth-century copy of wall paintings, formerly on altar wall of St Stephen's Chapel, Westminster, showing detail of Adoration of Kings above the sons of Edward III. The painted decoration of the chapel post-dates the plague (photo by courtesy of the Society of Antiquaries).

8. Winchester Cathedral, west front. The front, started in the episcopate of Bishop Edington, may have been left incomplete for years after his death (photo: P. Lindley).

9. Exeter Cathedral, west front. The sculptures of the first tier of niches belong to three different campaigns, the first abruptly terminated by the plague and resumed only a quarter-century later (photo: P. Lindley).

10. (above) Corpus Christi College, Cambridge. The college was founded in 1352 by the guilds of Corpus Christi and the Blessed Virgin Mary. Old Court was completed by c.1377. This photograph shows the east side (photo: P. Lindley).

11. (left) Wall painting of St Christopher, Paston (Norfolk), probably from the second half of the fourteenth century (reproduced from H. C. Whaite, *St. Christopher in English Mediæval Wall-painting* (London, 1929), plate 7).

12. 'The Three Living and the Three Dead' (c.1300), from Walters Art Gallery, Baltimore, MS W 51 fols 1ᵛ-2 (photo: The Walters Art Gallery, Baltimore).